CLEARANCES

To my old friend Wendy
with love as ever —
Mairi

CLEARANCES

A Memoir

MAIRI MACINNES

Mairi MacInnes

PANTHEON BOOKS, NEW YORK

Pantheon Books and colophon are registered
trademarks of Random House, Inc.

Permissions Acknowledgments appear on page 276.

Library of Congress Cataloging-in-Publication Data

MacInnes, Mairi.
Clearances : a memoir / Mairi MacInnes.
p.   cm.
ISBN 0-375-42068-1
1. MacInnes, Mairi.   2. Authors, English—20th century—
Biography.   3. British—Foreign countries—
History—20th century.   I. Title.

PR6063.A35 Z467 2002   828'.91409   [B]   2002022430

www.pantheonbooks.com

Book design by M. Kristen Bearse

Printed in the United States of America
First Edition
2 4 6 8 9 7 5 3 1

TO JOHN

[L]ife and the memory of it so compressed
they've turned into each other.

—ELIZABETH BISHOP, "Poem"

CONTENTS

PART ONE

BEGINNINGS

LOOKING FOR GEORGE

Here, as darkness fills out,
absolute circumstance also
begins to bloom

County Durham in the north of England is not a famous county. I've known an American scholar of English Studies question its existence. "But I was born there," I said to the man.

"You should check it out," he said. "It may have been eliminated." He meant, simply, that he had not heard of it, which made it as good as a hole in space.

And then there was the woman from Northamptonshire who rang up with a book of my poems in her hand. She was looking for Irish women poets and had read from the little biography on the back that I was born in County Durham, which, with my name, in her view made me Irish. "No, County Durham is in the north of England," I explained.

"So you're not Irish?"

"No, alas."

"And your name is not Irish either?"

"It's Scots. I'm of Highland descent."

"Even your first name? Not Irish?"

"No, it's my grandmother's name. And her grandmother's before her. It's Scots Gaelic. They were Gaelic speakers." I pronounced it for her. "Mahri."

"And County Durham is in the north of England."

"Yes."

"Too bad," she said, and rang off.

Obviously the nature of the poems—their worth, damn it—
did not concern her, only my sex and origins.

In any case, County Durham has not gone away. It's intact
within me, and on the map as well. When abroad, where for a
long time I'd longed to be, I wondered what it was I'd come round
to missing. I didn't picture the place so much as feel for it, which
was just as well, for it was not on the whole pretty, that land of
farms and industrial towns between Yorkshire and Northumber-
land, facing the North Sea, with exhausted coal mines and spent
fisheries, with a hinterland of old stone-built towns and of moors
and hills reaching west and north to the Debatable Lands for centuries fought over with Scotland. The exceptions, the great beautiful places, are the reaches of upper Teesdale, with its high moors
and deep valleys of ancient oaks and pasture, and the castle and
cathedral of Durham, built high on a rocky islet in the river Wear,
one of the grandest sights in Europe.

Now that I live in England again I must be more candid. My
County Durham is only a village near a market town that when I
was growing up was little more than a slum, the archetype of all
other slums in the Western world—moldy with damp, dirty,
overcrowded, diseased. Many spoke "Geordie" like the people
of Tyneside up north rather than "Yorkshire" like the people to
the south, and, despite the conditions they lived in, radiated a
sunny good humor, not the contrariness and hardness of Yorkshire people. That turned out to be important. When I was growing up we were constantly told that regional differences of speech
and behavior were disappearing fast and that soon we'd all talk
and behave in a smooth and uniform way, which, we understood,
would be all to the good. Not so. The differences remain; we
don't talk the same, we don't act the same, we face the world in
characteristically different ways, and it is a matter of local pride

to stick to the distinctions, as I was to find out on a visit after many years away.

"I'm looking for a man called George Bell," I said to the postmaster through the grille. "I know he was living here in the village two years ago, but I don't know where. He's lived in the village all his life. I wonder if you know his address."

The tiny post office was so crammed with customers that I was appalled to think how personal my question was, how irrelevant to postage stamps and money orders and pensions. Perhaps I should have begun my quest at the police station; but I hadn't seen a police station or even a policeman, and anyway George might have resented my associating him so freely with the police. A hush fell on the queue behind me, and I turned to find everyone's eyes on me. I smiled, and everyone smiled back. So what was George to me or I to George? What was it between us? A debt? In a way. Friendship? Love? No, something more delicate, something you couldn't name, something far too easily called into question.

The postmaster was considering, surveying the backs of his hands like a map.

"She's looking for a George Bell," a woman's voice explained.

"What age of a man is he?" asked another.

"In his late sixties." I blushed. I was nearly sixty myself. Everyone was suitably entertained, I could see by the faint smiles. An assistant pushed a telephone directory under the grille and tapped a column of Bells with her forefinger. It hadn't occurred to me that George had a telephone. I was dwelling in a past when private telephones were a rarity in the working class.

"There was a George Bell worked for Hall's garage after the war, as a mechanic," said the postmaster. He pronounced "garage" to rhyme with "carriage." I felt a pang of delight. I would have to reply in the same way, not in the American style, to rhyme with "barrage," as I had learned twenty-five years ago. But what on earth did it matter? "That's my man, that's George!" My father had taught George to drive so he would have a trade when he left us. We heard that he got a job as a lorry driver. So he must have become a mechanic in due course, perhaps trained in the army during the war.

"Mrs. Hall lives at number seven, The Green," said the postmaster. "I'd go and see her. Take down these telephone numbers first, though, now you've got a list." There were columns and columns of Bells, none of them G. Bell. There were some called G. in combination with other initials, though, and these I took down. When I returned the directory everyone looked happy for me.

"If all else fails," said a man in the queue, "you could ask the milkman."

The queue stirred in agreement. A milkman? So there were still milkmen? "How long is it since you saw this George Bell?" asked the man in the queue.

"Oh, quite some time." It was in fact more than forty years, a fairly weighty fact I had no intention of dropping into the delicate network of glances in the crowded room. In truth the last time I'd seen him had been at the start of the war, one wintry evening in late 1939 or early 1940, when I was running to the dairy for a pint of cream, an errand of the sort George had performed. George had just left us, but there was still cream: which pinpoints the date. So there I was, haring up the pavement with a jug in my hand, when I ran slap into George with a couple of other young men. He seemed huge and jolly as he collared me and laughed at me for doing his work, which I knew he had been glad to be rid of. On my side I was pleased to think of my competence. Presently the heavy bombing began. In 1941 we went to live in the south, and by then I think George had gone into the army.

Now I walked up the High Street with its fine Georgian houses and on to the green, where I found number 7 and rang the bell. It was an eighteenth-century cottage with a slate roof, facing into the sun, handsome in its dark handmade brick and white paintwork, overall North Country plain, with well-polished brass knocker, bell, and doorknob. The doorstep was beautifully white, just as ours had been every day; and there were discreet net curtains to stop people on the pavement, people like me, from peering in. A line of wallflowers—red and yellow, such as I hadn't seen for three decades, with such sweetness of smell that I felt giddy—grew underneath the windows at the foot of the wall.

No one answered my ring or my knock, so I wandered off, crisscrossing the green on the sheep trods I had once threaded on my brother's bike, the OK Perfection that he let me use when he was away at school. There was a red telephone box on the north side, where I worked my way down the list of Bells taken down in the post office. Only one person answered, and he was a Geoffrey. Eleven o'clock in the morning of a fine day in September with the children back in school was not the time to find people at home. A retired man might well be out for a walk with his dog, or shopping with his wife, supposing he had a wife.

I was overcome briefly at the thought of coming face-to-face with George and recognizing him instantly, only to be constrained by the presence of some old biddy who'd been his life partner. And how would he receive me? I had only the airy expectations of childhood to go on. He might well remember me with displeasure. His duties with my family were not endearing. He was simply our odd-job boy. Ours was the first place he went to on leaving school at the age of fourteen. He washed the car every day (wearing dark blue overalls and black gum boots). He swept the brick yard and the steps. He mowed the lawn in summer, and he tended the conservatory boiler in winter and brought in coal for the open fires. He mucked out my pony and groomed her and took me out on her, escorting me on his big sit-up-and-beg bike. At about five o'clock he delivered medicines from my father's dispensary to patients all over town. Though he'd loomed large in my life, I was ready to understand that I had been trivial in his. And yet I was out to meet him, for reasons I am only now putting into words.

To return to the question of his appearance, so hatefully important now: he might have thick spectacles; his hands might be knobby with arthritis; he might limp; his stiff-bristled hair might have fallen out or gone white; his wildly crooked teeth been replaced by perfectly matched National Health dentures. As for his clothes, he might be clad in smooth, comfy pseudo-athletic gear instead of the thick tweed three-piece suit he wore to work as a growing boy, with its trousers ending a couple of inches over hob-nailed boots, the sleeves inches from his wrists, his shirt collar a frill up over his tie of knitted black cotton. And his voice, would it be gruff still, and loud, the same as the voice I remembered; or had it been tempered into a commonplace imitation of genteel southern English, not grounded anymore in ancient and authentic "Geordie"?

Hell to think of not recognizing George. But I had to be prepared for a shock. I'd miss the teeth, to begin with. Nelly the cook, whom I'd questioned about them long ago, said he'd been kicked in the mouth by a horse. I didn't know whether to believe her; she wasn't straightforward. She and Betty, the housemaid, kidded me at leisure. It stood to reason therefore that they found George a joke. George was not refined like them, and it was George after all who set me free from their official housekeeping activity and their private lives that encroached on it so mysteriously, with plots for followers and rivalry about winning over—or outwitting—my mother. He removed me also from the teasing and ridicule by which (behind my mother's back) they reduced me to order. I saw George's teeth as a relief rather than as a disaster or sign of poverty, because they made him be like me—a bit of a mess. They made it easy for me to be friends with him, just as they made it easy for the maids to laugh.

For the last two years, ever since my discovery that George was

alive and in the village, my mind had settled on him as secretly as
a bird on its nest. Attempts to talk about him in America had
only aroused cries of ridicule there, or else displays of bookish
expertise in the English class system. I couldn't find a way of
describing how precious the relationship had been, or why I respected him. We had known each other in a universe without the
words to hint at deeply felt convictions, a universe without reason, even without discussion. The vocabulary of the imagination
was missing—I didn't know it existed. When at last I got to know
it, and to realize that others used it, I loved George more freely
than ever. In America, when I described George's function in our
household, my listeners thought I was describing inferiority. Of
course I should have begun with a description of his teeth, which
they would have understood perfectly, and which would have covered the same implications but in an unpolitical and more acceptable form. Now back in England, where the relationship between
George and I had existed on purely human terms, I excused my
doting upon him on the grounds that I wished to know what had
happened to us both and to this part of the world since we'd
parted. Change after all meant choice. Even when you had changes
thrust upon you, as by age or disease, you changed in a manner
that showed something about yourself. So let George confirm my
experience and also make it new. And let me understand both the
old and the new.

If far off in America I had been ready to dismiss my interest in
such changes as morbid or silly, on the well-remembered green
they looked deeply important. The green, after all, was where
George was in his element. He had been born in one of the houses
like Mrs. Hall's, but on the side facing north. He'd been to the
boys' elementary school down the High Street. He'd worked here,
most of his life, probably, and here he was probably living still. So
here he was boss. On several occasions he'd let me know exactly
how to behave and how not to. We'd soon find our level as we
talked. Yet—here we were again—how would I set the scene so

that we'd both feel at ease? "You'd ask him to your hotel," said a friend in America to whom I'd proposed the difficulty. Yes, that's what a journalist would do, I thought with relief: we'd sit in a bar, and I'd switch on my tape recorder, and George would feel that every word of his was gold and begin to pour forth. But wait: would George really do that? Wasn't I looking for him simply because he was the touchstone of integrity and would not be misled by the sight of a red carpet? The hotel where I had found the only available room in the neighborhood was very much a red-carpet proposition, a brassy place, an expense-account hotel, one of a well-known chain where you had to pay for the night the moment you stepped over the threshold from the street, and where they had looked at me coldly, an oldish woman traveling alone. It was dislikable in the realm of decency where George was king, and I couldn't imagine him expanding there.

If I approached him through Mrs. Hall, many of these difficulties would vanish. I went back to her house in the lunch hour, and again she was absent.

As I told the people in the post office, I thought George was alive because I had heard of him two years before. I had been traveling alone then too. The weather was fine, and I'd come up from Scotland unexpectedly quickly, too soon for an appointment in Derbyshire. Rather than fit in a visit to Lindisfarne or the city of Durham, I thought I'd spend a few hours in my birthplace. No one I was in touch with lived there now. I would be a ghost, invisible. I'd amuse myself wandering about and then take off laughing, thanking God I was away from the slums and the decrepit iron foundries and the big stinking chemical works at Billingham (and I smelled again the sulfur and ammonia and remembered the columns of bicycles with their small front lamps sweeping brightly home from Billingham past our house at five on a winter's evening).

Norton surprised me. The big circular green hemmed with pleasant old houses, and the island in the middle of the green where the blacksmith's forge used to be, with a sweetshop next to it; the typical North Country banks of neatly mowed grass between the delivery lane and the road itself; the pond, the ancient church with its Saxon tower, the fine high street with double rows of trees and houses opening right on the delivery lane: a pleasure to look at. Sheraton the great cabinetmaker had lived his forty years in Stockton-on-Tees, and there was a fine house named after him in Norton where I think he was too poor ever to have lived himself. Even the house where I was born still stood, a row of hollies in front, a pear tree espaliered to the southern wall. A pretty house of about 1820. I'd had no idea. Now the years had added a sense of themselves. Somewhere in the tide of time the house was built, and my family came to occupy it and then left; the date of our occupancy seemed remarkably unimportant. After one war and up to another. Two enormous wars in my parents' lifetime.

So the heart of the village had not changed much for two centuries. That was my first impression, readied by a lifetime away in another country where there wasn't much of the past in the landscape or its architecture. My second was that the little modernization that had taken place was crude. The churchyard looked as if it had been taken over by Laura Ashley and rearranged with too much neatness, the little memorials for babies pulled up and set out flat in the shelter of the outer walls, like a stone hem. The church—where my brother and I had been christened—was stripped of its Virginia creeper, which in former Septembers had been a blaze of red; its huge elms had been dismantled—gone too therefore the rookery littering their crowns and the crowds of noisy rooks. The duck pond was now lined with concrete. A ring road behind the green roared in the distance as if the green were a toy left by a child, not the focus of a place where flocks and herds could be driven in and safeguarded from attack by Scots raiders in the Middle Ages, and where later the villagers could walk and ride in safety. The village had apparently gone up in the world; it was gentrified and turned into a place that people drove from in the morning and returned to only in the evening, a dormitory rather than a community of wakeful, gossiping, self-regulating citizens.

That phase of change was under way when I was a child, and of course it was part of a bigger evolution. What had happened to the hall—the big house—on the green and to the mill at the end of one of the lanes was an example. The hall had in the late twenties become a club for the executives of Imperial Chemical Industries, that affiliate of I. G. Farben and DuPont: they lived nearby and went off to work at Billingham, two or three miles away. Some of those we'd known had become nationally famous at the furthest reaches of their yuppiedom. I walked by the hall door and saw it was still a club. The mill, on the other hand, already outdated by the turn of the century, was a ruin by the time I rode by it as a child, and now it had disappeared, together with its rushing beck and sloping sandy banks. In their place was a raw housing estate.

Most of the changes in Norton were the result of changes in Stockton, two miles away. From eighteenth-century market town and port and shipyard, Stockton very early had become industrial. Iron brought from the Cleveland Hills was smelted with coal from the huge South Durham coalfield, and this in turn led to rolling mills and blast furnaces; to which the world's first railway was a revolutionary addition when Geordie Stephenson from Newcastle drove passengers and goods from Stockton to Darlington in July 1825. Gradually Norton became detached from the places of work; it became the home of gentry and house owners. Farms no longer backed on the village. Cows didn't slouch across the green twice a day to be milked. Trams came instead, clanging their bells, to an insistent timetable. To this separation of Norton and Stockton my parents unwittingly contributed when they went there to set up house in 1919. My father was joining another Scot in medical practice in Stockton, but he and my mother bought a house in Norton. She was Australian. They'd met in 1917 in Number 50 British General Hospital at Salonika in northern Greece, set up during the Balkan campaign against the Turks. So they were very much outsiders in County Durham, starting from scratch in an understood way.

During my earlier visit I had run my small hired car up and down the village high street and its back alleys, marveling at the lack of change. The floors of the alleys touched me particularly, laid in a pattern of glazed bluish brick, scored to prevent horses from slipping. I had ventured to the single-track railway beyond the green, an old goods line serving Billingham. Wagons and hoppers used to crawl over the crossing, fifty, sixty, seventy of them at a stretch. The rails still gleamed from use. Beyond the lines were two short stiff terraces of workingmen's houses built for quarrymen in a now silent quarry nearby. Then came the fields where I used to ride as a girl of eight or nine. A farm track still led through them. A grassy ridge remained in the middle of the track, though with taller grass than I remembered. I bumped along, noting with adult educated eye the ridge-and-furrow corrugation of medieval fields that I had once found a puzzle which no one would explain. Up the pasture I drove where once a horde of a dozen shire horses had thundered up to me and my pony, to tower over us, all monumental yellow teeth and mad eyes and hooves like dinner plates, then to escort Dolly and me in plunging anarchy to the far gate, which to my relief they did not crash through, smashing us to pieces, but reared and nipped and kicked and took off in a farting, whinnying charge. Now I drove across in deadly calm. The same five-barred gates across the track, the same stony scramble up to the farmhouse on the hill, the same brick barns, the same mud in the yard, but a new silence and solitude. No animals now, not even a dog to bark at me; no farmhands. I got out and knocked at the farmhouse door. A man of indefinable age answered, a small man. Most Durham people were small in my day, from malnutrition. Behind him I could see a new staircase made of varnished pine.

I wished him good morning. "Please—could you tell me—can I drive through to Wynyard from here?"

"Naw, that's plough up till 'edge."

"I used to ride through very often. Does the farm still belong to the Hawes family?"

"Ay, it does."

"My father used to be your doctor. I used to come out with him when he came to see Mrs. Hawes. Then I came on my pony."

He began to smile and chuck his head in disbelief. "Yer cum riding that roan pony o' yourn, many and many's the teem." He clicked his tongue and shook his head. "Well! You've changed."

No wonder novelists do not try scenes of this sort, so full of banal amazement and emotion. "I live in America now," I said by way of explanation.

He obviously did not hear me any more than I heard him, as we pronounced on the passing of the years and similar drolleries. The real meaning of our exchange lay beyond words, and I don't know that we made any more sense than if we'd stayed silent and simply smiled at each other. So, what with our sighs and head turnings to this side and that, it was a relief to hear Hawes mention an actual name.

"That lad that cum with yer, that George Bell, 'e worra nice lad, wor that George. A nice lad, and a nice chap 'e turned out to be, everyone says that. Everyone 'e knaws likes George. A fine man 'e is."

My heart exploded within me. "Ah, George, is he still here? He came back from the war? Can I go and see him? Where does he live?"

Hawes was a small dark Celtic-looking man in spite of his very English name. While we grinned at each other with the name of George on our lips, our common liking for him giving us a footing, I wondered whether he was the son of old Hawes, the farmer of my childhood, or the grandson. Was he George's age? These questions crowded in with a dozen others, leaping up out of nowhere and falling back unanswered as I tried hard for coherence. They seemed to have nothing really to do with us as we stood at the door of the farmhouse on that bright September day. Later I wondered how I could have been so careless of fact. But I felt such strong emotion that facts appeared beside the point. So what was the point, exactly? It was real enough, but I have trouble putting it into words, perhaps because I had known George before words came so easily and so distortingly.

"I 'aven't seen 'im for a year or two. More, like. Could be four or five. When I last 'eard, 'e wor working at Kia-ora."

The name wasn't new, but it wasn't familiar, either. A New Zealand name? A lemon drink? Now a place, and a place I'd once known. A place with George in it.

"At Kia-ora, at the car 'ire, that's where 'e wor."

"And he's still there?"

Hawes did not know. Behind him was a table laid for the midday meal. Was there someone else—a wife, for example? Why didn't he ask me in? A woman would have done so. It occurred to me that some woman not his wife was there, some woman whose presence he wished to hide. Or he'd quarreled with his wife and she was sulking in the background. He must want his meal. I started to back away, making polite noises, and he didn't detain me, though he smiled insanely, as I did myself, nodding and tossing our heads from side to side like ponies. So we exchanged this bit of silly information and that, and I backed away and got into the car, calling goodbyes while he remarked on the change in me. Well, I had been a shy and inept child, and here I was a shy and inept old woman who suffered from difficulty in getting to the point.

I drove back to the village wishing the water in the beck beside me would wash over me and cleanse my soul. Before I got there I pulled to the side of the cart track to compose myself, and realized I was going to be late for my appointment in Derbyshire, and wished I had more time to dig George out but was thankful I hadn't. Suppose I postponed that appointment and turned up at Kia-ora, wherever that was, and found him, in the blue overalls and black gum boots of forty years ago, and he was no more generous of himself than Hawes: what a letdown, how irretrievable that would be! Accordingly I left the district and reserved our encounter for a future when I had more time and command of the situation, and forgot even the name of Kia-ora.

I must confess, though, to cowardice. I was afraid of blundering into certain episodes of the past with my big blunt adult consciousness, changing what didn't suit, ignoring what was tacitly there, donning theoretical spectacles to view the scenery of the past, dominating with my physical presence, my height and well-being, my clothes, my wrinkles, my motherhood, my wifeliness; and dominating that past with my worldliness and education and experience.

Once, on Hawes's farm, George had propped his bike against the brick wall of the fold yard and sent me off to the wood, saying he'd be along. I had been reading about an Indian who ran alongside his white master as he rode, holding on to his stirrup as the horse galloped. I tried this out on Dolly, urging her up a hill as I ran alongside clutching the leather. Dolly hated it and let me have a hoof in the stomach. When I came to, George was holding me up and bending me over so I could gradually get my breath back. How had he come so swiftly from the farmhouse kitchen to the dark part of the wood? Was he being neglectful? No, oh no. I said nothing to my parents, and nothing was said about the incident. Even if George told them of it, they would not have fussed. And George trusted me, he was the only person who did so, and I had to prove worthy of him, even now, flinching from the thought that he might feel lessened from the figure he had once cut in my world.

Of course the years had gone by, and we'd both have been foolish to discount them, and with luck we might have felt friendship, love, respect, but certainly we would have had to create a new relationship. Not that back then George wasn't already expanding the narrow walls of our common world. Presently he showed me violets in the bank. It was spring and the wood was just coming into leaf. He pointed out rosettes of leaves, in the middle of each rosette the dark violets held in the crook of the stem. He held up one to be sniffed, the first violet of my life. I leaned down from the saddle, surprised by the smallness of the flower, its scent, its importance to George. He was teaching me to use my eyes and nose. Later he showed me birds' nests in the hedge and identified each one. In summer we turned up during haymaking, and I showed off to the rakers by galloping in and out of the stooks. He showed me where cherries grew in a grove behind the farm, and nuts in a hazel coppice.

Then, by my tenth year, when I could ride reasonably well, George got permission to take me to nearby meets of the South Durham hounds. The master was a charming woman called Nelly Brown who lived in a handsome old house with creamy rendering overlooking the green. It was still to be seen on my recent visit: not a house to be casually knocked down or made into a shop. Miss Brown rode sidesaddle and was remarkably graceful and slender, her body inclining and swaying with the motion of the horse, her slender straight back in its well-tailored habit rising to her stock, her head surmounted by a topper and netted in a veil through which you could see her freckles and pretty dark eyes. She had apparently chosen not to marry, which was interesting, I thought. Years later someone explained that she and a delightful doctor in the village were in love and could not marry because as a married man and a Catholic he was not free. Perhaps for this reason and for her beauty and elegance my mother respected Miss Brown, and so I was allowed to follow the hounds, out over the hedges and ditches and roads too, where you might see a man from Stockton walking a whippet as you trotted by, or unloading a basket from his bike with a racing pigeon inside. All these activities were a great change from the quiet life at home, and I owed them entirely to George. I could believe no evil of him, and though I can see now what pleasure he got out of them too, that makes no difference. Ensuing complications have made no difference either, even though it has become clear that he gained a great deal of power through the odd way I was brought up.

At nine I had still not gone to school. A governess taught me in the mornings (and very well too). The rest of the time I looked for something to do. I read and reread all the books in the house, from surgical manuals to the plays of George Bernard Shaw. I accompanied my mother to market or the shops. I built tree houses and climbed over the roofs of the chapel next door. On Wednesday afternoons my father drove us to Newcastle, where my mother looked at more shops and we had tea at Tilley's and went to the pictures. Very occasionally my father escaped and played golf with his friend from student days in Glasgow, Walter Connolly, another doctor, who now lived and worked in a town nearby. He had a charming wife, but my mother didn't really respond to her and was too unathletic to play golf, and the friendship faltered. There were rows. A crash. A cut-glass jug thrown on the hearth, glass everywhere. A bunch of black grapes, a present for my father from my mother, cost a fortune, flung on the coals because she refused to sample even one, blistering and sizzling to extinction. Departures: my father leaving in the car and not coming back for so long that I visualized him dead, a suicide, the car deliberately launched off a particular wooden bridge over water on the way to Seaton Carew; my mother leaving in Hall's taxi (the same outfit George was to work for, the one owned eventually by the Mrs. Hall who lived at number 7, The Green). "Go and say goodbye to Daddy."

"I don't want to go."

"Do as I say."

There he was kneeling on the lawn, knifing dandelions out of the lawn. "Goodbye, Daddy."

"Go if you want," he said, not looking up. "But don't expect me to say goodbye."

I should have hid. Instead, I stood and howled. "Come along," called my mother from the gate. We got into the huge boxlike car and side by side in its dove gray interior were driven to Darlington, where we spent the night in a hotel. The next day she rang him and he came for us and drove us home.

My cousin Mary MacNab, who was twice as old then as I was, recalls parties in those days when carpets were rolled back and bare floors sprinkled with crystals to form a smooth surface for fox-trots and quicksteps. Music equally smooth sang from the windup gramophone. One night Mrs. Mcgonigal took a fancy to my father. "And no wonder. Such a handsome man, though he never admitted it. Oh, he was a beautiful man. Mrs. Mcgonigal was a real gypsy—coal black hair, bright red dress. Your mother, poor soul, had chosen the wrong dress and sat out most of the dances."

The Mcgonigals came to be considered fast. "We weren't like that," said my mother, nodding at me in my early married days, establishing complicity. I thought of Mary, who was very fond of my father herself. No doubt many women held a grudge against my mother, but Mary had a way of appearing throughout my life like a Greek chorus, commenting on her inadequacies.

Then there was the locum called Dicky who was going out to West Africa, "the white man's grave." He dropped in to say goodbye. At eleven that night he was still there. "I'm off to bed," said my father. In the morning they were still there, my mother and Dicky, laughing and talking. Dicky was still there at lunchtime, and at teatime. When my father appeared at eight after evening surgery, Dicky was still in place and they were both wiping tears of laughter from their eyes. "Good God, Dicky, you still here?"

Whereupon Dicky went off to catch his ship and disappeared for good.

My father never forgave his own rudeness.

How interesting life was for them, how full of scandal and flirtation and rows and excursions. I longed for my brother's return from boarding school so I too could have an interesting life, but he and my mother became bent on my reform. I mispronounced "monument," which became "modgement"; "tuckbox" became "touchbox." He reported riotous behavior at a children's party. My table manners caused them to recommend that I eat in the stable. Everything I did was wrong. I made no effort to set things right. What was the point? They objected to my true self. So I looked to George. For one thing, his interesting life had an impersonal clarity about it, as Latin had when I finally went to school. One foul winter day he let me melt lead in a tin cigarette box on top of the conservatory furnace and then pour it into molds for crude soldiers. One day he produced a revolver, and we shot at a tin can set up at the far end of the greenhouse. He produced a ferret and let it loose down a hole in the stable; it caught nothing, but its sharp rapacious face bewitched us both. He chided me for flinching when the huntsman smeared my face with fox gore after the kill. "What are you ducking for?" asked the glorious Miss Nelly Brown from the saddle of her huge hunter. "Didn't you know what happened to foxes when they were caught?"

"No," I said, and the crowd laughed, those on their great horses and those on foot. They thought I was a fool. It was true, I'd never thought of death but as something quick and simple, not that dismembering of the fox, the casting of the corpse to the hounds and award of mask and bush to novices like me after we'd had our faces daubed in the ritual of blooding. It wasn't altogether shocking. In a strict world, you could kill, couldn't you?

George also accused me of putting on airs when I left my name with the maid at a friend's house as Miss ———. Such lessons you don't forget. His comments were unmalicious, unbookish. They came out naturally, like water from a tap. About birds' nests, for example: in spite of what I'd read in boys' comics, it was wrong to take eggs. He didn't, and I was not to do so either. Some lads did, of course. I knew which lads he meant. Lads without shoes and without fear, lads with slabs of bread and strawberry jam, who swarmed past our house every morning on the way to school. If I was opening the gate for my father to back out into the road, they'd pour into the drive and battle over the shutting of the gate with its long iron bar, screaming and yelling like maniacs, jumping up and climbing over it and then opening it and escaping or running along the top of the high brick wall and leaping down the seven-foot drop to the pavement.

"Need whipping," said George, rescuing me.

"Why, George? They haven't done anything wrong."

"They'll steal the rowan berries next and the flowers as soon as you turn your back. Teacher whipped a lad when I wor at school, for stealing holly."

"How unfair!"

"No. It's fair. You've got to larn 'em."

The same boys swept out of school at close of the school day and overwhelmed my pony and me if we happened to be trotting past. Sticks and stones appeared from nowhere and fell like a storm on Dolly's poor flanks. "Ride 'im, cowboy!" they screamed as we tore down the middle of the road between two opposing streams of traffic. "Need beating," George grumbled, catching up and letting me through the gate into safety.

His principles, so much higher than my own, were matched, I thought, by his kindness. He didn't have to be kind, I knew that. Our friendship (if I may call it that) was all the odder because my mother was very particular about whom I knew. The discovery that George had other friends surprised me. Ted Toulson didn't seem to count because he was older than George. Toulson was a butcher who kept horses and rode to hounds. He had given me a few riding lessons on one of his ponies before Dolly came, and George and I occasionally met him in the fields and he would comment to George on my riding style; George would indignantly convey the criticism to me later.

Gunner was someone who set the whole notion of friendship on its head. He was a gardener who undertook to make something of the clay soil our garden was cursed with. I think my father was taken in by his talk of sweetpeas and carnations, flowers my father loved for their sweet scent, flowers that never prospered in our garden. I can't remember if Gunner managed to grow them, but I remember vividly how his presence alienated George. Snickers and chat rose from the greenhouse now, whistles and strange cries when the two males emerged, swaggering and laughing. Was Gunner "throwing his voice" as heroes did in boys' comics? No one explained. A far lonelier life began.

Corrupted perhaps by Gunner, George started acting up when my brother arrived home for the holidays. Life got so intense as to become oppressive. The boys' red faces and big pale hands and robust smelly presences delighted me. But Iain, my brother, inclined to my mother's point of view, as I have said. My glee over melting lead and shooting at tin cans must have struck him as out of hand. And when I talked of the paradise of the countryside as revealed by George, he yawned and went off on his bike, telling me not to come with him, or he hit a punch bag in the garage.

One rainy afternoon I was helping George groom the pony when to my joy Iain joined us. But somehow or other there was a challenge thrown out between them, and another and another, to do with strength, and with people who needed beating, to larn 'em. What was happening I wasn't sure and didn't wait to find out. My father and mother were reading by the fire in the sitting room when Iain came in and threw himself down in a chair, red in the face and groaning with rage. He refused to answer questions and presently my father, nonplussed, went off to afternoon surgery. I locked myself in the bathroom, extremely frightened, and swore I would never marry.

So those years drew to a close. I went to school in the village at last and had less time to go riding. Then one day I rode downhill too fast, Dolly stumbled, threw me over her head, and bloodied her knees. My father bound the knees with a new gummy bandage that kept the air out of the wounds and caused a dangerous accumulation of blood and debris. The pony became very ill. After he took off the bandage she recovered, but she had been weakened and had to be pensioned off to two old ladies who drove a trap. And presently I was sent off to boarding school to see to the manners business once and for all.

Back in Stockton on my second visit, holed up in the wretched hotel with its smell of air freshener, I sat by the telephone again and rang through the list of Bells I had procured at the post office. As in the morning I drew a blank. It was then that the word Kia-ora presented itself to my mind again. The receptionist on duty did not know that name. So I rang my one remaining friend from the old days in this neighborhood—a woman in her seventies now living in Liverpool. She'd come to Norton as the seventeen-year-old bride of an ICI man. She had fair hair in a chignon then, and looked like the goddess in Botticelli's *Birth of Venus*. She and my father had been in love and used to meet in the fields. She'd always been kind to me.

Yes, my friend said, she knew the name Kia-ora. She couldn't place it, but she knew who would be able to: Olive—Olive her maid who had married the milkman. (It was like her to have kept in touch with her maid. We had lost touch with ours and with George.)

So I called Olive and identified myself. To her, as to the people in the post office, there was nothing untoward in my looking George up. Unluckily she didn't know him. As for Kia-ora, it had been torn down a twelvemonth since. And worse, the kind voice went on, her husband the milkman had died, he who knew everybody. A whole archive had gone. Olive's voice became anguished, for me, for her husband, for George, for herself. "I'm not from here," she explained. She was from a pit village twenty miles away, another world.

It had been a great pleasure to send Dolly over grass, swerving down grassy tracks, mounting and sliding down banks, crashing over hedges, wading through becks. Mastery of action was sheer delight. Life without my pony lacked flavor. Now I drove about Stockton, a machine within a machine, down new roads knocked through slums a hundred or two hundred years old, past new buildings erected in their stead, and could see little but the back of the lorry in front of me. This was slavery, and mostly due to the increase in road traffic since my family lived there. It was true that poverty like that of the school urchins of old had disappeared. Well shod, well clothed, well grown, well housed, and huge, Stockton people looked pleasing enough, though it was not clear what interest the town offered them. The new architecture looked like a garish malignant growth on the old habitat, and many old buildings had been knocked down that more sophisticated towns would have paid a fortune to keep and restore.

In Norton Mrs. Hall answered neither telephone nor doorbell. So I went to the rectory, to look for the clergyman. If he knew nothing, I would try the police. The rectory itself, an enormous handsome house of Georgian brick, had, rather amazingly, turned itself into an opera school run by a descendant of Richard Wagner. As I was searching for the new rectory just behind it, a man coming out of the door of the old place told me that the opera school had failed and been replaced by a school of dance; and true enough, a certain thumping and calling and insistent music sounded in the distance, and through the garden gate crowds of girls appeared running to and fro. The new rectory was a cheap little bungalow. No one answered the two-tone chimes. I went to the church: it was locked. I was marching in exasperation back to the green when the man I had previously spoken to caught up and asked if he could help.

"Try the newsagent before you try the police. He could tell you where Kia-ora was too."

He watched me as I hesitated at the edge of the green, and pointed to the newsagent next to where the blacksmith had shod horses and repaired tubs and wheels with iron bands out in the open air. You used to hear his hammering as you walked up to the green, as his forge was on the raised and inhabited island in the middle. Trams used to run up to the terminus there with a clang of the bell, which sounded again the second before they set off again on the long journey back to Middlesbrough. Now all was quiet. The newsagent's was a big sunny shop with a surprising range of newspapers and magazines. I bought the *Times, Spectator, Private Eye,* and at last addressed one of the two women behind the counter. Did she know of a George Bell who had lived in the village most of his life? No, both women said in turn, thinking carefully. They appealed to the boss, who was setting out new issues of magazines.

He glanced at me and straightened up. He was in his mid-thirties, a smart, businesslike sort of fellow with his jacket off, showing his fresh blue shirt and navy tie with a little gold design on it. "I know a Chris Bell, he's a friend of mine." He paused. "He had a dad called George who lived with him. A little old man was George Bell. He died last year."

A little old man? A little old man, with a smart son like this newsagent? "Ah. I'm too late then." And I turned from the three alert faces, thanked them stiffly at the door, and walked out of the shop. How could I ask any more of them? After forty-odd years of neglect it was impudent enough to have pursued George as far as I had. What would I say to his son if we met, supposing him to be bright and up-to-the-minute like the newsagent? The important thing was that he had a son. Yet I did not think I could bear to look at him, another stranger, mystified, dragging out of his mind something his dad once said, ashamed, resenting my interference; or even proud of his dad, saying what a grand character he was:

how could I have told him honestly what I knew of George? I couldn't even pretend it was accurate. So I just left it at that and walked back to the car. As I'd felt with Mr. Hawes two years earlier, the facts—whatever they were—struck me as beside the point.

PORROCK

A cold religious air blew from the past. . . .

One morning we woke in Norton to find that the gale in the night had blown down the ten-foot wall at the end of the garden. Over the chunks of brick and mortar lay a vision of undreamed-of back gardens, with orchard trees and bushes and bean rows and sprout stalks divided by rickety fences. These gardens belonged to the terrace of Victorian houses next to the Methodist Chapel, which must have been built about the same time to accommodate the newly enfranchised classes of clerks and shopkeepers of the mid-nineteenth century. They were tall thin houses reaching up from a handkerchief-sized square of garden in front, with a railing and bushes separating them from the street, lace curtains at the front windows. After dusk that night I clambered over our fallen wall and crossed the gardens from end to end over the fences, as far as the single railway line which at night reverberated with trundling wagons and engine hoots. Apart from the thrill of trespassing unseen, I remember the astonishment of looking up each strip of garden to which it belonged, into the uncurtained, lit back room where a family sat at table having supper, or where children studied, women sewed, men read the newspaper. It was an altogether strange vision of intimacy, with each separation, each small world, each group of lives being carried on side by side, oblivious that it was being stared at. I returned with the sense of revelation, unable to understand the terrific importance of that set of separate worlds.

For in 1941, the second year of the war, our own interior world at Norton was dismantled, dragged out, exhibited, wrapped, packed, and presently set up in entirely different and unrecognizable surroundings, in the usual but unforeseen way. We were moving to Windsor, in the south, because my parents thought of bettering their lot. They believed that my father was overworking while his partner was marking time; his wife and little boys had gone for the duration to the Lake District to escape the bombs, and he would go at weekends to visit them, leaving his patients to my father, who was senior to him. And our house had become engulfed by a tide of council houses, in which people from the most miserable parts of Stockton were installed, their old houses demolished. So the green fields were gone, the traffic increased, and the big copper beech on the pavement outside the house was occasionally hung with boys. They were perfectly harmless boys, yet everyone except me considered them a threat.

"We've lived here twenty-two years," my mother told everyone when we prepared to leave, as if that were noteworthy. The house where we lived had been built in 1902 by a master builder called Foster, who made it square and solid, with stained glass in the stair window and the lobby, carved wooden panels in the hall, marble columns by the big sash windows, brass fittings on the heavy doors; drawing room with conservatory off it and furnace underneath; a double kitchen with pantry and larder, tiled in red and cream, with a black cooking and heating range; cellars with tiled table for keeping food cool, and wine racks for dozens of wine bottles (you could enter the cellars through a trapdoor in the hall floor if you despised the designated stairs, as Iain and I sometimes did on rainy days). There was also a living room in two parts with plenty of plaster swags of fruit and bunches of flowers on the ceiling and a device for communicating with the kitchen by means of a whistle, an earpiece, and a mouthpiece attached to a

flexible pipe that you spoke into. Outside in the garden were two
little summerhouses, one thatched and full of insects, the other a
proper little room with table and benches and a locker for board
games, footballs, cricket bats and balls and stumps; a washhouse
with fireplace and a vast copper for boiling clothes and drying dol-
lies overhead; stables with loft, a big greenhouse. Even now I can
feel my way past my parents' bedroom, down the staircase avoiding steps that creaked, holding the broad smooth banister, and
make my way into the warm kitchen, open the larder door, and
steal currants from a blue and white pottery jar with lid called
SUGAR.

The next house never lost its foreignness. It was a big 1930s
Tudor building with black and white pseudo-timbering over a
half story of brick. Some windows were leaded, and one room was
even paneled in dark oak, but the house was no more Tudor than
it was Gothic except in those special features. It is true that I was
allotted a room of my own for good instead of being made to mi-
grate from nursery to my parents' dressing room, to Iain's room
and back as my mother constantly renewed the possibilities of her
old house, but I had never minded that. In a way the shifts let me
get to know each of my bedrooms well. And now, pleasantly surprised at the view over the garden, I had inklings of what was
later to trouble me about the new town, that it was somehow ide-
alized, not the jumble that was Stockton and Norton, an organic
heap in the mutilated landscape of the North Country. The ideal-
ization in Windsor involved imitation, as of the Tudor style, to
make a rather snobbish statement, or at least a statement with a
lot of leisure about it. It didn't really make much difference to
day-to-day living, but it seemed humbug. Witness the doctor's
surgery and waiting room tacked on one end of the main house:
what was Tudor about them? You wouldn't have had Tudor in
dirty old Stockton. People would call it "stuck-up." My father

would have called it "stupid." "Stupid" was one of his favorite words. I might have called it "snobbish" by the time I left the district: silly snobbish, petty bourgeois. Such terms were becoming familiar.

So with the old things distributed throughout, the house still stayed strange, though my mother set to and polished and prettified till she was exhausted. No George, of course, no Nelly to cook and run the laundry, no Betty to keep the house. No pony, no dog. Outside the house, no friend, not even an acquaintance. Iain was now at Oxford. As for me, at sixteen, I'd compounded my isolation by deciding to leave school for good and work at home with tutors for an Oxford scholarship. I longed also to join the services when I was old enough and do my bit in the war effort. I hadn't the least idea of how lonely I would be, and in any case my feelings didn't matter when so many were being wounded and killed. Girls were irrelevant or seductive. As a girl I hid myself; people understood that, and were kind. So occasionally I struck out for myself.

Porrock was the first dog in our family that everyone thought of as mine. He was a small black and tan terrier, all curls, ravaged by fleas, who cost me five shillings at a door in a back street. He was promising from the start, overjoyed as he was to meet me and charmed to sit on my knee and be driven from his birthplace like a grandee. In two days he was housebroken. In three he learned his name. Porrock was an old detested nickname of my father's, abandoned after our move away from the exuberant silly man who thought such nicknames a form of endearment; he'd seen some resemblance between a movie character called Porrock and my father and blithely transferred the name from one to the other. My father thought the name better suited to the dog, and the dog learned to look up at the sound of it, searching for the source of my voice, which he duly discovered in my face high above. When he saw me smile, he'd curl back his ruched lips in imitation and reveal his tiny white teeth. So I would laugh and he'd wriggle for joy.

We went everywhere together. He learned to walk on a lead in hours; he loved learning what I had to teach. Because he was just a pup and tired easily, I taught him to sit in a basket on the front of my bike and be carried to places of long grass and wildflowers where I'd lie and read one of my prescribed books while he stumbled and bumbled to and fro and eventually came back to sleep with his small hard head on my foot. For a long time—for the year and a half between my leaving school and entering university—Porrock was my only friend.

In our old town there appeared to be two sorts of people—the industrial working class and the rest in ascendancy. In Windsor we were the working class and there appeared to be three lots set over us: the court, who lived in the castle, the clergy of St. George's Chapel in the castle precinct, and the Guards in their barracks nearby. My mother seemed not to understand. She remembered going to Norton as a bride in 1919 when she and my father set up house and everybody in the ascendancy called on her and left cards and invited them to dinner. So every afternoon, freshly made up, the house tidied, she waited for people to call on her, and none did. It is not hard to see why. France had fallen, invasion threatened, U-boats sank terrifying numbers of merchantmen, bombs flattened the East End of London, the British army fell back across North Africa, the Japanese took Singapore. But there was a kinder tradition in the north that the disintegration of convention did not disturb and that hasn't disappeared even yet, and she looked for it in the soft atmosphere of the south as the war raged on even as you might look for a blue sky in summer. She was so aware of the danger that she'd booked passage on a ship for Australia for herself and me in 1940, meaning to leave me with her family there and return to England. (I'd refused to go.) But she expected people to behave in a certain fundamental way even

in extremis. When people didn't call on her in Windsor she simply changed her tactic, being a witty and resourceful woman and
able to attract in other ways, and bridge players began to crop up
like mushrooms in her friendly soil, not of the court, or the clergy,
or the Guards, it is true, but decent enough, and serious enough
too, I daresay, though they played cards while half the world
burned. My father quickly got to know the medical fraternity and
became acquainted at the hospital. My brother went on being a
medical student. I alone felt the need to speak to the dog.

Something was wrong with me. In the effort to get to grips
with it, I wrote to a canon of Winchester Cathedral whom I had
met. I told him that after I'd been thoroughly convinced of His
existence, God had become a blank, no more than a wall to Whom
I prayed without the slightest sense of a quickening in response.
The canon wrote back to say that I was entering the second stage
of conversion, in which God appears to withdraw from the beloved. But there is no love in me, I replied by the next post: not
for God, or parents, or country. I didn't feel for anyone except my
dog. The canon sent me C. S. Lewis's *Screwtape Letters* and said
that I needed to talk to someone nearer at hand. He offered to introduce me to a canon of St. George's Chapel in the castle: at
which I broke off the correspondence in panic. The exchange of
letters had taken place in secret, the postman being intercepted at
the gate, all traces of my passionate and possibly romantic activity
being hidden under the floorboards of my bedroom. I could not
make my needs known, because that would involve talking about
God with my parents, who did not go to church. When I was
eleven they had sent me to a school conducted on strictly Christian principles, a delightful place that nevertheless made religion a
taboo subject at home. That's to say, I could make my parents
laugh by describing the Wellington boots that the chaplain wore
under his cassock, but when I told of a teacher who became a missionary to the people of Melanesia in the Pacific and another who
became a nun, they grew alarmed. The actual teaching of Christ

they appeared to assume was right; on the other hand, the forms roused doubt. How, not what, mattered. Efforts to question or receive reassurance were knocked on the head.

Then there was the girl, slightly older than me, who drove me out in her dogcart on two or three occasions and once arranged a party for my brother and me to attend a local dance with her and a partner. The prospect as it drew nearer caused me to fake a violent illness. My brother was angry, my parents puzzled.

"In our life alone does Nature live," wrote Coleridge, and when I read his words, prescribed as they were, and therefore hallowed, I wondered what Nature lived in me, so far from the world I had lost. Even now my friends in the north would be preparing work in the sixth form, talking and arguing and attitudinizing, while I went unsteadily on by myself, unsure and unsupported except by a puppy. Of my old dense life, barely anything remained. Even my physique had changed. To look at, I was now a woman. But it felt odd to be inside that woman, housed in ridiculous splendor when I wanted something simple. Coleridge, the man of chaos, offered a revelation of how to think in orderly fashion. "Not only this," I told Porrock, "but also that. Moreover. Ever yet. Let me venture to add. In the first place. In the second. A third class of circumstance." My understanding crept sideways like a crab. Suddenly it would arrive, and without a process of thought. I did not think. I jumped. I landed. I fell over. Coleridge showed me how to appreciate at least some of the ways by which one arrives at an opinion, even retrospectively. Once a process of understanding is consciously gone through, the pattern becomes easier to repeat. So I began, quite timidly, to learn.

My schooling hitherto had been mechanical, and so it continued to be in Latin studies until I made some progress. It was otherwise from the start in English, where I began to see the skeleton under the flesh of words, and saw how certain writers manipulated the skeleton, and how the genius of language mysteriously affected us, as figures in a dance affect us differently when performed by different dancers. No one had previously talked to me about art, and no one gave the name of art to these considerations even now, but my new tutors talked frankly and openly and critically about them as if they were talking about food and drink, and smiled at me with great goodwill and a great excitement breathed over me as if puffed from the mouth of Apollo himself.

For escape I walked in Windsor Great Park. An avenue bordered by a double line of lime trees ran from the southern gate of the castle three miles to an opposing hill on which there was an immense statue of a toga'd Roman on horseback, crowned with a laurel wreath and with a hand extended benevolently over the land. The plinth bore an inscription in Latin and declared that George IV put up the statue to his father, George III—fat Prinny put it up to his poor mad father. How ludicrous the statue was compared with the classical figures in lead that I had seen dotted about the eighteenth-century parks of Studley and Duncombe in Yorkshire, which weren't out to dominate or impress so much as to embellish the landscape. In those parks little Grecian temples worked in the same way at the end of vistas. You could sit by one of the columns and eat a sandwich and the landscape quietly went to work on you. It was not very different from examining a poem by Wordsworth, letting it work and then seeing how it worked. The gross statue of the king was of a lower order altogether, and I allied it with the weight of gentility in Windsor compared with the mixture of frankness and tolerance in Norton, where it seemed to me that nearly everyone tried to avoid coarseness or "commonness" and condemned the "cheeky," whether they were high or low.

As I walked, the dog rabbited ahead. The country was very fine, though for me it lacked the power and reticence of the North Country. A huge castle, flowers everywhere: not my taste. Nor was the lassitude of the Thames Valley. Coleridge said, "In looking at objects of nature, I seem rather to be seeking, as it were asking, a symbolic language for something within me." That was it. And:

"To see is only a language." I looked about me with anguish at the objects of nature: they were indifferent to whether I lived or died, whereas I cared passionately for them. To love and be loved, man to woman, woman to man, must be perfect. I was only slowly associating such perfection with my huge physical desire. Love in the movies had absolutely nothing to do with my own experience, or with those of the other moviegoers, any more than the looks of the actors had anything to do with the looks of people on the street.

"Give us a smile, bonny lass," said the young sentry in a sweet Geordie voice as I walked past pretending to be invisible. I was pushing my thoughts in the wrong direction. So I paused and grew visible. "I'll talk on the way back, because I'm late," I said, and made sure to go home another way.

Meanwhile Porrock grew. He'd learned to catch a ball in midair, and proceeding from that to toss the ball up for himself with a jerk of the head and to leap up and catch it. This he'd do over and over, jumping and twisting like an acrobat. I'd look out of the window and see him at it even when there was no one outside to take any notice. He'd amuse himself too by hurling himself into my arms as I walked up, so I'd have to catch him. The memory of that skinny, awkward little body with its thrusting legs is still marvelously with me.

I used to take the double-decker bus into town to shop for my mother, and Porrock would go with me, scrambling up the steep stairs to the top deck. When I came back, laden with groceries, I let Porrock off the lead so I'd have one hand free to grasp the rail, the other hauling the loot; Porrock managed perfectly well to keep his balance in the jerking and cavorting of the bus on the empty streets of those days. In fact he managed so well that sometimes he took it into his head to go into town by bus without me, hanging about at the bus stop and hopping on with people and letting himself off at the High Street before the conductor could find out whom he belonged to. So I was told by those who'd witnessed this extraordinary performance. I was told too that he visited butcher's shops and made off with scraps of bone or gristle. He would also drop in on various well-meaning householders who would feed him and make him welcome with tidbits nicer than the regular stuff I gave him at home. Eventually he would come back by himself and resume a common dog's life.

"It's a pity he's so damn ugly," said Iain after Porrock had reached maturity. "He isn't a bad dog, as dogs go." Iain preferred cats. In recent memory, in the lifetime of our previous dog, an unlikable Sealyham, we had nearly come to blows. The dog barked at the cat and made to steal the cat's food. So Iain booted the dog and I screamed and squared up to him like a boxer. For two pins I would have hit him. "Look at her! She thinks she's a man!" he jeered to the audience of my mother. But I wasn't man enough to hit him. For Porrock, the cat was negligible, which in our household, where emotions ran high, was a blessing.

For months these high-running emotions became directed at Iain, who kept failing his exams. He failed anatomy and physiology three or four times and later midwifery, obstetrics and gynecology, surgery, and all the other branches of medicine you can think of. Every time failure was announced my father would roar and bury his head in his hands and ask aloud where the money was going to come from to finance another go. Medicine was hard, and Iain should work at it hard instead of reading Proust or fooling about learning to dance or listening to opera on scratchy expensive records. How ironic it was, my father said, that as a young man he dreamed that his baby son would grow up to be a famous surgeon and play rugger for Scotland. What a hope! He couldn't even pass anatomy! Then we'd all go around with long faces for a week, until we began to think of something else and cheered up.

As far as my mother was concerned, emotion expended itself in enormous measure on domesticities. She made clear that the two or three hours a day I'd mentally allotted to her were not enough. She said that the house was falling into filth and decay, the ironing overflowed the laundry baskets, the brasses were dull, the shopping had to be done, food provided, dishes put away, the lawn to be mowed, the windows washed. None of these imperatives struck me as important. There was a war on, I pointed out. People were killing each other on various battlefields and some were bombing civilian populations. Planes droned overhead every night, sometimes dropping their bombs so the house trembled and one's ears cut out. In any case, housework bored me to death. "I don't know what's wrong with you," said my mother in utter bewilderment. "You always have your nose in a book. Let me tell you something: men don't like bookish women."

I wrote to my old school friends describing the scene. My mother lived in a frenzy, I said, preparing for visitors who never called, while my father behaved like a god whom nobody prayed to.

My mother intercepted these letters and read them. "If I'd written letters like that when I was your age, I'd have been *beaten*."

In the midst of these domestic confusions, Cousin Mary telephoned to say that she and her husband, Hector, were in London on business and she'd like to call on us the next day. My father happened to answer the phone. By this time my mother and Mary's mother—my father's sister—no longer spoke to each other. My mother therefore decided that she would not be at home to Cousin Mary either. So as the time of the visit drew near, my mother tidied the already tidy house and withdrew upstairs, forcing me to go with her. We watched from a bedroom window as a taxi drew up and a good-looking woman in a trim navy suit approached the front door. After a cup of tea with my father she crunched away over the gravel and went off in another taxi.

"What is this farce?" I demanded. I would have liked to meet Cousin Mary again. At five or six I had been a bridesmaid at her wedding in Edinburgh, where there had been more kilts than I could count, and she gave me some pretty beads. "Little do you know," said my mother, keeping me by the window in case Mary returned unexpectedly. "Your cousin is not a nice woman."

"I don't see why you have to pretend you're not here."

"Little do you know."

"Tell me then."

"You shouldn't speak to me like that. One day you'll understand."

"Understand what?"

"Never you mind."

"What a farce this is you lead."

Presently the domestic pressures created by my mother met my resistance head-on. "I don't know what you're crying for," she said. "I'm the one who should be crying."

They sent me off to stay with a friend in Yorkshire for a few days. When I came back I bought a charming black and white rabbit to fill a gap not entirely stopped by Porrock the dog. The rabbit escaped from the hutch I built him, and while he was eating cabbages on a neighboring allotment, the allotment holder cornered him and hit him with a stick. The rabbit was squatting by the cabbages unresisting when I was summoned to fetch him, and soon after I carried him back in the hutch he shut his eyes and died. But before natural death intervened, the desire to kill him with my two hands swept over me. I itched to strangle him, to throw his body on the ground and break its bones. Later my mother came to the door of my room and began to complain. "Go away!" I screamed at the top of my voice. My father came and sat on my bed and listened to me tell him between wild sobs how much I hated her. My mother stood at the door with a half smile. She said she knew I didn't mean it. "I do mean it!" I shouted, so she left.

"What's brought this on?" asked my father. "Is it some man?" A startling thought. A young solicitor I'd talked to at the bus stop had asked me for a drink in a pub, but I'd not gone, and a handsome young sailor had chatted me up on a train, but I'd not agreed to meet him again either. "You're much more reasonable than your mother," observed my father, still sitting by me on the bed.

A huge understatement, I thought, flattered all the same.

"You know, you have to put yourself in her shoes," he added.

"Why? She doesn't put herself in mine."

"No. I don't think she ever went to school, you know."

The jump in reasoning brought me up short, and normally I would have leaped on him for it, and the conversation would have ended. But now I needed him, and I listened closely. He said that my grandfather did not believe in women's education.

"So she doesn't either," I said.

She wouldn't talk about it, he said. The grandfather was a difficult old man. "I've always held it against your grandfather that he never gave us a penny when we got married. He's a rich man, and we had nothing. Not a penny did he give us."

He spoke with feeling and I understood that he was on my side, and felt immensely cheered.

"She's a very brave woman, your mother."

Did he mean that she had married against her father's wishes and was brave to do so?

In 1917, he went on, she left her home in Sydney to volunteer as a nurse with the Australian troops, with not the slightest idea of the hardships she was to undergo. Had I seen her medals?

I had rescued them from the bin where she'd thrown them more than once: war decorations with important grosgrain ribbons in moiré reds and blues dangling from a clasp, in a leather box from Spink of Piccadilly, like a soldier's. "She was very brave."

But never went to school. Must have had a governess. Probably shared the governess with half a dozen sisters. Wrote a beautiful hand, full of character. Was amazingly good at mental arithmetic. Could make my brother laugh till he cried. Sang well. Hadn't a clue about history. Didn't know the Bible, didn't think about it. Could recite Wolsey's speech from *Henry VIII*: "Cromwell, I charge thee, fling away ambition: / By that sin fell the angels. . . ." Sewed beautifully. Adored her husband. What a pain my mother was, rich man's daughter, immensely loving and lovable and unpredictable, sexy obviously and frigid probably. I much preferred my father. I think everyone did. She insisted on his perfection too. However, he was devoted to her.

These days I have extra knowledge of her, now that it is too late. I'm aware of her departure from Melbourne in June 1917, on a troopship bound for Cairo. The horrors of Gallipoli, where so many Australian troops were slaughtered, had roused my grandfather to lament that he had no son to send to the war. So she'd said, with dreadful bravado, that she would be his son, and she volunteered as a nurse to go with a batch of troops from Melbourne. Her nursing unit was eventually dispatched to Salonika in northern Greece, where in Kalamaria, a hut hospital that operated under appalling conditions of cold and wet in winter and scorching malarial heat in summer, she met my father (as I've said); he was a major in the Royal Army Medical Corps attached to the Argyll and Sutherland Highlanders. He had been on a hospital ship off Gallipoli. In late 1918 she sailed from Alexandria to England to marry him. "When she looked down from the deck of the troopship at Tilbury," an old cousin wrote to me recently, "she saw your father waiting on the dock and was shocked. Out of his major's uniform, wearing a mean suit, he didn't look worth it. She thought she couldn't possibly marry him. She felt nothing for him." What in the world had she done, giving up her home, the family of sisters and the powerful old father, and her old fiancé, who became famous as a cartoonist, the creator of a character called Ginger Meigs. I know him as the donor of a handsome traveling clock which she kept by her bed always. She must have had it in her luggage at her moment of doubt. And it was probably raining. Orderlies carried her trunk ashore, she walked down the gangplank, she met my father in his mean suit and they embraced, and they went off and got married.

She didn't return to Sydney for ten years, when my brother was

seven and I was four. I don't remember much of the long visit except the end of it, when my brother and I stood beside her on the
deck of the ship that was to take us back to England. Below us on
the quay stood Clare, the most dear to her of all her ten sisters. My
mother pressed rolls of paper streamers into our hands and told us
to hold one end and fling the rolls unraveling and spiraling down
to the quay far below, which we did, and the steamer drew away
from the dock and the streamers parted and fell lifelessly down the
ship's side or draped the quay and sagged into the water, while the
hooters frightened us all to death. The sisters never saw each other
again.

The day after my conversation with my father I painted a wall
of my room with huge figures dancing in a landscape of tall thin
poplars and rounded busty hills. It astonished me to see how sexual the painting was.

Within a few months my mother had painted it out.

We all leaned formally on the idea of compassion, especially because none of us, with the exception of my father, was compassionate. Porrock, for example, came in for a great deal of verbal
abuse because he was ugly and good-natured. Kind words came
from my father, probably because he was the only member of the
household who lived his life in composed and dedicated fashion.
As he'd always rushed, his constant rushing didn't suggest to me
that he was under a strain. Just as in the old days, I used to go
with him when he paid a few visits on a Sunday morning; I sat in
the car with Porrock while he dived into various houses to see how
the sicker patients were doing. The streets were better kept, the
gardens were neater, the houses really finer than the ones I'd grown
up seeing, and there were no foundries or ironworks or men hanging round street corners waiting for the pubs to open, no slums, in
fact, and the river had walks along it and flowering trees, not abandoned staithes and crumbled wharves. My father should have been
happier, and perhaps he was; he kept his own counsel about happiness. In his book, hard work brought its own rewards. He used

to hum or whistle to cheer himself along, and this device among others, and his willfully sunny nature, made me think he was someone to laugh at as well as be fond of, and my brother and I used to get hysterical at his simplicity. One Sunday the small Morris my father used to visit his patients broke down half a mile from home, and we decided to haul it to the house with the help of the bigger car he kept in the garage. There was a thick rope somewhere in the garden shed. I spied it behind a heap of tools, the mower, the roller, flowerpots, string, netting, and my father—a great strong man—reached in and began to haul the rope out in powerful heaves. It wasn't a clever thing to do. The smaller objects flew about, the flowerpots smashed, the mower fell over, the rope came out inch by inch. My father exerted more and more brute strength: the shed came away from the wall and tottered. Terrible rending noises ensued. At any moment the window would pop out and shatter and the roof and walls slide down like playing cards, one on top of the other. At last the rope came free and my father staggered back with it in his hand. Porrock had long ago fled into the house. I looked at the debris of the shed and then at my father, trying to grasp what was happening. "Sorry," he said, panting and surveying the damage. By the time we'd got the other car out and hauled the Morris home, he was again calm and humming one of his two tunes, "My Blue Heaven" and a Gaelic song that goes:

Hoo-roo my nut-brown maiden,
Hoo-roo my nut-brown maiden,
Hoo-roo, roo, maiden, you're the maid for me.

The words made me blush, they were so silly, and yet so sweet, and the tune was pretty. The oddity of my adorable father filled me with misgiving. Why, for example, didn't he relieve his expenses by giving up smoking? "Cigarettes cost you a fortune. Think how rich you'd be without them."

"True," he'd admit, and light up. Often he regretted how he'd sold his stocks and shares on the outbreak of war. Sometimes I think he also regretted leaving his huge working-class practice in the north for the small middle-class one in the south. The Stockton practice provided a sure and steady income, and it was a two-man practice. In Windsor he worked alone and shouldered the responsibilities alone. Certainly the National Health Service in Stockton would have paid him well by his large register of patients when it was introduced after the war, and he had a commitment to poor people that would have been amply rewarded there.

He was so hard pressed financially at one time that he and my mother took to not declaring all their few assets for taxation (causing themselves even further anxiety). My mother confessed to me once that they buried some money in a pot in the garden in order to avoid a declaration of income to tax inspectors, until the tax inspectors pressed them so hard that they had to own up and get a spade and unearth the pot. Not that there would be much in it. But this was after the introduction of very high income tax by the Labour government after the war in order to pay for that war.

Well, said the tax inspectors, they'd never seen anything like that pot in the garden. My mother laughed triumphantly as she told me, and I listened amazed and ashamed. The business was over, they'd paid up and been forgiven, but what characters they were, her husband and herself: that was the bit of story she enjoyed.

Those were exceptional times, though passionate indignation is the norm in families and exceptional times merely raise the temperature. The war grumbled away in the near distance like the weather, or at worst a dragon that occasionally bothered the neighborhood. We didn't think crisply about it, any more than we thought about fate. And yet we considered each other's conduct. If only one behaved better! If only one were kinder! If only we had more fun and weren't so glum! "You're all so glum!" my mother said repeatedly. "How I laughed as a girl! All my sisters laughed their way through life."

A depressing thought. Only Porrock was jolly, and she disliked the dog for so effortlessly displaying the cheerfulness she demanded of us.

The illogicalities of her train of thought were set off by my own routine. Twice a week I biked three or four miles for a session with my Latin tutor, which was followed in a different part of the town by a session with my English tutor. There should have been a French tutor also, but he fell away after a couple of meetings, bidding me study by myself. The Latin and English tutors were much more conscientious and demanded swathes of material— prepared texts, unseens, essays, commentaries. I knew I hadn't the slightest chance of a scholarship.

"What is the point of Latin?" my mother asked.

"I like it," I said, and my father, with authority, said, "Wonderful training for the mind." Ludicrous assumption. My mind was netted by the language into which I'd blithely flown. And somehow or other I was frightened that I'd be exposed as a fraud when the great moment of the scholarship and entrance exam came along. My fondness for Latin was like a fondness for sweets. I was wasting my father's money. What hard work those fourteen months at home were! We had few books at home and I had no book allowance. Nor was there a decent public library in Windsor. I remember thirty-minute bus rides to Slough Public Library to read contemporary writing: Auden, Isherwood, MacNeice, Ivy Compton-Burnett, Henry Green. The bus passed through Eton, and it is tempting to depict resentment at how well off the Eton boys were in comparison, with their rich libraries and their hosts of masters; but it did not occur to me at the time to think poorly of my situation. I did not see how I could learn any better than under my excellent tutors, who insisted principally on close study, with the library at Slough providing what breadth it could. I've never found a substitute for that primary wrestling with the subject that I was forced to undergo, and subsequently write about, regardless of whether I cared for the subject or not, or had anything to say about it.

The only real pleasure of my life was my relationship with Porrock, who would dash with me alongside the bike as I tore to Latin and back to English, waiting for me in the hour-long sessions, guarding the bike, enchanted when I emerged with my file of papers, barking with joy at the prospect of the next lap, the race with me along the pavements till I finally swerved into the graveled drive of our house with him skidding beside me.

I thought a lot about morality in those days, and the morality of loving a dog more than my family was one of the many issues that gave me pause.

I took the Oxford exams in the family drawing room with a defrocked clergyman as my invigilator. He was one of my father's patients, a thin, harsh, unfinished man who'd run off with someone's wife and now lived with her in sin. He sat on the sofa and read while I scribbled at a card table. The exams stretched over three or four days, at the rate of a paper in the morning and another one in the afternoon. One was an essay, which my clergyman read through when time was up. He shook his head: "No, no. You can't say that. It's rubbish. Go on, do it again. Go on. It's all right. Don't worry about the time. I'm not going to say anything." I'd written for all the time allowed and said everything I wanted to say about simplicity, the subject I'd chosen for its appeal in a confusing world. The clergyman made me sick because he assumed he was my superior and had better judgment. I was tired of not being taken seriously. It was clear that the man was unwise as well as dishonest. So I declined his offer, letting him cluck in dismay.

My essay was the best thing I did. It didn't win me a scholarship, but they offered me a place at Somerville. (I had applied to Somerville alone, because it was the only women's college that was secular, and admitted women of all creeds or, like me, of no creed yet.)

My father said: "I don't know if I can afford to pay for more than one year, but at least you'll be able to say that you've been to Oxford." So he prized what I prized? And yet he'd have me throw it away? Why couldn't he throw the house away, or the garden, or a car?

At this juncture, when the end to my time at home was in sight, something happened to Porrock that changed him. It was late spring and the front door stood open on the graveled circle inside the gates to the garden. One morning he came through it howling and yelping, tore up the stairs as I was going down, passed me, and disappeared into the farthest bedroom, where I found him under a bed. When I put a hand out, he showed his teeth. Later, unable to fathom what had happened, I dragged him out in spite of the bared teeth. He was quite rigid but had no sores or contusions. Much later, he crept downstairs and drank from his water dish, but he wasn't his old self and took no notice of me. The next day he went out on the road and raced after a car and tried to bite its tires as they spun by, so I suppose he'd been hit by a car previously and was trying to punish the aggressor. I had to keep him on a lead, because he became insatiable in his pursuit of wheels. Only gradually did he come back to normal. We went out together on the bike, with him sitting in the basket in the old way or running on a lead beside me, but several times without warning he yanked the lead out of my hands and tore after another bike, dangerously snapping at the feet of the cyclist, or after a car, yelping hysterically all the while and traveling like the wind. Once a car stopped and the driver got out and told me off for keeping such a dangerous animal. Yet on the whole, in spite of such incidents, I thought I was checking this mad new tendency and believed it would wear itself out with kind handling. At the same time something told me that I'd let Porrock down and he wouldn't change back into the innocent creature he'd been. He was only a dog. You could not expect him to go to town on a bus or steal from the butcher's or walk alone into people's houses for a meal or wander down the street by himself without things going wrong. The human world wasn't geared to him. Even the dog world wasn't geared to him; he was much too intelligent to be content with its smells and meals and grooming rituals. If he were only a dog he wouldn't teach himself to play his ball game, or to smile at me with bared teeth.

So what was I to think? I didn't think. My mind had shifted away from him, as his had shifted away from me.

When I came down from the university at the end of my first term, I looked forward to the old scene: my parents, my brother, my dog. But Porrock was not there to meet me. "We had him put down," my mother said. "That business of chasing after traffic got too much for me. There was no one to look after him."

I remember not replying. A reply would not have been adequate, it would have been hurtful, and it was too late. Simplicity had arrived, like a razor. Porrock didn't belong in the house except through me, and I'd gone away. Therefore they felt free to kill him off. I had used him, and his usefulness was over. My mother said I would be thinking of other things now, and it was perfectly true, my world had become fascinating and full of friends and talk and opinion in which Porrock had no place. And yet he was the halfway point between, on the one hand, the baffling world of green places that did not respond to me, and, on the other, the world of ideas. But that was not quite right. There should have been a place for him, and I should have found it, and not given up till I'd found it. "You must respect the animal," my father said once when I was younger and had dressed an earlier dog in a bonnet. So I respected Porrock. He had his own life, and it impinged on mine. He was the fur, the lick of the tongue, the heavy sigh with which he'd collapse beside me before going to sleep, the desire for physical companionship expressed by pushing against me. We were two animals with an animal world in common but a generic barrier between us. Or we were two kin souls if there is a world of souls, as I sometimes think there is.

Many years later I reminded my mother of how Porrock used to throw balls up into the air for himself to catch on the way down. I laughed with delight at the memory, but my mother looked puzzled. Then she remembered who Porrock was. "Fancy your remembering that. After all this time." Her voice was full of reproach.

LOOKING FOR HEROES

Time hath, my lord, a wallet at his back,
Wherein he puts alms for oblivion,
A great-siz'd monster of ingratitudes. . . .

Troilus and Cressida

I went up to the university fresh and green as a salad. "I'm glad you are not a burnt offering," my tutor said. When I looked round, however, and took in those who weren't as green as myself, I envied people who had been subjected to more intellectual heat. It was clear that my schooling had been slack and genteel and girly until the home tutors of the last eighteen months.

My parents had wished the best for me, and after the early governess and two years at a good day school for boys and girls, they had decided when I was eleven years old that the best was femininity. Suddenly I could no longer race Patrick Anderson down the paths of the day school, or compete with David Merson at Latin, or act the part of Robin Hood when the boy actor caught measles. I was sent off to the charming boarding school at Duncombe Park in North Yorkshire where from a world of large and exciting uncertainties I passed into one of little certainties and small scope. There I was made to study courtesy, piety, music, sewing, dancing, deportment, and to repeat the schooling of the previous two years. Its great benefit was its scene. The school lay in a secluded landscape garden, made in the beginnings of the eighteenth century and one of the earliest in England. It lies on level ground situated high over limestone cliffs. You can look down on the valley of the little river Rye that loops and ripples through grass and rocks and big trees, where sheep and cattle roam, and once, when I was there, herds of red deer and fallow deer roamed. It is still one of the loveliest places I've ever seen, a Forest of Arden where we lived in romantic exile from the industrial world. It worked insidiously, infusing the scenery with godliness and the notion of privilege, which I knew, going home to Norton, I'd no right to. Nevertheless I liked the idea of boarding school, and was as naughty as possible in the boys' school tradition that I'd learned from my brother's school stories, walking on the roof on summer nights by creeping out of the attics, carving my initials on pianos and even those of a friend whom I wanted to be in my boys' world with me. She couldn't believe I'd acted without malice, and of course my fantasies were too complicated to explain when the crime was discovered and she was accused of vandalism. Opinions were not tolerated there, opposition was suppressed. Some of us learned silence and stealth and cunning.

At thirteen I won a scholarship to a thoroughly bad school nearby where the girls were directed to achievements well within their power. When I was fifteen my brother went to Oxford and suggested I go there too in time. The headmistress asked why. Others on the staff told me simply that it was impossibly hard to get into. Easier the University of Leeds, so much handier.

I'd like the best, I said. Oxford's the best.

Not necessarily, said the headmistress, a massive figure in cardigans who had me down as someone good at games.

I was the first in that school to win a place at Oxford. Of course it was indeed hard to enter then: one place for a woman for every eight places for men, when only five percent of the country as a whole went to university. And it was hard to face down the contempt many felt in the north for clever women or hardworking women or women who wanted what their brothers had. Yet the school fell in my esteem most of all over its self-righteous mediocrity. For I wasn't very clever. I just wanted and was prepared to work hard for something more interesting than the nice husband, the pretty suburban house, the middle-class household, the emptiness, the Emma Bovarydom that the school held out as prizes to its prettiest, most charming girls.

Once in the university I found myself missing the two sixth-form years in school when I'd have been part of a little intellectual community that debated the things that bothered me in the isolation of home and that broadened its horizons in general study. Never mind, I might catch up if I tried. Unfortunately I didn't try, I had a good time instead. I made good friends, went to the theater and the cinema, enrolled in dramatic societies, philosophical societies, poetry societies, talked and listened, learned to drink and smoke, went punting on the river. As for the academic work demanded in that alarming present of long ago, I began to practice the art of writing an essay once or twice a week on the prescribed literature, without necessary recourse to the bulk of scholarship on the subject, without bibliography, footnotes, or other scholarly apparatus, but showing how it engaged the reader. I didn't get far with the art, because it is an art, and I didn't then take enough pains to develop it. It was the heart of the Oxford education, and I didn't profit from it for some time. My tutor was austere, I was childishly shy. Two lots down.

The war meantime demanded more than my minimum as justification for not serving in the forces. It is curious how a great demand is more often answered by apathy than by the heroic. So better join the forces and be useful now rather than in some hypothetical future, I thought. At that point it looked as though the wars would go on for years. When they were over, I'd return. In fact the war in Europe was drawing to a close when I went down from Oxford after a year and joined the Women's Royal Naval Service as a driver.

———

After training I was posted to a holding depot at Chatham in Kent and then to Newton Ferrers outside Plymouth, over three hundred miles away, where I'd learn my final destination. Contrary to all reason and information, I became convinced that this destination would prove to be Italy or perhaps India and that I might not be back for years. Puffed with apprehension, therefore, I telephoned my mother to meet me at Paddington and say goodbye. She dropped her eternal housework and came up, mystified, on the noon train. The train I'd been ordered to catch went off without me, and we sat in the station buffet for hours among servicemen and -women and mountains of kit bags. It was hard to think of anything to say. When finally she said goodbye and I boarded the next train for Plymouth, it crawled out of the station and stopped dead. After half an hour it set off again west in a series of jolts, little runs, and blasts of power.

The bathos of our parting hit hard. I did not mean to copy my mother's departure for her war in 1917, only to show fondness in the midst of my usual irritation, doing the right thing by her, volunteering just as she'd volunteered, being I hoped with the lowest of the low—anything to be unprivileged, anything to help win the war, anything to cope. I wanted to do the very humblest tasks, eat crusts, drink water, like other people. Under these unworked-out determinations lay possible salvation. On another level I suspected that my contradictions and incongruities didn't make much sense, and that my mother probably would not have cared even if she acknowledged them. Life for her was straightforward: there was a right way and a wrong way, and she was not afflicted with self-doubt. Nor, lucky as I was, should I be. Our differences were important, and irreconcilable, but I wanted to make it clear that I was determined.

The wretched train reached Plymouth at midnight. The packed corridors and compartments emptied out, the station exits jammed, and suddenly everyone had gone. The engine expired in tremendous clouds of steam. Someone took me by the arm and pointed me in the direction of the YWCA through blackness like the bottom of a swamp. I slung my luggage on one shoulder like a sailor and spread a hand along gritty brick walls and groped my way forward, calling out for help when someone approached, not understanding that I saw less at night than most people. At last the dim sign showed over a door. Two women opened up, gave me hot milk, and watched me drink it; leaning forward absorbed, their elbows on the table, as if I were a small child. In the morning a lorry took me to Newton Ferrers, the holding depot, where I found that I was of course not going abroad but to a Fleet Air Arm station in Dorset, for which I took a train back one hundred miles in the direction of London. I found myself at an airfield near Henstridge, a six-house village in a muddle of lanes. Signposts had been taken down everywhere at the first threat of invasion several years before and nowhere did you see the name of the village in letters. Did it merit a name, poor Henstridge? Petrol was so severely rationed that there wasn't much traffic, and few people drove by who might have been ready to take Henstridge into account. It was hard to see any original cause for the village, such as a bridge or a crossroads. And perhaps that let everyone off the hook. The airfield was made up of a huge flat grassy expanse crossed by landing strips and encircled by a perimeter track. There was a control tower, hangars of various sizes more or less camouflaged with grass sods, a bunch of huts where the day-to-day administration went on, a farmhouse where the captain lived, and two camps of Nissen huts, A and B, a mile apart, where personnel slept and messed. The business of the station was to train pilots for the Fleet Air Arm. As far as I know, they came with the rudiments of flying and added refinements such as the art of precise landing and taking off which they'd have to employ on aircraft carriers pitching in the sea. The fliers' world was entire to itself, with its own protocol, its own language, its own jokes. The tone was set by the aircrews, who thought life was ludicrous. Like the other drivers, I used their catchphrases and imitated their attitudes in a straight snobbery that the regular sailors resented. The student airmen were very young. Wrens spoke of the occasional one who lost his nerve on a solo flight and flew blindly about until talked down by his instructor. Another managed to fly into a hillside soon after I arrived at the base. Very green myself, I drove a salvage crew to the site to recover the body. It seemed a perfectly ordinary thing to do, to fly your aircraft into a hillside and die and be dug out by men in fireproof suits and put in a bag that a Wren would drive back to the base. Day after day other planes taxied slowly round the perimeter track and one after the other took off, one after the other they landed, new batches of student pilots coming as others went. The drivers transported them, just as they transported the girls who prepared the parachutes, the catering officer who went to market and neighboring farms to pick up supplies, officers going on duty to various functions. They met personnel at the railway station and took others to catch trains. They took observers to observation posts on the hillsides miles away. They shuttled endlessly between A camp and B camp.

Between jobs the cast of Wren drivers, seven or so in number, stood on call in a large hut in the Transport Section. They seemed to have known each other for years, endlessly gossiping and laughing, given to placing bets with Percy the chief mechanic on the races at Wincanton, making jokes, teasing, carrying on long conversations on the telephone with their boyfriends in other parts of the station. To my disappointment and relief I couldn't say any of them were vulgar. They seemed sixth formers of some pleasant undemanding school, from the powerful Eleanor who spoke undiluted cockney, and Elizabeth, one of the most beautiful women I have ever seen, with her black eyes and pale skin, to which were added the gentlest manners, and Lucy the general's daughter, who might have stepped out of the *Yellow Book,* so soft and corrupt she looked, to red-haired Clare who was engaged to one of the instructors, a sanitary engineer in real life. They were all kind-hearted girls, absurdly frivolous like the airmen they courted. It was a shock for me one Sunday to be called before the captain for reckless driving. It was true that I'd been driving faster and faster in the effort to be dashing, but I wasn't aware of having done anything transparently wrong. After lecturing me on the perils of the road, the captain said that I wasn't the driver he'd seen transgressing, and let me go. I take it now that he was giving me a shock and a chance to reform, in accordance with the fairly benign spirit of the place.

There wasn't much to do off duty. Without buses or maps, the surrounding country was a mystery. I halfheartedly enrolled in a German-language course taught by a gentle young man with a strong German accent. He asked me to go for a walk with him one evening, and afraid of being laughed at, I refused, though he was intelligent and educated, and would have been interesting to talk to. No, I wanted a handsome daring man, headlong love, by and with a pilot if possible. I went to the weekly hop only to find out that you were supposed to bring a partner, and I had none. Once Americans at a nearby army camp invited Wrens to a dance and a dozen of us went, for something to do. The tents were pitched on a hillside in a park overlooking an extraordinarily beautiful Georgian mansion in a saucer of grassland where clumps of vast trees stood back to let the house appear to perfection. None of the soldiers I spoke to knew the name of the place, nor did they apparently care to know. The dance took place in a Quonset hut and was fairly decorous to begin with. One of my partners pulled out photos of a hearse, a very long and distinguished black hearse, with him standing beside it. He was an undertaker in civilian life, or mortician, as he called it. This was very interesting, and so was another partner who claimed to work in Hollywood and was struck by how much I resembled Joan Crawford. When it was time to leave, Wrens and soldiers climbed into the back of a truck which rattled us off into the dark, tossing us to and fro as it shot down

the lanes. The moment it set off, the soldiers went mad and tried
to rip off the girls' clothing and, if not actually floor them, wrench
their heads into impossibly prolonged kisses, bent back and maintained bent by viselike grips round their thighs. The Joan Crawford man had to be diverted with kicks, but it was my mortifying
amusement that really safeguarded me. Other Wrens were not
so lucky. One was unloaded in uncontrollable tears. Others were
in shock, clothing askew, bruised. The next day a girl who'd been
with us stopped me walking to work and asked if I'd ever known
men carry on like that. We stood there in the open, pondering.
Why didn't we know? Why had we been taken by surprise? Were
Americans different? Weren't they just men like the sailors and
airmen on the station, who never behaved like that? Years afterward I listened in surprise when Americans told me that women in
Britain had a reputation for loose and lustful behavior. "Jump into
bed as soon as look at you," a man said. "Can't take their hands off
you." He spoke wryly, though he might have been flirting.

"Goodness," I said. "Was that your experience?"

He didn't answer and shuffled his hands. One of those chasms
between cultures or between men and women yawned between us.

A woman said earnestly, "Everyone knows that Englishwomen
are very very promiscuous."

In a few months the drivers were knitting baby things in their
leisure hours. The red-haired Clare and her fiancé were expecting a
baby. She would shortly be leaving the service in order to get married and set up house. Unlike the other women's services, the
Women's Royal Naval Service permitted a girl to leave it without
calling her a deserter. It was said that a house existed somewhere
for pregnant Wrens with nowhere else to go. Rumors began to
reach me concerning a certain inn favored by aircrews, and it was
there, clearly, that Clare and her flying instructor had found a bed
and conceived their child. Others, too, went up those stairs: X
from parachutes, still other drivers with their fellows, nameless.
Lucy knew about it. But where was it? Did it exist only in hearsay?

Was she involved? Impossible to discover. Her faint weariness and worldliness was provocative, and she talked of nightclubs in London, an alluring married sister and her set, Ascot, Henley, dances, and a society that was probably Society, whose activities and births, marriages and deaths were reported in the *Tatler* or the court section of the *Times* as if they were important or enviable. The connection between Society and the goings-on in a village inn that offered accommodation to courting couples was not an obvious one, so perhaps Lucy's world extended beyond Society, or the inn simply provided a needed substitute. The odd thing was that Lucy seemed to know and accept what I still found mysterious, and she knew that, and enjoyed her status as informant.

August came, and my father, who was in desperate need of a holiday, was spending a few days at a glover's in the neighboring village of Marnhull, in a novel arrangement I'd made with the glover's family which both sides enjoyed. He and I walked and talked and ate together as much as possible, and then one night as I lay in my bunk after my return to the camp, a bosun's whistle sounded on the Tannoy, followed by an announcement that the Japanese had capitulated and the war had come to an end. The camp was in an uproar. The girls in my hut hastily got dressed and went outside. Men were already dancing and singing outside their huts. Very lights whooshed and popped over the airfield, and a modest bonfire outside the men's mess soon swelled to a mountainous dazzle and crackle as ideas of revolution took hold and mess tables and benches were broken up and tossed on top. At the control tower, on the top level where my friend Jean worked in the meteorology office, a crowd pushed to and fro, and Jean herself had no sooner turned to speak to me than she was grabbed and twisted into an embrace by an officer in his shirtsleeves, who kissed her full on the lips as her hands wriggled and flapped behind her like a seal woman's. The man was a tall lean type, not so much handsome (he explained to me later) as "a near miss."

Jean was deeply offended by the kiss. Freddy knew she was en-

gaged to Geoffrey, she told me after in her overbred voice. Hence
Freddy was no gentleman, unlike Geoffrey. Geoffrey would have
protested if he'd been there, even though Freddy was his superior
officer. The kiss itself did not enter into our discussion, which was
as well because I could not condemn it. I had never been kissed
like that, knew only boyish kisses, little affectionate pats and
hugs.

Later the met officer drove three or four of us over to the
glover's and I banged on the window and my father came out in
his dressing gown and poured us glasses of celebratory whiskey in
honor of the peace.

Some weeks afterward a lorry driver dropped Lucy and me
halfway to Sherborne, where we were going for some diversion,
a cinema or fish and chips, and we were picked up by a naval car
driven by Freddy of the kiss, whom I now knew as the chief flying instructor and a lieutenant commander. His passenger was a
younger fair-haired sublieutenant called Dicky who was going
into Lloyds when demobbed. They took us off to a football match
between the air station and a nearby village, and the moment it
was over, on a pubcrawl. I remember surprise at the extraordinary
amount of beer the men swallowed at each village pub and the
smooth frequency of their visit to the lavatories, while Lucy and I
stayed amazingly witty and composed with our tots of gin; bun-
dling into the car time after time and dashing headlong through
the night to Freddy's cries and whoops. Lucy reassured me all the
same that Freddy was an excellent driver. How did she know?
What she sensed was my fear, as he flung us together this way and
that, careening through country lanes. Very late, I was aware we
were moored somewhere in the camp itself, and now Freddy and I
were in the front of the car together and he was kissing me with
the same appetite he had shown for Jean on VJ night—an assumed
appetite in both cases, I now think. Lucy and Dicky were scuffling
in the back and presently snoring. Freddy propelled me home
through the dark to Wrens' quarters and let me go. I climbed into

my bunk in a haze of love and longing and drunkenness. For the next few days I could barely eat or sleep.

Lucy sought me out. After he'd seen me home, Freddy had returned to the car, where she was by now alone—Dicky having sloped off to bed—and made a pass at her. She thought she'd tell me in case I got ideas. Freddy was not very nice.

As she cautioned me, he became even more alluring. I met him leaving the officers' mess and flashed him such a besotted smile that he asked me out for a drink with another man and his girl, who both disappeared early. In his apologies, relayed to me later, the other man said I was just the thing for Freddy, and a cut above the tart with him. A tart! A vulgar girl at last! I'd tried to be friendly, she'd smiled blearily: disappointing. Now that we were identified, Freddy and I talked endlessly, that night and others, about his war service on an aircraft carrier, his childhood in Newcastle, the death of his father, his two elder married sisters, his mother, how he broke a leg and was snatched out of a hospital in Alexandria by a chum and carried back to his ship; about myself too, about the future. And here, to my surprise, Freddy came to say he was falling in love with me, we got on so well, we were drawn to each other, he could see us together. It was amazing. I wasn't one of the golden girls. He had appeared to be one of the golden boys, but it was an easy act to stage. The man who shouted and whooped and kissed girls when he could, talked of children and earning a living in the aircraft industry after he left the service. We saw more of each other. He rang me in the drivers' room and I blushed to hear his voice.

Once, prompted by some idiotic undergraduate facetiousness, I confessed I'd been at Oxford. "Yes, I'm frightfully clever," I said.

Silence. "God, I hate you when you talk like that," he said.

I told Jean I was in love. Of course I was fair game, she would think that; but curiously enough Freddy was fair game too, an innocent in love, a man whose experience of sexuality was suspect and haphazard. Jean said earnestly that she was glad for me

and said nothing more. A Wren officer who met Freddy and me
out together took us in with a friendly glance and a friendly comment to me afterward. "I didn't know," she said. No one knew, I
thought, largely because there was no formality to be acknowledged. He was to be posted to Cornwall within the month. "I'll
be back. We'll get some posting together somehow. I'll arrange
that." His lovemaking was passionate. Seriously as I took his declaration, secrecy was my habit. There was very little time left, and
I was thankful he seemed not to know of the inn where Wrens and
airmen went upstairs and conceived children, so we had nowhere
to go except into his narrow cabin, where the danger of being
caught by senior officers, and of court-martials and reprisals, and
of conceiving a child, was so terrible that I could not think about
it for long. Certainly I could not tell him the terror I felt. "But
suppose I become pregnant," I said merely. He said that the
pitter-patter of tiny feet would be a delight, and he laughed. This
was either entirely frivolous or entirely serious, and now I think it
was serious.

Soon after Freddy flew off to the west, I met Elizabeth walking
back from the office of the commanding officer. I told her how
slim and elegant she looked in her best uniform, and Elizabeth
smiled that it wouldn't last. She was leaving the Wrens to marry
Sam. Oh! So she was pregnant, dear Elizabeth. Presently I was
posted to the Admiralty in London. Letters from Freddy followed
me, one after the other, and as I replied I began to wonder if I
might not marry him and live happily ever after. Then the letters
ceased.

In the long days and weeks of silence that followed, I found to my
relief that I wasn't pregnant. What if I had been, though, in this
silence that might mean, must mean, that he had broken things
off and no longer cared for me? How could he possibly turn his
back on me after all he'd said and sworn? I wondered if I could

have gone through pregnancy and childbirth alone. I imagined the disgrace I'd have brought on my parents and the burden I'd have been to them. And then I remembered my father pointing out a woman in Windsor who by chance cycled past us, who, he said, was entirely admirable because she had insisted on giving birth to her illegitimate child and bringing it up herself, without a husband: refusing first abortion, and then adoption. As I didn't know that abortion was ever an option for him, I was surprised. And I had certainly no idea that he would approve of a woman's flouting convention in these matters under any circumstances. So I looked on him in a new light after that. All the same the idea of illegitimacy was frightening. And the child—suppose the illegitimate one said, "Tell me about my daddy," what then?

Meanwhile my family took it for granted that I was and would remain a virgin.

I think of my Admiralty posting, which took place soon after Freddy's departure, as a banishment from the green world of Henstridge to a bleak unpainted subterranean passage with pipes running along the ceiling, somewhere in the catacombs of the official building off Trafalgar Square. Seated on a bench there waiting for my passenger to appear in order to be taken to a railway station or a naval depot or dock in the East End, I once found myself with another Wren driver whom I'd seen but didn't know, a very quiet private girl who never joined the competitive talk and exclusive gossip of the drivers' pool. She was delicate and fair-haired and neat, and looked as well as any girl could in our depressing uniform of navy suit, white shirt, black tie, thick black stockings and blunt lace-up shoes, and round navy cap with ribbon and a gold-lettered H.M.S.

"When will these fools come?" I said after a few minutes' silence.

"I don't care if they never come," said the quiet girl. "In fact, to

tell you the truth, I'd far rather be dead than sitting here waiting
for them. I wish I were dead anyway."

My mother would occasionally say something similar by way of
protest at her drudging life. My brother had a stock of answers:
"Who do you want at the funeral?" "Shall I send a wire to anyone?" Because he was close to her, she'd soften and laugh. Whereas
I wouldn't say anything. She had nothing to be desperate about.
My inquiry of the quiet girl, on the other hand, pierced us both
with knives. Her boyfriend was dead, she said. After the shock I
said I thought my "boyfriend" might have been killed too because
he'd stopped writing, and knew instantly that I had no right to
speak: he had simply stopped writing, nothing to do with death,
he had jilted me, he had chucked me. I wondered how dear to each
other the quiet girl and her boyfriend had been. This seemed very
important. If they hadn't been to bed together, the situation
might be saved. This was so in my case. I therefore asked her if
they had been lovers.

She shook her head, frowning.

"I know I have no right to ask."

"That's right, you haven't. You want to tell me of something
that happened to you, in exchange? In exchange?"

"No." I was horrified.

The perfection of love is its inherent chaos and disgrace. I did
not want to risk any criticism. I could have written to Jean at
Henstridge and asked her what, if anything, had happened to
Freddy. Working in the control tower, the center of intelligence,
she would know. Her disapproval made itself felt in advance.
What's more, Geoffrey, her fiancé and Freddy's junior, might be
scandalized either by me or by Freddy, supposing he'd cast me
aside, and in any case my inquiry wouldn't do Freddy any good.
Lucy, so sophisticated and knowledgeable in the ways of the
world, might be more reliable. Why didn't I write to her? Because
she had warned me against Freddy in the first place. My mother
was of no help either. From the first she had treated the idea of

Freddy as a joke. When the joke stopped writing, she said, "Good riddance." So I went on, chaotically, disgracefully, at the same time driving about on various assignments, being useful. Driving was always a solace. At least I was in charge of the vehicle, as I'd been in charge of a horse once, and I got the same sense of freedom and authority from dashing through the thin traffic and maneuvering the streets and lanes in the effort to find shorter and shorter cuts between one point and another. And there were new friends, who lived in new worlds, which made it easier to leave off the old ones and have the illusion of starting afresh. It would seem callous now to push aside the world of grief, but I had for a long time lived in duplicitous fashion between the official, religious, and public world and the secret, imaginative, private one.

Lesley, one of these new friends, asked me to visit a large fashionable store with her one day when for some reason we had the whole afternoon free. It turned out that her father ran the store, as became clear when she rushed me to see a new red suit that she was thinking of spending all her clothing coupons on. She was greeted with kindly intimacy instead of the hauteur that invariably greeted me, and she had no sooner put on the pretty suit and was parading in front of a mirror when a distraught man in black coat and pinstriped trousers came rushing up. There was an immediate row of the subdued kind, with much whispering. The red suit was put on one side until Lesley and her father could settle the questions of payment, expense, good behavior, and so on.

Such conflict was typical of London in those days, when parsimony and the longing for the things wealth brings went side by side. Paintwork had been neglected for six years, windows hadn't been cleaned or pavements swept. The parks were trodden gray, people were shabby, food was tasteless. There was no entertainment that I could afford except a film now and then; though on my lunch break I could walk over to the National Gallery to hear a free concert by the magnificent Myra Hess, and look at pictures in the gallery. The people borne to and fro on the buses and the tube suited the thin blue landscape of still-smoky London.

Certainly the other men I eventually went out with had nothing heroic about them. I got into trouble out of sheer negligence, once failing to get the dispatcher to cover for me (as was usual) when skipping duty on a quiet Sunday morning, and once mislaying my shirt and tie after a party in civilian clothes. Charges followed. Confinement to barracks meant learning to operate the telephone switchboard, and kitchen duty meant learning to gut herring and peel potatoes like lightning, useful skills. The bad side was putting up with the triumph of the petty officer on the latter occasion. She was what is now usefully called a Sloane Ranger, who had found out that I had been at Oxford and was resolved to get the better of me, which was not hard.

In 1946 I went back in Somerville determined to work eight hours a day, exultant that I was well supported by an ex-service grant and that therefore my father did not have to pay my bills.

The bursar had assigned me a lodging far up the Woodstock Road, which called for twenty minutes' hard biking to reach from the college and twenty minutes to get myself back. My room was half a bigger room cut in two by cardboard that let though every word uttered by the woman in the other half, and she talked day and night. By some fluke my mother came to visit me and discovered how it was, and to my horror made herself known to the bursar. "My daughter cannot be allowed to remain in such a ramshackle, disgusting, inappropriate place," she said. "That is not good enough for my daughter. It may be good enough for some, but not for her." While I stood by in agony, the bursar, without a word, gave me a very pleasant room in college, and I stayed there contentedly for the next two years. "Who are these ghastly women?" my mother cried before she went, eyeing the charming and distinguished French scholar Enid Starkie going by in her odd getup of pajamas and beret. "A dowdy lot of old maids. Let me out of here."

One day my friend Angela, who'd been an aircraft mechanic in the WRNS, invited me to a party to meet a man who'd recently been demobbed from the air station in Cornwall to which Freddy had been posted. Had he come across him, I asked. Yes, said the demobbed man, indeed he knew him. Freddy had been flying a single-engine plane over the Channel when the engine had packed up and the little plane had come down in the sea and he hadn't got out.

Oh, I said. I'd wondered what had happened.

Everything went on as before. I went on thinking of Freddy as usual, every day, several times a day, as I had for a year, his life now unraveling at my fingertips. Another year passed before I discovered a week had gone by without a thought of him. Thank God the business was drawing to a close, I said to myself, eager to get on with my life. I repeated to myself that he'd been killed so as to get used to the idea as quickly as possible, though now and then wishing he'd junked me and gone on living instead, so at least he'd have his life. Three or four years later he appeared at my bedside, absolutely silent, as the dead are, warning me by his huge physical presence not to take up with a booby I was drawn to. And long afterward, in the third year of my marriage, I went with my husband and his old father, who lived with us, to the showing of a Russian film called *The Cranes Are Flying*. As far as I remember, the film ends with shots of a girl going to meet a troop train on which she believes her soldier is being brought home. She runs up and down the platform till the station is empty and she realizes that he is not coming back. It was a sad film, and I began to cry and couldn't stop. The lights came up, I was in floods of tears, my father-in-law made his face into a mask and banged his stick on the floor with irritation, we walked on to the street, where my husband, whom I loved very much, opened the car and we climbed in, and still I sobbed. We drove home, we left the car, we entered our house. Our little son was asleep upstairs. My husband took the baby-sitter home. My tears ran out. "What was all that about?" my husband asked when he came back. I tried to think through the devastation, and remembered Freddy's death, having forgotten him for years. Already I was older than he was at the age of his death, thirty-one to his twenty-seven. Ten years had passed since he'd died.

Lest there be misunderstanding, let me say clearly I was overwhelmed not by the memory of sorrow, which is purely sentimental, but by sorrow itself. It stormed through the years and took me by surprise. So that was sorrow! Once I'd recovered, that was all. The young man lay at peace within me for good.

I wish I had something intelligent to say about his death, its terrible uncertainty and then its terrible certainty. Stuart Piggott the archaeologist said to me once at a dinner table and unprovoked that it made not the slightest difference who won what battle over whom, or what cities burned and were lost, or what civilization: history continued throwing up its tides like the sea.

The statement was tremendous, and obviously true, though not of a truth to dally with at the dinner table. I should have said simply, "Mr. Piggott, there's a providence in the sparrow's fall." His retreat into vast commonplaces temporarily stunned me, but afterward I thought of the various disasters I'd known, and they were none of them world class, and yet they were disasters all the more for their being small and solitarily apprehended. I only am escaped alone to tell thee, says the messenger to Job after his children, his servants, and his flocks and herds are wiped out. Only I knew of the death of Freddy, so it appeared. Whoever else mourned him was unknown to me. That is what was so frightful. I might have made him up. Even now my account may be spurious. Only the sorrow strikes me as genuine, as I look back and barely recall his face. Perhaps that is the true sorrow about disasters, the fact that they fade.

There's an envoy to this account of my early life.

In June 1982 I was traveling from Heathrow to stay with friends in their cottage near Bath when I made a false turn and fetched up near the great house of the Pembrokes' at Wilton, which I had wanted to see for a long time. As my plane had come in low over southern England early that summer's day, the young man next to me had asked if they went in for agriculture in a big way there below. We peered together through the little window of the aircraft at the neat woods and small green fields on rounded banks and hills lit by the seven o'clock sun, and in some amusement I said, yes, they were keen farmers, and had been at it for many hundreds of years, and bit by bit they'd tidied and planted the woods and hedgerows and drained the marshes. He then asked me if I was an admirer of the English landscape. I tried not to laugh. Was I an admirer of the sky? Of the ocean? Surely the landscape was a given. And immediately I saw that through those workers in the woods and fields you might be permitted to look on landscape as something made by an infinite number of choices, in fact as a style, as much a style as any style in the true arts. The young man must have been taught something of this sort about the English landscape, and precious as he sounded, he was asking a perfectly serious question. So—all in a matter of seconds—I came round to being moved, and said yes, I admired it tremendously, it was Arcadia.

"Arcadia," said the young man, smiling. "I've read that word."

Immediately endeared to me by this response, he nodded with another burst of delight, and so when I found myself at Wilton, by the sort of crude chance that no novelist would dare incorporate into his plot, I saw no reason to protest: because it was here, at Wilton, that, in about 1575, in the days of Elizabeth I, Sir Philip Sidney wrote his famous pastoral romance about knights and shepherds, the *Arcadia*. John Aubrey the antiquarian says that Sidney rode thereabouts in the still-unhedged open fields carrying a notebook, in which he'd scribble while on horseback, prompted by what he saw. Wiltshire shepherds, like the shepherds of ancient Greece, wore the old white woolen cape which came halfway down an even-longer cloak, and carried a shepherd's crook, a sling, a scrip, and flute, while a dog ran beside them. Sidney also saw meadows, shades, green banks, stately trees, gliding rivers, "*romancy* fields and *boscages,*" and he crystallized all these things in *Arcadia*—properly, *The Countess of Pembroke's Arcadia,* a gift to his sister. It is a dreadfully ornate and rambling piece of prose, written by a poet in an age of poetry. I had yawned my way through it at Oxford. Here, it seemed quite rationally to me in my exalted state of jet lag and homecoming, I should find the Arcadia of the countryside seen from the plane realized in the Wilton of the tourists, which was also the Arcadia of long ago as seen by Philip Sidney, hero of his age.

The present Wilton was ravishingly beautiful—a big tranquil unadorned stone house of subtle color, the very place I'd missed, though I had never seen it before. Mind, I was jet-lagged and had been homesick: yet still it was moving, with its discreet domestic quality. It had nothing to do with my own history in particular, but everything to do with the history of all us creatures, aggrandized and Arcadian. I thought I'd like to see the interior, and joined a group of visitors at the entrance. Our guide turned out to be a small, neat, and businesslike woman. The tour, she announced, would take about thirty minutes. She eyed us coldly. We were five or six women and two men, none of us young or exceptional or even keen-looking.

What we saw, the guide told us, was not what was there in Wilton's heyday. It was converted from a convent after the dissolution of the monasteries and given to William Herbert, a swashbuckling Welsh supporter of the Welsh Tudors who was made Earl of Pembroke for his services. The house quite soon became famous under the rule of Mary Herbert, Countess of Pembroke, William's daughter-in-law and sister to Sir Philip Sidney: "Sir Philip Sidney, Knight, whose Fame will never dye, whilest Poetrie lives, was the most accomplished Cavalier of his time," writes John Aubrey roughly a hundred years later. Brother and sister were devoted. "He was not only of an excellent witt, but extremely beautiful: he much resembled his sister, but his Haire was not red, but a little inclining, viz. a darke ambor color." When he died, aged thirty-one, all England mourned. The countess became patron in his place to many of the wits of the day, in this very place, at Wilton. Moreover, she became celebrated as a poet in her own right for her considerable part in the translation of the Psalms that her brother began. The guide read from her notebook the words in front of me now, from Sidney's dedication of the *Arcadia* to his sister: "Here now have you (most deare, and most worthy to be most deare Lady) this idle worke of mine. . . ."

I wished my brother had said that to me! One of the women that day at Wilton said as much out loud.

"No you don't," said one of the men.

"Why not?"

"Ha! Why not? Because they went to bed together."

"What, Sir Philip Sidney and his sister?"

We all woke up.

"That's gossip," cried the guide. "Gossip repeated by John Aubrey, who had a family grudge against the Herberts. Sir Philip Sidney was the hero of the age, without flaw. His sister likewise, without flaw." Something about her turn of phrase reproved us, as sermons do. We looked at each other indignantly.

The man went on blithely: "When it was time for the stallions to be put to stud, she'd arrange to watch through a little peephole in the wall, and that would excite her, and off she'd go to one of her lovers."

We gasped. The owners of Wilton had, after all, allowed us to pay our fee and stare at their belongings.

"That is pure gossip, malicious gossip." The guide glanced around for help. "John Aubrey wrote down all kinds of items that he heard. No truth in it whatsoever."

"Where'd you hear all this?" demanded a woman. Another sighed that this was not what she'd come to Wilton to hear. I agreed with her. If I wanted gossip, I'd read the newspapers, I said.

The guide nodded at me. She said loudly that Mary Herbert, the Countess of Pembroke, was a very learned lady. She knew Latin, Greek, and Hebrew. She was very kind, and beautiful, and good.

The anarchist gave a faint snort. "That's what they'd say, isn't it?"

"But supposing she really was kind and beautiful and good?" protested another of us. Here the guide turned again to her notebook and read out crossly:

Underneath this sable hearse
Lies the subject of all verse:
Sidney's sister, Pembroke's mother;
Death! ere thou hast slain another
Fair and learn'd, and good as she,
Time shall throw a dart at thee.

"That is what one of her poets wrote for her epitaph. You can't say that's not meant."

"It's meant," said the anarchist, "but it was an age when poets depended on patronage, and he had to do what was expected of him. He meant that he really did need his bread and butter."

"With due respect," said the guide, "I will conduct you now to the staterooms." And she walked furiously off with us following, the anarchist included, though as soon as he could, he ignored interiors in favor of the *romancy* fields and *boscages* visible through the window.

The rooms were each more glorious than the last and culminated first in the Cube Room and then in the Double Cube Room, a classically beautiful design thirty feet in height by thirty feet in breadth by sixty feet in length, which contained great gilt sofas upholstered in red silk brocade and giant console tables and mirrors, also gilt, with walls hung with a stupendous collection of Van Dyck portraits in huge carved and gilded frames. None of these great rooms would have been there in the days of Mary Herbert, Countess of Pembroke, since they were thought to have been built to the design of Inigo Jones. Glorious rooms, we nodded, exhausted with the grandeur.

Only last week there was a roller-skating party in the Double Cube Room for the Pembroke children, the guide concluded. On the ancient polished oak floor. The furniture of course removed.

And the earl did not object? asked someone ingratiatingly. Or the countess?

The earl and countess were separating—in fact, divorcing, divulged the guide sternly, as if she were proffering a scientific reason for the party, adding, with mysterious choplogic, "We must move with the times."

The anarchist grinned at me as we wandered away down the passage, and I couldn't help grinning back at the lack of deference we were showing in this immensely historical place.

In the tearoom one of the women confided to me that she preferred going over country houses without a guide, so she could linger where she wished.

But they are afraid one will nick the spoons, I said, that is why someone is in charge of us. It was bad taste to make jokes of that kind, I knew immediately, because she lowered her eyes to her plate.

All that gossip, she said. How can you have heroes when you have gossip?

I drove off thinking how Philip Sidney's story had been in my first reader. Someone brought him a cup of water as he lay wounded on the field of Zutphen and he gave it to a dying soldier, saying, "Thy need is greater than mine." Much to my sorrow, a scholar has discovered that the story is an invention. One prefers heroes to be heroic so when they die, one can go mad with grief. I drove through the town of Shaftesbury without realizing where I was, feeling jet-lagged, obscurely put out, and thinking ahead of my friends and the cottage near Bath where there'd be understanding and jokes and hot baths. The country was of course delightful, I had forgotten the extent of the pleasure it gave. The steep hill down from its ancient fortlike prominence brought some excitement with the speed it lent my wheels; the thrill of looking over the wide expanse of Wessex that shrank with descent. And so the sudden appearance of the name Henstridge on a wayside stone made me jump. A curious coincidence. At first I wondered whether to allow another break in my journey, a break in my thoughts. I might look at the tiny village, though, and identify the thatched cottage where Jean and another friend and I had rented a room to have somewhere of our own to brew a cup of tea and read a book. I might look at the pub where they'd served rough cider. I could have lunch there, if it served lunch. I had plenty of time. So I turned off the main road without much curiosity and acknowledging to myself that one should never go back. The thatched cottage wasn't where I left it. The inn had pleasant white iron tables and chairs and a new sign in front. I thought I'd follow the lane a little farther in and see if I recognized anything. Henstridge had been a small station, and relics of the naval quarters in Nissen huts, the command in a farmhouse, A camp, B camp half a mile away in a wood, must have been cleared away long ago, but I found myself looking right and left, recognizing nothing. I'd walked back from our cottage to A camp once in the dark (for the blackout was still on). I had no flashlight and hadn't realized I suffered from night blindness. Stars that would have been sufficient for a countryman didn't stop me from falling into ditches and ensnaring myself in hedges before I saw the sentry in the distance and he challenged me. So now I crept down a narrow lane, just as blind; drove up and over a cheerful little humpbacked railway bridge with a line of single track running underneath, and in a mile or so found myself among a dozen great silvery grain silos with ventilators humming in the afternoon air like planes. And beyond them, years and years beyond them, lay the old perimeter track encircling the level grass of the runways, and humps in the grass outside the perimeter like tumuli, except they were really former bunkers and hangars, and far over the grass was an apparition from another world—the old control tower of brick with sheets of glass round the observation deck: a useless building now, Freddy's once, from which he'd conducted by radio the education of fliers. Some men in black leather and crash helmets were riding motorbikes far away on the tarmac aprons.

I stayed there for a long time, run through with grief and longing. What it costs, to survive! It was murder. My survival had murdered Freddy.

Was he a hero, Freddy, or had I made him up?

A man in a tweed jacket and a flat cap eventually walked up, two liver and white spaniels at heel, and remarked that I looked lost. I said I wasn't, and I had been a Wren there many years ago— a straight answer hypocritically short of the truth. He looked across the field and said it was the control towers that always gave such places away. I agreed. Then, because the spell had been broken, I said goodbye and backed the car out.

Antonio Machado, who lost his wife when she was only eighteen, wrote a poem about her called "Los Ojos," which I translate as follows:

When his beloved died
he thought he would grow old
in the closed-up house
alone with his memory and the glass
in which she used to see herself on a fine day.

Like gold in a miser's chest
he thought he'd keep
yesterdays as one in the clear glass.
For him now time would not run on.

But after the first anniversary
what were they like, her eyes,
he asked himself: brown?
Black? Green? Gray?
What were they like, dear God,
that I can't recall?

One day in spring he walked out
bearing in silence his double grief
within his closed-up heart.
From a window in a dark recess
he saw eyes flash. He lowered his own
and carried on. Yes, like that!

That's it exactly. You come away with a new yardstick, by which you measure in time even the past, as I do here. It is a gift beyond plain knowledge. Because it is new, it causes you to doubt and confuse both the things you have known and the things you come on for the first time. By degrees I became used to the measure. I am a skeptic about myself, not a cynic.

CUTTING LOOSE

Over the hills and far away,
Over the hills and far away,
Over the hills and a great way off,
The wind will blow my topknot off.

—*Old song*

"I often think that your despair is *voulu*," wrote Rosemary from
Italy in one of those penitential moments when unsolicited opinion verifies your suspicion. I loved Rosemary for her mind and
charm and enterprise. When we went down from Oxford, she
took a job as governess to a noble family in Milan in order to learn
Italian. She got out, as I longed to. Our tutor at Somerville had
told me that she had a man's mind. One could still say such things
then. To have a man's mind meant simply that you had an eye to
what was important, and you had a range of interesting ideas that
you weren't afraid to try out. Women have got bolder, but there
are still many who become bogged in convention and are conse-
quently afraid of asserting the truth as they see it. Rosemary,
clearheaded as she was, found the grandmother of her Italian family playing football with the children in the long gallery of their
palace, transgressing the rules they had agreed upon. So she resigned her post and went to work elsewhere. It would not have occurred to me to resign, because I would have instantly become

bogged in the sweetness of the scene. Secondary things have always captivated me.

Yes, my despair was cozy. I'd left it behind, but every now and then sought it out again and sank into its forgiving warmth. Now, obviously, as others had spotted it, I had to turn my back on it and walk away. In the autumn my mother and I went to Paris for a week's holiday, and at a dinner party I met a man who worked for UNESCO, recently set up in that city. If I wanted a job, he said, he could give me one, provided I learned shorthand and typing. Go away, he said, learn them, and get back to me. The moment we returned home, I enrolled in a grand secretarial school near Queen's Gate and spent months plodding after seventeen- and eighteen-year-olds who picked up skills and speeds with ease.

I might have been walking away from despair in my own determination, but commuting daily by train and tube through that hard winter, from Windsor to Gloucester Road, reminded me of it. Trains were slow, late, cold, and dirty, and the engines gave off a peculiar metallic and gaseous smell that lingered at the back of the throat. The newspapers throbbed with the scandal later picked apart in the Lynskey Report of January 1949, to do with the series of transactions, supposedly, in which bribes were offered to public servants in return for political or commercial favors. A certain Sidney Stanley was said to have acted as intermediary, entertaining, lending money, giving cases of wine, a gold cigarette case, a musquash coat. The parliamentary secretary to the Board of Trade, Mr. John Belcher, was supposed to have been contaminated by these gifts. His plain, serious, and undistinguished face often appeared on one side of the page and Sidney Stanley's melon one with its huge grin on the other. In the end John Belcher's minor parliamentary post was taken away and he disappeared into obscurity, accused of nothing more than indiscretion. Mrs. Belcher, a decent quiet woman, said, "I think the tribunal's findings are a disgrace." I thought so too, disgusted by the self-satisfaction on one side and weakness on the other. When the time came for Sidney Stanley to be arrested, he jumped bail, disappeared, and to everyone's amusement turned up in Israel. Nevertheless the leader of the Opposition said piously in the House of Commons that the tribunal had vindicated "the honor and reputation of the system by which we carry on government."

"What can you expect of people like that?" demanded several of the Windsor commuters, shaking open their newspapers as I opened my current Conrad novel. To this day I associate Conrad with chill and spiritual denial in a complacent world. There was a talkative old Etonian on the train, a man in his fifties, to flirt with. He took me out to dinner once at a restaurant on the King's Road in Chelsea and confided to the waiter that he was fifty-four, and the waiter told him he didn't look it. Silly as that was, the dinner was bad and he looked older. I could think myself into a Conrad character and speak endlessly through its voice the thoughts that ran behind my eyes; I surely couldn't think myself into a public-school man. Even to speak to a public-school man involved disbelief and elaborate acting. So I found ways to avoid the debonair eye on the endless slow cold journeys.

In the spring I left the secretarial college without completing the course, and wrote to the Blumenthals, who had introduced me to the UNESCO official. I had studied shorthand and typing, I said: would they let him know I was eager for a job? By all means, they replied: ring us up when you arrive, we'll go out to dinner and arrange something. By the way, we've just had another baby, a sister for Hervé.

So in due time I took the express to Paris and late in the evening arrived at the Gare du Nord, that great sleeve of light and steam, glass and iron, blackened and filthy with smoke and loud with the noise of the shunting and whistles of departure. I went by taxi to my hotel on the Left Bank only to find that my booking was for the next day. They had no room and I was feeling ill, so I sat on my suitcase in the tiny lobby and let the tears flow. Furious Monsieur at the desk, clicking his tongue, found me a room in a brothel up the street, where people tried my door all night and I was sick in the bidet. In the morning I itched. The sheet was a riot of running black bugs. Over the new day and the next few days the itching developed into a torment of red and hideous bumps. I had to go to dinner with the Blumenthals wearing a long-sleeved jacket to conceal them, though it was July and very hot. It was a black silk jacket with a pattern of little yellow flowers borrowed from my mother. Other guests included a very masculine hairy man glowing with health and vitality who had spent the war in Argentina. He told of the mobiles of Alexander Calder, which he had seen for the first time that day.

Mobiles? Alexander Calder?

We stood on the balcony of the apartment and he pointed out the hand of Viollet-le-Duc in the west facade of Notre Dame, and brought up the character of Henri IV whose statue rode nearby, *le vert galant*.

Le vert galant?

When I too lived in Paris, such knowledge would come running to me like a pet and change my life. I'd become conversant with art and architecture, slim and amusing, sophisticated and independent. The attractive man was asking me if it was useful to know the names of things. Or was it better to leave them nameless, the unnamed parts of a recognizable whole. Was it useful to know the names of the parts of an artichoke, for example: the hay, the choke. As well as the leaves that you dip in drawn butter, thus.

It was late when they dropped me off at my hotel with instructions to telephone the next day to discover what arrangements they had made for me with the UNESCO man.

But in the morning my telephone call met only tears and incoherence. The Blumenthals had returned home to learn that their little baby had died in its cot during their absence. I knew nothing of cot death. It seemed to me that for a child to die without reason meant something was terribly wrong with our behavior. It struck me as the most terrible judgment that the tiny creature should cease to breathe in their absence, even while watched over by its nurse. "You can never see them again," said a friend who helped me buy a little white wreath for the funeral. I wondered if I could decently stay on and perhaps meet the UNESCO man later, but decided it would be indelicate. There were other factors. Money was very short, the Blumenthals were my only friends. They had already given me far more than I could give them. (The life of their baby.) So I gave up and went home.

I became the secretary of a Third Program talks producer in the BBC and found myself a room in Bayswater. The salary was pathetic, to balance the pleasure of working for a clever and kind man. He commissioned twenty-minute talks from various intellectuals which a minority audience all over the country listened to, sometimes—in areas with poor reception—with their ear pressed against the radio. It was a brilliant service meant unashamedly for an elite of ordinary people who loved ideas and wanted to inform themselves of the latest theories and movements in the arts or sciences, or those of the past, sometimes late at night when the rest of the world had gone to bed. How was it killed off? Why hasn't it been replaced? No wonder I loved the job and my office up on the maids' floor of the old Langham Hotel opposite Broadcasting House. My fast, inaccurate typing and shorthand that I couldn't read back appeared forgivable. I was allowed to attend studio recordings and make suggestions as if the place were open to them, and there were other hints at greater openness in the future, that programs might soon be broadcast live, some with the public phoning in, and on-the-spot reporting. It wasn't a bad first job, except for the pay, which I couldn't live on, and I was contemplating how to better myself when, a few months in, a friend of the family called me late at night in my Bayswater room to say that my father had had a heart attack while playing golf with him. He had apparently recovered enough to drive home, cancel his evening surgery, and take my mother to their solicitor to make their wills. Then he drove her home and had another heart attack.

By the time I got home, very late, having called my boss and resigned my job, packed my possessions, and put paid to my few commitments, my father was resting quietly in bed. A colleague had come and ordered him to hospital, and presently ambulance men were maneuvering his great length down the stairs on a stretcher, sweating profusely as they did so and shouting instructions to each other like furniture movers. My brother had called to say he was on his way home from Belfast, where he was doing his national service as a medical officer in the navy. He had compassionate leave and would act as locum for an indefinite period. He had understood immediately that a second heart attack would follow the first, and, when his commanding officer hesitated over granting him leave after the first attack, had wept in front of him. Meanwhile we were alone, my mother and I, and for the first time in my life she said she was glad I was there: not that she was cold-hearted, but so open an expression of love wasn't her way. Why had this happened, we asked. My father was never ill. He went without coat or hat or gloves in the coldest winter. He ran rather than walked. He didn't get colds, never got out of breath, had low blood pressure. Of course he coughed, but that was because of smoking sixty cigarettes a day. So it must have been worry that caused his heart to let him down. He was worried about the practice. And money of course. The stocks and shares they'd sold at the beginning of the war would now have been valuable, and oh how regrettable that they'd been sold.

But supposing the Germans had won the war, what would have happened to the investments then?

Well, there was that. Silly to worry about money in any case. "If Daddy died, I wouldn't want to live," my mother said. "I wouldn't know what to do." This struck me as no less dreadful than my father's heart attack. What indeed would she do? She had no interests outside her family.

At midnight we rang the favorite cousins in Australia, and the brothers and Aunt Ann in Scotland. We had a comfortable whiskey afterward and washed the glasses and plumped the cush-ions as usual before going up. In the morning I put a notice on the waiting-room door canceling the day's surgeries and explaining why. All morning I heard people walk to the door, read the notice, and turn back. At lunchtime Iain arrived in his naval uniform and took charge. "Six weeks in bed," he ordered my father.

"Jaybers, what rubbish," my father said as he lay in the hospital bed. As soon as he got home he got up a little every day, explain-ing the heart needed exercise and so did he.

Memory has thrown the weeks and months together, and I re-call only that we anticipated each other's needs to a hitherto unheard-of extent, as if to express once and for all our devotion before it was too late. The big house was sold to a builder who planned to turn it into flats, and we bought a smaller, much nicer one to live in, and set up the surgery in a terrace house with a housekeeper-receptionist. My father engaged an assistant and, after Iain left to finish his tour with the navy, resumed work in a calmer frame of mind. And then, with life flowing along in a sweeter way, my father showed the second result of the heart at-tack and spoke of visiting Skye.

To me it was heart-wrenching, as though he spoke of returning to the Age of Gold.

To my mother it was as though he spoke of returning to the Middle Ages.

To an old friend it was as though he were an aged elephant seeking out the elephants' graveyard to die there.

My father himself told me, however, a sad truth that had noth-ing to do with these fancies: he had never particularly wanted the life he had. He had arrived at it for the sake of peace. For peace, he told me, he had given up everything he prized: his friend Walter Connolly and his wife, Greta, whom my mother didn't really get on with; the regular twice-weekly game of golf (for as a Scot he regarded golf as a birthright); his brothers and sisters, whom my mother had quarreled with; and Skye, his home, its beloved mountains and lochs and seas, where he had not visited for a dozen years because his people were unkind to her there—or so she imagined. All for the sake of peace, said my father, making those sad lamenting noises in Gaelic that weren't even words for me to make out. Ah-ii. Ay, ay. Ah-ii. You mustn't think, said my father to me, that this is what I choose freely. I choose it for the sake of peace.

When I had taken these words to heart, absolutely astonished, I began to persuade both father and mother with all my power of persuasion that they should leave the assistant in charge, since he was a capable young man, and that my mother and I should stay at home, supervising in case of need, and make excursions to interesting places by car, myself at the wheel, and have days in London together; while on his own he would visit Skye, taking the night train from London to Glasgow and north up the west coast of Scotland, by Shiel Water and Rannoch Moor, through houseless country of loch and mountain and distant sightings of the sea, stopping at rare stations of small stone houses with black slate roofs and dormer windows, ending at Mallaig, where he'd take the ferry over to Armadale of the great trees. There his brother would meet him, both of them without a doubt in tears.

And so it came to pass. He went. He had a marvelous time, was driven all over the place, talking to people he knew, and in that part of the world everyone knows everyone else and their families for generations back; chatting and learning the latest, reminiscing, looking, looking, looking. There are great distances in Skye ending in far-off mountains. Your views are blocked not with roofs or woods but with weather. This has an effect on your sense of life's wholeness, as I learned for myself years later. He came back with a gold brooch for my mother and a silver one for me with a golden stone that I had made into a ring. Eventually he saw something of his other brothers and sisters. He took up golf again, regularly, on Thursdays. But the main thing was the return. Can you read a man backwards? What unknown deprivation had it meant to him, to leave his home forever, as he had in 1914 when he went off into the Royal Army Medical Corps? It meant everything. Why? It wasn't just the house by the ford, or the Benjamin's happy childhood, and the long-dead father and mother, it was those hills and seas and the islands in the Minch, and their associations, the culture of the place and its history, a place of innocence and purity and poverty, when speech wasn't chat but necessary talk establishing kinship or enmity, and there were no classes except between the young and the old, and between men and women, but all were equal, and lived simply, climbed mountains, sailed seas, ate herring, oatmeal, milk, and salt, and were hardy as a result. I pored over the photographs. Well, no wonder! You cannot live on scenery, no matter how sublime, but when it is yours, through your family, for ages back, it feeds an allegiance and a godliness. And there I was, already longing to escape from my own home. Was it money made the heart grow fonder of that early poverty? Was it closeness to the land (because my grandfather had a croft that was still in the family)?

When I think now of my father's longing for what was missing, I look sharply at my mother, but that is wrong, she was not to blame, she had her own history and agenda. The missing comprised a strong local society like Skye's, though in Skye that society was much taxed and exploited by the lairds (and perhaps grew all the stronger for that). We didn't have that kind of society in the Windsor of the court, the army, and the church.

As for infinite longing, my father was lucky in knowing what he longed for. Whatever relation exists between a place in natural surroundings and a place in society, he was rooted, as Yeats says of John Synge:

> *that rooted man,*
> *"Forgetting human words," a grave deep face.*

An American used to the English framework of society and not knowing the Scottish once asked me as a put-down if my father loved a lord. A bitter joke, had he but known it, given the Scots society from which my father came, for the old heads of clan, who used to hold the land on behalf of their clansmen, had gradually assumed the rights and habits of English lords and landowners, and in doing so helped destroy their ancient society. My American did not begin to understand. Far from loving lords, my father and his kin felt they were superior to such unprincipled creation.

"He's the salt of the earth," my mother said to my brother and me and anyone else she could trust, detaching him from what she regarded as the ignorance and religiosity of his family. Perhaps for a few years there in Windsor he suffered a lessening of himself, in the frenzy of worry about which way the war was running, his horror of Nazi Germany, and our personal finances, my brother's slowness in qualifying as a doctor, my inconsequence. And then when the war was over, with the installation of the National Health Service, of which he was the most vigorous and convinced supporter, the salt in him began to gather strength. The visit to Skye confirmed him in what he was. He spoke his mother tongue, he walked as a well-set-up professional man where he had run barefoot as a boy, he was recognized and honored by people he loved, and he renewed his allegiance to the brother and sister who'd stayed behind in the croft and the post office that his parents ran. "Every man has a lurking wish to appear considerable in his native place," wrote Samuel Johnson. It is also easiest to travel alone. So he came back a happy man.

As for my mother, now I'm prompted to look back, I see her in the grip of something stronger than reason as in his absence we put on our best town clothes, our high heels and gloves, she put on her hat, she counted her money, and off we went on the Green Line coach that deposited us on Hyde Park Corner, the world lying be-

fore us, where to choose, whether in the refined and middle-aged
Harrods of those days, the narrowly elegant Harvey Nichols, or
the scattering of little dress shops where my mother hoped to
negotiate a bargain. There was never much money involved and
there was always a great deal of consideration over quality, work-
manship, cut, durability, smartness. After the careful selection we
would have a coffee and a sandwich with the crusts cut off and
cress hanging out, in some smart café. Just before the rush hour we
would board the coach for the return journey along the Great West
Road, through the miles of brick semidetached housing with tiny
gardens in front, past the concrete offices and decent smokeless
factories, turning off at Slough, chugging through narrow Eton of
the red-cheeked boys, up the hill past Windsor Castle, sighing to
a stop at the bus station, a few hundred yards from home. She was
happiest then, thinking I was happy too. More like two sisters
than mother and daughter, she'd tell strangers who admired the
two of us. It was a charade, and sometimes glamorous, with the
perfumed shops and the slim women behind the counter and
the haughty old bags sweeping past and the nice women holding
doors for you and smiling as if they shared a secret with you. That
was the world she expected me to marry into. We drove out to a
grand National Trust house in the country with photos of old
Queen Mary in her weird toque and pearl choker and the next king
and queen in silver frames on the grand piano in the big dingy
drawing room.

She never cared for him, said my mother. Bit of a pip-squeak.
He's done well for himself, I'd say. She's been the making of him.

So boring, so drab and chintzy, the lot of them, I said, so thoroughly pretentious and second rate.

My mother identified the antecedents of the last lady of the
house. Where did her money come from, I wonder.

Who cares, I said.

Was it brewery money?

All spent now, I said. Here we are, riffraff, in her place.

I've got to go and get a job, I said.

My parents looked at me in dismay. I could so usefully become my father's secretary, they said. I could be my mother's companion. They needed me. At such moments I remembered my brother saying to me that we could never leave them and, as always, thought, what rubbish, of course we must.

As it was, I went off to London to a combination and succession of jobs: morning secretary to an M.P.; private secretary two evenings a week to a prominent psychiatrist; secretary to a sociologist investigating the success of the new towns started from scratch after the war; secretary to a charity that provided dowries for Greek village girls. The manufacturer of an apple drink considered me for an administrative job, and the World Council of Churches for a secretaryship in Geneva, but the consideration extended over months. When I applied to the local paper for a job, the owner called on my parents and said journalism was no job for a woman, and I couldn't persuade him otherwise. Meanwhile a publisher of magazines and the management of Imperial Chemical Industries both offered jobs on a permanently clerical level because on principle they did not promote women, and on principle I had to refuse because I needed a future. After months of this experience I was too ashamed to go to a dear friend's wedding. My parents then offered to finance my path through medicine or the law, and I refused, thinking that I wanted to write, after all, and was writing a novel, and poems, and that was primary.

At this low point I was living in a room at the World's End. One day an estate agent sent me notice of a little flat in Kensington Church Street, rent-controlled at a few pounds a week, on the attic floor of a building opposite the side entrance to Kensington Gardens, opposite the North Thames Gas Board and over a laundry. The property had been at one time occupied by the maids who worked in Kensington Palace. It comprised two small rooms, a lavatory, and a bathroom-cum-kitchen (lid to be dropped over bath when meals were being prepared). My mother came up on the bus and had a look at it, paid the deposit, sent a man to paint it for me, dispatched some furniture from home, and went with me to choose curtain material, out of which she ran me up two pairs of curtains. My father, whom I felt closer to, never understood my needs as clearly as my mother. Or, if he understood them, he left to her the management of a daughter, which for her included the censure of my friends. One was poor, one was dirty, one was foreign, one had no taste, one was dowdy, she said after meeting a few of the best. Yet one weekend in Windsor she admitted, "There's nothing here for you, I see that," while at the same time razor-keen to identify possible lovers. So when X turned up on my new doorstep with a grin, wearing a suit and leaning on an umbrella, it was no surprise. He was a tall ugly man who'd married someone else after our Oxford friendship had faded, and there he was again, ready to revive it. As if I couldn't look after myself! Her suspicions were so far short of the truth that when she discovered a contraceptive in the bedroom of the flat one day, she was so distraught that she went to Windsor, returned on the next bus to London, and turned up again in the flat to levy one accusation after another, which I didn't answer. I was twenty-six years old.

One morning I happened to look out of the window while racing to get ready for work, and saw in an upper window of the North Thames Gas Board over the busy street a man's face. I paused. It might be a dummy's head, it was so still, and the eyes bulged in an unlifelike way. I left and came back. It was still there. In the evening it had gone. In the morning it was back again, eyes popping. I called the Gas Board, who were incoherent, and in the future got dressed in the back room. Rosemary came to spend a few days on her return from Italy before taking off for her women's college in Baghdad where she was to teach: we looked together at

Popeyes. "It's a man," she said finally. As we looked, the starer was rudely snatched to one side of the window and a hand twitched a curtain back into place.

There were other points of interest. I could throw a stamped, addressed envelope with a letter in it out of the window so it landed on the pavement below, and in a matter of minutes a passerby would notice it, pick it up, read the address, and march it to the pillar box down the street, all observed by me as I craned out of the window. Thus I came to love my flat and use it as a vantage point for the conquest of the world.

Before she left, Rosemary introduced me to Alessandro, tall, thin, thirtyish, pale, a mad cadaverous smile. She went to fetch something from the other room and Alessandro bent forward and kissed me on the lips in the second before she returned, and then, as they prepared to leave, with her back to him, mimed a series of other kisses.

I had recently sent some of my poems to Hugo Dyson, a former tutor of mine at Oxford, who forwarded them to John Wain, my contemporary, who was teaching at the University of Reading. Now Wain had inaugurated a series of poetry pamphlets there with his own work, and wished to follow it with an outsider's: that is, not with his friends'. He wrote to me directly asking if he could publish fifteen or twenty of my poems—a flattering prospect. A few more poems were needed, to make up a quota, and these I set out to write forthwith.

About then, too, I read in an anthology or magazine a poem ludicrously entitled "Le Monocle de Mon Oncle." It included the lines

If men at forty will be painting lakes
The ephemeral blues must merge for them in one,
The basic slate, the universal hue.

To men of forty, the poem said, all attractive women are attractive for their youth. Hyacinth (who died of love for his own image) showed their scope. In other words (if I read correctly), men loved the reflection in women of their own youth and beauty, however attenuated their youth and beauty became. And

> *The fops of fancy in their poems leave*
> *Memorabilia of the mystic spouts,*
> *Spontaneously watering their gritty soils.*

If those lines meant what I thought they meant, they referred to the poet's phallus, its work, and the poems that celebrated it. The poet that wrote this poem was just "a yeoman, as such fellows go." But he knew what instrument was in question, and the tree that resembled it.

> *It stands gigantic, with a certain tip*
> *To which all birds come sometime in their time.*

I must have laughed in amazement, as I do even now, at the frankness and the comedy with which this poet treated men's holy sexuality, while he held back from treating women's. I laughed, and I revered. The poet was Wallace Stevens, whom I'd never heard of. Bookshops didn't know his name, and neither did the U.S. library in its beautiful Georgian house in Grosvenor Square across from the brutal new American embassy for which other beautiful Georgian houses had been destroyed; however, the librarian looked him up and gave me the titles of his American publications. He was to be published in London in the following year, thirty years after his first book had appeared in the United States. Meanwhile the London Library turned up single poems, diamonds, in various anthologies: "The Snow Man," "Anecdote of the Jar," "The Emperor of Ice-Cream," and "Sunday Morning."

With Wallace Stevens's binoculars I saw my scene far off,

an amusing spectacle. The comprehension in "Le Monocle de Mon Oncle," right from its absurd title, drew me in, whereas T. S. Eliot—the only comparable figure in contemporary poetry—stared me down. The exhausted decadence of *The Waste Land* was based on disappointment, the absurdity of "Le Monocle de Mon Oncle" on libido, which I well understood. (Alessandro was particularly good at the game of "ephemeral blues," which he always contrived to win.)

A friend suggested I should go to the Salzburg Seminar in American Studies, where the entire oeuvre of Stevens would be in the library. They had fellowships available. So I wrote off to the director and applied to be admitted, citing the interest of Mr. Wain in my poetry and my own interest in Stevens, and in due time was invited to an interview on a Saturday morning in Harkness House in Portman Square.

I was late, having changed my mind several times over what to wear: the brown suit? A mark on the skirt. The navy dress with a stripe and white collar and cuffs? It didn't fit well. I had hardly any clothes. Finally I put on the navy dress with the stripe and rushed down for a bus, which edged off and then stuck in traffic. The man who eventually joined me at the big conference table in Harkness House did not seem to mind my lateness. A quiet man who moved quietly and reassuringly across the floor, he was about thirty, of medium height and build, with a high forehead and thick wavy dark hair, gentle greeny brown eyes, and an unusually deep voice. To my relief he didn't fool about discerning what attitude to poetry we were dealing with. I was able to speak openly, and he listened. He was interesting, even striking, and he didn't talk down. He knew about Wallace Stevens, but also about Ogden Nash. So the Salzburg Seminar might be enlightening, or wonderful, and I left the interview hopefully.

Two months later my train crossed the French border and entered the German-speaking world where I had last been as a child of thirteen in 1938, accompanying my family on holiday. That was just after the Anschluss in which Germany had marched into Austria and declared the two countries were one, in a vast Germanic unity. Uniforms were everywhere, black and brown and field gray, with Nazi insignia; and Nazi salutes were exchanged, even in shops in quiet villages bordering the lakes of Karinthia in the Austrian south. Fourteen years later, on the train packed with American soldiers bound for Munich, a well-tailored American lieutenant offered me a cup of coffee. He waved my protest aside. At least it was coffee, not the ground-up acorns flavored with chicory of 1938. And I was going to Obersdorf, the recreation center for troops? No, Oberdorf, a tiny village high in the Tirolese Alps near Gmunden where a friend had rented me some rooms from his sister so I could write. Later I'd go down to the Salzburg Seminar in American Studies. And would the lieutenant like a cup of coffee on me?

In 1936 we'd gone to Berlin to see the Olympic Games. We simply arrived by car via the ferry from Harwich to Antwerp, were assigned a guide and handed some glossy pamphlets about the National Socialist regime portraying girls clutching sheaves of wheat and young men wielding spades in a sunny land where all worked hard for the common good. The guide was a charming medical student who took us to lakes where we could swim and outdoor cafés among the pines. We'd been assigned lodgings with a worker's family in a new apartment block which the unemployed in Stockton would have thought paradise. We never saw the Games. You needed reservations and perhaps more money than my father thought we could afford. It didn't matter. The sun shone, the new age of Nazidom flourished around us, lean and promising young people smiled at us, banners flew, brass bands pom-pommed, and everyone greeted each other with the preposterous Nazi salute and "Heil Hitler!" Later we drove to the Isle of Rügen on the Baltic where the Hitler Youth had its headquarters, and we played on the sands as beautiful young men leapt athletically along the tideless sea. Like ancient Greeks, we thought.

Their health and innocence had something in common with my father's childhood in the Hebrides, and it was moving, as idylls are, and sad with a tinge of the artificiality I swear we felt even then, and faintly ridiculous, so Iain and I giggled, and were called to order.

There were other, more frightening events in those years. Once, in Nuremberg, soon after one of the enormous protomilitary rallies of the Nazi Party, we had booked into a hotel and were taking an innocent evening drive on the outskirts of the town when we found ourselves engulfed in a thousand or more young men in black and khaki uniform, on foot, bearing pitch pine torches, who swept past us without a smile or sign of recognition, souls apparently uplifted, eyes high, as we sat meekly in our car facing the wrong way and unable to turn round. A second incident took place the next morning after breakfast, when we left the hotel on the main square with its old buildings and cobbled surfaces, and walked over to our car in the center, carrying our luggage. No sooner were we organized and ready to drive off than two or three men came over to have a look at us, then six or seven or more, a dozen, twenty, thirty—till we were surrounded. They rested their arms on the car roof and jammed their faces up to the windows. None of us spoke, as we waited for an explanation. "Toot," suggested my mother, frivolously bold.

"No," said my father sternly.

"No!" my brother and I cried.

After ten minutes' mystification my father put the car in gear and moved it forward an inch, the crowd shifted, we moved forward another inch, and another, till the crowd of men parted and let us go. I have no idea what they were after. These incidents took place in another world, impossible now. In the mountains I met nothing but kindness. Perhaps it was because there I played the part of the poor student, so well understood in the German world. I wrote some verse for John Wain that reads now like the translations of Arthur Waley from the Chinese, and began another novel, feeling now and then I was on to something.

The Seminar in American Studies was held in Schloss Leopoldskron, a former palace of the Archbishop of Salzburg just outside the city. Max Reinhardt the theatrical impresario had taken it over in the twenties. A daughter of Chaliapin has told me she remembers staying there in those days, and how grand and operatic it was. When I came, it was still everything the wooden village house in Oberdorf was not—tall, stone, stuccoed, ornamental, with Meissen candelabra and a giant Meissen clock, lots of plasterwork, a gracefully spiraling staircase, huge doors with huge knobs, tall graceful windows, black and white marble floor, and many other features very good of their kind. Outside on the south side was a broad terrace with shallow steps leading down to parterres and dusty run-to-seed gardens, and a big shallow milky lake, with steps where punts could moor and crouching animal statues in stone on each side. Over to the south lay the considerable mountains of the Tyrolese Alps, capped with snow.

Into this palace of the eighteenth century I tiptoed with my suitcase and typewriter, surprised to find no one to receive me. I left my luggage in the great hall with its black and white marble floor and walked in the direction of a hubbub of voices. There, in another vast room, I found hundreds of people at lunch, a great mob all talking at once while plates clattered and glasses clicked. At last I spotted an empty place and sat down, and to my alarm discovered that my neighbor at table was none other than Alessandro.

Or rather, a minute or two later, pseudo-Alessandro. The same pale cadaverous Etruscan face, the same grin and refusal to be impressed. No, of course, not the real Alessandro. Yet he kept appearing and disappearing, superimposing his features on those of the replica. The fake lost no time in suggesting a walk by the lake in the dusk, where he kissed me just as the real Alessandro had done, so I should have known better. Furthermore, a few days later, pseudo-Alessando and I were with a group of people from the schloss straggling over the rough path home after a concert in the town when without warning he flung his arms round me in the dark so that we both fell painfully to our knees on the dried-out roots and stones of late summer. Not sure what was happening, I thought he was helping me to my feet when I felt his mouth close to my ear whispering, "Miriam, be mine!" and understood I was part of a farce.

The schloss lent itself to charades like this; within its theatrical shell it resembled an empty stage. The vast bedrooms, with their cornices and porcelain-tiled stoves and huge sash windows and double doors, contained only a few iron beds, and the long corridors a few makeshift showers and washbasins and lavatories. There were no curtains or screens. The great saloon was equipped like a naval mess, with deal tables and a variety of iron chairs, though they were set out under chandeliers, on a once shining parquet floor. The people in the seminar, too, had something theatrical about them, each nationality producing a different behavior, different mannerisms, and different expectations, like foreigners caricatured on the stage. An Englishman, just such a caricature, told me years later that he had always been faithful to his wife "except at Salzburg, which didn't count."

Such hypocrisy was more characteristic of the "fellows" than of the American lecturers and the American students who'd come to help, who by contrast and of course deliberately represented high-souled old America, America of the mind, not the America of the armies housed in the barracks half a mile down the road. Fellows and faculty both wanted, however, to get behind what Henry James calls "the fatal futility of fact," in accordance with the imagination of some Harvard students and their mentor F. O. Matthiessen just after the war, when they feared the ideals of the great republic might not be represented by its armies. Hence the foundation of the seminar, and its openness, which I believe now has disappeared in the confines of social and business studies where to be accountable is all.

It was delightful to discover that the bijou library, with its Meissen chandeliers, pretty rococo windows, spiral iron steps, and balconies of books, contained the entire works of Wallace Stevens. I had plenty of time to read them. Robert Lowell's course in American poetry, to which I was committed, consisted of his reading favorite anthology poems aloud in a gravelly voice and answering criticism with anecdote. When his students deserted en masse he became a presence on every scene, disheveled as if he never slept or ate or washed or changed his clothes, red in the face, waving his hands, pacing the dry gardens along the milky lake with a critic or disciple, an unappealing figure at odds with his poems, straight from

the kingdom of the mad,
its hackneyed speech, its homicidal eye. . . .

Tentatively, unsure what was going on, I showed him some verses I'd written in the throes of Stevens intoxication. I hoped to be told whether the experiment worked or whether it should be abandoned. He called it "distinguished verse," which conveyed his disapproval unambiguously in perfectly polite form. However, as if he hadn't made his point and conviction couldn't be held back through the crystal-clear vision of mania, he soon went further.

On the other side of the lake, approachable by a short walk along the right bank, was a bar which served beer in a sandy outdoor place with iron tables and chairs, and there one day Jørgen Sonne, the Danish poet, and I went for a drink, to find Cal Lowell present with Claude-Edmonde Magny, the critic, and Brian Foss, a sociologist from London University. Claude-Edmonde was reading palms, and the three of them screamed together like little girls. Brian rushed over to say Jørgen and I must have our palms read too. When we trooped over to their table, Claude-Edmonde Magny gave a great sigh of irritation, and Lowell snapped to me, "You're no poet!" Yet a lot of poetry is essentially experimental. The poet makes and remakes a poem until he considers it finished or abandons it. Lowell chose to be scathing about my experiment. He was kind to me later, but his kindness, like his condemnation, was beside the point. The poem didn't work, it was a poor pastiche, and eventually I saw that for myself.

The schloss reminded me of school, with its large important building and monastic interior, with simple food, simple plumbing, scholarship in easy bites. American ease, however, astonished me. The unbuttoned friendliness of the distinguished scholars soon led me to think poorly of the narrowness and deference of my upbringing and student life.

There were misinterpretations as well as reinterpretations. The psychologist Jerome Bruner was alarmed by the number of uniforms still on the street. It was the Tyrolean costume that misled him. Those olive green boiled wool jackets with leather tabs and horn buttons and flashes of red were indeed a kind of uniform, though no more military than the dirndl. Events overtook his fears, and presently he was engaged in full-time discussions with a young Frenchwoman about Cal Lowell's aberrant behavior. Lowell himself had begun courting Giovanna, an elegant young Italian woman. (The Italian poet who had been courting Giovanna, and Mrs. Bruner and Mrs. Lowell, were swept aside.) I stumbled on the director and his wife kissing madly on a back stair as if they were embarking on an illicit affair. She was being wooed by a German journalist, while the director was pursuing the journalist's wife. With the end of the six-week summer school, relationships fell back into place, except between the dean, John McCormick, and his wife. He was off to teach in Berlin, while she and their small son headed for England.

I remember very little now of the multitude of people who swarmed in and out of the schloss, across the stone terraces and through the parched gardens, who sang or played the guitar in the evenings or recited verse, or those who played parlor games, or those met at concerts in the town, where the famous festival of music had begun, or those with whom one conversed for hours, and about what. The dean gave a memorable lecture on Faulkner's *Light in August,* covering a blackboard with chalk tracks and arrows. Others I came across later in exalted positions, including the psychologist, one of the musicians, two philosophers, and several poets, but the majority, who in some ways meant more, have slipped away. The endless talk has vanished, like my essay on Wallace Stevens's poetry. Some events remain sharp, chief among them a scramble over the mountains to Berchtesgaden, Hitler's old mountain retreat, and from there to Königsee on a pilgrim route. There were four of us at the beginning: Catherine, who proposed it, Hans the German journalist, Jørgen the Danish poet, and myself. Catherine was an Irish girl of great charm and seriousness who taught Italian at University College, Dublin, and who was contemplating marriage. Jørgen, the Great Dane, as Catherine called him, was a tall, big-boned man in gold-rimmed glasses, kind and gentle and given to shrieks of laughter. Hans appeared much older, probably because he'd been a prisoner of the Russians. He was a stringy dark fellow, balding and narrow in the face, who kept his thoughts to himself except when Catherine was present. Unfortunately the bus had no sooner dropped us off at the foot of the mountain and we'd started scrambling upward than Catherine turned her ankle and became so lame that she made up her mind to return to the schloss, insisting that we three others carry on. Without her, Hans reverted to silence, even during the brief halts made so I could recover my breath. I remember thinking we were making good time until another of the seminar fellows passed us so quickly on a steep gradient that he appeared to be running on all fours. In any case, by evening we were up on the snow line at a hostel where we were given hot soup and bread and sausage, and a place on the crowded floor of the dormitory under the eaves, very uncomfortable and very cold in spite of the blanket each of us was issued. Jørgen held me close and gradually we warmed up; Hans kept to himself, though it would not have been in the least indecent if he'd clutched me too. There had been a terrible moment earlier when he'd taken my tiny knapsack and peered within it for a map, to find, besides money, passport, and so on, a lipstick, and he had exploded at my inappropriate behavior.

The following day we crossed the almen where cows were grazing. Hans bought milk from the herdsman, warm and delicious like the milk of my childhood, and then because we had lost the track between the pines and the overhanging cliffs he said he would scramble a little way down a dry streambed to see if we could descend there. He started off gingerly, sliding the seat of his lederhosen down the smooth worn rock and braking with his feet from one obstacle to another until he disappeared from view. Jørgen took my hand and we talked on and on, lying in the warmth on that peculiar cropped grass, a grass thickly interspersed with thyme and other herbs and moss, which gave off a faint dry odor of summer like the huge terraced lawns of country houses in England where for centuries they have brought in the sheep to keep it in some sort of order. Some twenty minutes later Hans's balding dark head showed down the lip of the streambed, and we took it in without alarm. He moved very slowly, clutching roots and bumps of rock. Then Jørgen exclaimed, climbed down, extended himself in Hans's direction, held out a hand. I anchored myself on a tree root and grasped Jørgen's boots, and slowly Hans climbed up and took his hand and climbed up his body and then over me and up the bank, where he collapsed on the famous grass.

Apparently he had found himself on the lip of a precipice, where in spring the snowmelt would hurl itself off the mountain. When he turned to climb back up, his boots refused to grip the polished stone of the watercourse, and he nearly went over. So the Furies were still after Hans. There are other fragments associated with it: Catherine limping away down the path on the way home, the icy water with which we washed at outdoor troughs in the early morning at the hospice, the dark water under the cliffs of Königsee where we took a boat to a pilgrim shrine, Jørgen's grasp of my hand on the boat coming back, how we had a beer at a kiosk and missed the last bus, how the waiter told us of a shortcut to the station where the last train would leave in fifteen minutes, how we ran through fir trees and cows and rocks and met a barbed wire fence, and heard the train glide away, and how we had to walk through the dark to a stop miles distant where eventually a bus returned us to Salzburg. Why do these fragments edge toward a wholeness false to the essential incoherence of the experience? The community at the schloss lives on in bright flashes.

We returned to the schloss very late. Cal Lowell had been taken away in an ambulance to a Munich hospital. Catherine had been waiting up for us, her ankle bandaged and resting on a chair. Someone was playing a guitar in the stairwell so the music floated through the house. People returning from a bar in town came in and listened. The place held delicately together with the modest moral intelligence that had conceived it. The U.S. barracks down the road where huge lorries driven by soldiers in fatigues went in and out whitening the trees with their dust, like the camp for German refugees from Eastern Europe which had formerly been a POW camp for Allied soldiers, now looked no more than the scenery of an old war. For six weeks, we'd honored the sanctity of individual human folly as if there were plenty of room for it. Sometimes folly looked madder than Cal Lowell. In a late conversation, the director spoke to me of the threat posed by Chinese troops who supported the North Koreans. The war had entered a bad phase. "We should drop the atom bomb on China now," said that elegant sensitive man. "Better deal with them now rather than later."

"But that would be *barbarous*."

"No, I don't think it would. . . ."

An idiotic argument loomed, of the sort doomed to angry

words, accusations of stupidity and blindness—even blows. Yet we munched our way through the meal, changing the subject in the nick of time.

One evening at about that time Jørgen asked me to have a quiet beer with him on the terrace overlooking the unruffled lake and facing the backdrop of the tremendous Alps. He had arranged saucers of olives and nuts and hard-boiled eggs and slices of sausage to go with the beer and flickering candles two inches high. He was expectant, but I was unwilling to propose whatever he had in mind. I had washed and ironed some shirts for him, that was all. After an enjoyable half hour I could bear expectancy no more and fled, leaving the saucers of delicate offerings and the glasses of beer untouched.

Catherine and I traveled to London the long way round, taking in Trieste, Venice, and Milan. At Milan we found ourselves jammed in a compartment with students returning to England after a season picking grapes in Sicily. Conversation ranged over the minutiae of Italian sensibility. "No Italian can pass by Lake Trasimene without feeling the most frightful sorrow," said one young man. And then, since we looked blank: "Because Hannibal defeated the Roman army there in 217 B.C. The Romans lost fifteen thousand men."

Back in London when I met Alessandro for a coffee I hastened to mention Lake Trasimene by way of tribute. "A place of sad association for Italians, of course."

"What?"

I explained.

"Nonsense. Italians do not know who Hannibal is."

The remark gave me great pleasure. Alessandro had grown much more severe during my absence. Why did I believe the silly things people said? It was not a crime to be skeptical. To make up for his harshness he lent me his antique bull-nosed Morris one week when he was away, with its huge oil consumption and the nuisance of parking it.

In return I told him about Jørgen, who in a few weeks after the end of the seminar at Salzburg had written to me to say that he had become engaged to Vera, another of the British contingent of which I'd been a member. Alessandro listened, frowning. "I thought he wanted to kiss me," I said. "But I had to make the first move. This engagement comes as a shock."

"Why didn't you make the first move?"

"I suppose I thought he should woo me. That's what men are supposed to do, isn't it?"

"Some men genuinely prefer women to take the initiative."

"Then women take the risk of being rebuffed."

"Of course," said Alessandro. "I rebuff them again and again."

"You don't always rebuff them."

"Let us say the spirit of contradiction is strong. And remember, I am not an English gentleman. I am not afraid of saying no to a woman. And since you won't have me, tell me, who are you seeing now?"

That I refused to answer. My ideal, I said (carrying on the line of argument), was an equal partnership between people of different sexes.

Alessandro bleated with laughter. "And yet you won't make the first move!"

Vera would no doubt be delighted to tell me more of the engagement. Jørgen himself might even be there. I looked forward to the drama. Meanwhile I was sharing my tiny apartment with the cartoonist Haro, who'd occupied it during my absence. That suited me very well, because he paid the rent. I had as yet no job and no other income, though I'd decided to settle on a business career that would pay bills. A woman at Salzburg had put me in touch with several large advertising agencies, where the interviews I underwent in due course seemed promising, and I was waiting to hear from them. On several occasions Rosemary joined Haro and the three of us drew and sketched, though I had no talent at all, and we stuck our drawings on the wall. They were of dancing figures at one time; late in the summer night, provoked by the images on the wall, we began to dance from one room to another through the tiny hall, round and round like banshees on a moor, leaping and waving our arms and swooping. My neighbor was deaf but the people below were not, and during a spirited cavort a hammering on the door made me open it to see a tiny man in pajamas whom I had never seen before, threatening to call the police.

The peculiar half-domestic, half-literary life came to an end when Haro finally left and Rosemary went off to teach in Baghdad. At Vera's party I hoped to find a flat mate to stand between me and my fatal attraction to another wrong man.

Before the party, however, Jørgen wrote to say his engagement to Vera had been broken off. He was very angry. The fault was all hers. Moreover she was unwomanly. Moreover she had not returned his engagement ring. It was not surprising. Jørgen was the sort of person who liked unexpected things to happen to him, and at one moment or another perhaps Vera was unexpected, and they'd both been carried away, and later returned to earth. She might even have proposed to him herself. My theory about unexpectedness was strengthened by a tale Jørgen told me in Salzburg about a hike he'd taken in Italy. He was walking along a road by an orchard wall and pulled some peaches off an overhanging branch and began to gobble them. He was half starved and they were delicious. He'd no sooner finished, and was about to gather more, than a hand came over the wall with several clusters of peaches, which a voice invited him to take. Jørgen was convulsed with delight when he recounted this story.

When we were both married he and I corresponded for a while and then lost touch. The last I heard of him, he'd taken up with an

Italian countess, and I thought of the peaches—gratuitous, delicious, part of life's bounty.

Vera's party was pleasant and well attended, as if, having been part of the Salzburg community, we could not bear to relinquish each other. We all stared a good deal, taking in the more formal clothes, the tidier hair, the shaven chins, the improved manners. We were now at home, none of us uprooted as we had been at Salzburg, less our very selves now that we came equipped with a familiar context. We were less brittle, too, gentler even, less presumptuous, easier to talk to, but also stupider and stuffier. I was not sure that the cushioning on show was commendable, now that my life was to be lived more forcefully. Nor did a flat mate turn up. I confided in Mary, a musician, that I really needed a buffer. She took me to see Maria Callas in *Norma* at Covent Garden and the passion onstage lent me perspective. I felt doomed, as much as any soprano in opera, but unable to get the audience on my side by means of my dazzling coloratura.

John Wain rang me up and invited me to a party in Oxford, at Wadham, where his summer school was winding up. I accepted and enjoyed myself, though disturbed by the implication that I was Wain's special, favored guest.

Alessandro used to drop in late at night from time to time on his way home from the hospital. His visits were not at all convenient. He would have a coffee, ask why he was attracted to me, and go. Occasionally I caught his interest.

"John Wain is a married man, you see. He says his marriage has failed. That may be just a ploy. Even if he is separated from his wife, as he says he is, he is still married to her."

"So if you are afraid of getting involved with this man, why do you go to this party in Oxford where you are his guest?"

"I love a party, don't you? He is not a man I would like to spend my life with. That's why I don't want things to go any further.

He's funny and interesting and he knows everyone who is writing
and he has an immense knowledge of American literature, and he
knows what is lacking in the present scene. He wants satire, and
form, and control. The party was fun. I met all kinds of interesting and amusing people. At the same time I don't want him as
a lover. Surely that is plain enough. After all, isn't it rather a masculine way of dealing with a member of the opposite sex? A man
likes a woman and perhaps fancies her, but he doesn't want to
commit himself to a long affair. That's quite common, in my experience."

Having explained so much, I began to suspect that John Wain
felt exactly this. Alessandro had a clarifying influence.

"Is he enough for you?" he asked.

"Well, I don't know, of course. What an extraordinary question."

"I like to ask this sort of question."

I'd glimpsed John Wain at Oxford years ago, once walking
down the middle of the Turl, a cadaverous figure with hair flop-
ping over his eyes, which were dark and sunken, a poetic figure
except for the way he clumped in his hefty shoes. I saw him also in
an undergraduate production of *Measure for Measure* in Christ-
church, in which he played Claudio, condemned to death for for-
nication. His sister Isabella visits him in prison and swears she'd
die in his place if she could.

> *O, were it but my life,*
> *I'd throw it down for your deliverance*
> *As frankly as a pin.*

But the hypocritical prosecutor Angelo wants not her life but her
virginity, in return for sparing the life of her brother. Indignantly
she refuses, and promptly informs her brother.

"Death is a fearful thing," says poor Claudio.

"And shaméd life a hateful," says Isabella.

"To expect one's brother to die on behalf of one's maidenhead!" I said to a friend at the time. "What a hope!"

"That's the point," said the friend. "One expects nothing of the sort now. Isabella is terribly high-minded. That doesn't mean to say she's wrong."

John Wain amused me at first by treating me with an unreal and extravagant courtliness. He might have been sixty years old. It was as if, having barely escaped with his life as fornicating Claudio, he had to handle a young woman with tweezers. Adding to my impression, he'd throw in little demurrals concerning my vulnerability—he wouldn't hurt me for the world, and I mustn't be alarmed if he said thus and so, and if he put such and such a thing coarsely, I should pay no heed: until I wanted to say that he needn't worry so much about the delicacy of his manners, they were fine, and I had knocked about a great deal, and wasn't easily upset.

Soon I went down to Reading by train to be introduced to the professor of English, Donald Gordon, who was about to go off to Italy, a man with a fine self-regard who laughed at me, because of my crude verses, perhaps. William McCance, the great printer, was amusing and courteous. After lunch John took me on his scooter to his bungalow down a bumpy unmade road on the outskirts of the town, and we talked, and walked, with John commenting on the talk and the walk. There were women's clothes on view in the bungalow, many of them thrown into a back room for sewing. The owner had gone—for good, said John. He talked of her a little and explained that she taught also in the university and in spite of that—or perhaps because of that—they went their separate ways and pretended not to be a couple. It occurred to me that they might not be a couple in private either, or she might have objected to his entertaining me in their house alone; on the other hand, they might be a very trusting and loving and open couple who had no secrets from each other. The abandoned look of the bungalow might not be visible to either of them. Order might be necessary for people on lower planes like me. Yet the only evidence of Mrs. Wain's character was the remarkable number of her things she had left behind.

Mysterious, too, was the relevance of John's own poems to his life. They contained no reference to his wife, nor to teaching in the university, nor to living in a bungalow in Reading, nor to riding a scooter. Nor were there any poems of feeling, except elegies for feeling. There were poems in tight form, tightly controlled, the resonance kept within bounds. He wasn't describing emotion, like me, nor the events that produced emotion. He was interested in spatial qualities, the distance one thought had from another, and in the public manifestations of poetry. Wain the critic cast his shadow on Wain the poet, the clarity of the first overlying the formality of the second. The sell in the poems was the presentation, the intricate rhymes. He knew what he was doing, which I did not, when I thought about it. If I didn't think about it, sometimes I came near to poetry. This often meant letting the words do the work, from lack of control and lack of craftsmanship. I was looking for the very essence of poetry, he was not, he was after the craft. What made him tick? What drove him to poetry? The desire for fame, mostly, and the belief that he was extremely clever at poetry, and the desire to reform the present state of letters, wrecked by the excesses of Dylan Thomas. He admired William Empson's knotty poems and the slight, graceful efforts of Robert Graves.

As I'd told Alessandro, he knew everyone who was writing in English, at home and in America and elsewhere. He knew the contemporary scene lacked wit and satire, and began moves that led to *Private Eye*. He knew everyone's work and, when he ran *First Reading* for the BBC Third Program, was able to introduce them to the public. From him I first heard of Kingsley Amis, whose *Lucky Jim* I read in typescript and didn't think funny. Nor do I think it funny now, compared with the much greater work that came later. He spoke, too, of Philip Larkin, whose *XX Poems* impressed me deeply, and whose novel *A Girl in Winter* was uncannily familiar ground. Through John I also met his disciple, Al Alvarez, no pooh-bah then. Younger than we were and better off, he used to turn up in a green MG. I met also the ugly, winning Wallace Robson, who went on to teach at the University of Edinburgh. I met Thom Gunn at Cambridge one wintry day with snow on the ground, and went on to admire his work. And there were others, including A. A. Hartley, who was to compile the Penguin anthologies of French literature; he disapproved of me. Through John, too, I went to a party given by Janet Adam Smith and Kathleen Raine where William and Hetta Empson were guests, where (I think) George and Paddy Fraser invited me to their house in Chelsea for Tuesday poetry readings. These were occasions when I was sick with fright at having to read out what I longed to read out, and heard competent, practiced work by the regulars: cooked to my raw, and more digestible. There was often a silence after I'd read, and never the criticism I longed for. The others appeared to me to have decided what they wanted to say and then said it—not always a good stratagem for poetry. The range of options, however, became clear, and the others were generous and hospitable to my efforts. George Fraser thought women were simply out of the mainstream. I didn't want to believe him. I preferred being thought temporarily incompetent. Paddy said I wrote what she secretly felt. I'd go home in a fret of exhaustion and love and hatred, and write for another hour or two. Some of these new poems were accepted in the *New Statesman* and the *Spectator*. The Institute of Contemporary Art included me in an evening of reading by several poets where John read, and Kingsley Amis, and William Empson (leaning forward like a blackbird poised for takeoff from the dais, his face thrust out toward the half-hysterical audience, his eyes shut, his beard a ruff, screeching).

These happenings were later ascribed to what he called "The Movement" by J. D. Scott, literary editor of the *Spectator,* in an article dated 1 October 1954. People have been made wise by the name, but it never had an identity. There was a shift in fashion, and that was all.

Meanwhile my new job in advertising gobbled me up. After a few months my salary doubled, pathetic as it was.

"A very odd thing has happened," I said. "Well, I suppose it was predictable. It was the way it happened that was so very odd."

Alessandro yawned.

"If you are bored you should go," I said.

"No, no, no. By all means, go on."

"He said he was in love with me."

"Fine, carry on."

"I said I was in love with him too."

"Not so fine. Carry on."

"Then he asked me to marry him."

"You tell me he is married already."

"Yes, exactly. That's what I said to him. But that's not the thing that troubled me most. I mean, it was bad enough. One can always get divorced. Not that I believe in divorce. I don't really want to get married, come to that. Marriage for the sake of marriage makes me think of going to prison for fun. When I admitted to being in love with him, though, he gave a great chortle. You know what a chortle is? Like this." I chortled.

"Horrible," said Alessandro.

"And he crossed from his side of the railway carriage—we were on a train, I forgot to say, all alone in this compartment, one of the sort without a corridor—he crossed over to my side, and put his legs sideways on the seat beside me and snuggled up, still with that awful shameful chortle of triumph, and squeezed my arm. *My arm.* Like a little boy."

"Disgusting," said Alessandro.

"Yes. Then came the proposal of marriage."

Alessandro frowned. "You can't take him seriously."

"A proposal of marriage is serious."

"*Quand même.* . . . How do you say in English *quand même?*"

"He must think me an earth mother, or a nursie."

"*Quand même, quand même,*" said Alessandro.

"'All the same'?"

"No, no, no. 'After all,' perhaps. Yes, 'after all.'"

"It bothers me. He has an idea of himself as a buffoon. As well as the cleverest man in the country. He thinks the buffoonery makes the brilliance all the more acceptable."

"He is a buffoon, certainly."

"Do you think so?"

"Of course."

"He has committed himself now, and so have I. I was afraid of this all along. Now let's see what happens."

"It is no good saying that or thinking that," said Alessandro. "It is very stupid. *After all,* it is very stupid. I suspect he will not be enough for you." When I said nothing, Alessandro raised his eyebrows. "So I am right," he said.

Meanwhile the business world wanted text and jingles that would sell a new shampoo that did nothing more than other shampoos, and a deodorant no more original than others, but people wanted new things, and the new shampoo and deodorant supplied that need, so almost any pleasant words announcing the newness of the products came into their own. The South-Western Gas Board produced some testimonials from local customers about the pleasures of cooking with gas; where local customers didn't turn up, members of the agency put on pinnies and were photographed grinning in mock-up kitchens, while copywriters like me wrote enthusiastic letters purporting to be from members of the public. Then the Milk Marketing Board was disbanded and my agency was told by free-market forces to extol the virtues of milk, so more would be sold, farmers would profit, and the public would thrive.

A plain description was no fun, however, and after a great deal of thrashing to and fro our art director thought up the slogan "Drinka pinta milka day" and photographers portrayed a very young and pretty model with a glass of milk in a series of fetching poses, and everyone was happy and drank lots of milk. I also performed more elementary tasks such as listing products for sale in Timothy White the Chemist's, and merchandise for sale at a big clothing store. I extolled oranges too, and bananas. I liked the people I worked with. So winter came, I saw John Wain from time to time, and we wrote poems that I am convinced were far better than either of us had written before. In the middle of winter Wallace Robson and Al Alvarez asked us to a party at Lincoln College, Oxford. At the last moment John said he couldn't go, so I went alone. It was a good party, but I knew few of the guests and felt intensely shy, and wished to leave long before it ended. The boardinghouse up the Iffley Road where I was to sleep was shut for the night when Al Alvarez drove me there. I was not allowed to stay in the college, being a woman, so was forced to take the milk train to London at three in the morning. It crawled, and I had to fend off the attentions of a drunken sailor who got on at Reading. At Paddington there were, strangely enough, no taxis present to take me home, nor buses running, nor tube trains, and I left the station angrily to walk a path I had never walked, still in my party clothes, to find the world outside the station smothered in night and fog. The streetlamps hung high like misty grapefruit, casting no light at all on the ground. I had to feel my way along walls and railings as I'd felt my way to the YWCA in Plymouth many years before, pausing at corners and searching for the names of the streets, meeting not a soul, grit of the bricks on my fingers, soot on the roof of my mouth (London people still burned coal fires in their grates). When I got home, shivering convulsively, I made tea and toast in front of the gas fire because I dreaded putting my freezing body into a freezing bed and staying frozen for good like a packet of peas. That the party should end with hardship and

solitude, without the presence of the man who would have justi-
fied my going so far and for so little, was ominous.

It still amazes me how happy the mind is to hold completely
contradictory beliefs. It must know how happy that ambiguity
makes the self, so it can look wrong in the eye and declare that it
is right. In the late winter John let me know that he was going
into hospital for another operation for a fistula, a long narrow
pipelike ulcer at his anus, a painful and embarrassing condition.
After the operation I took a day off work and visited him in the
hospital of the Pottery town he came from. He talked of how he'd
certainly visit me, on his knees if necessary and twice as far, if I
were ill. Again the courtliness struck me as dotty. We knew each
other very well. He was distancing himself from me, as if I had
been undignified to make that journey when he had his parents to
visit him and even his wife, who had returned. He spoke, too, for
the first time of taking a year's leave from teaching at Reading and
going to live in Switzerland, since the doctors had informed him
that there was a connection between the fistula and tuberculosis.

On the train home I wondered if I was in my right mind. On
the phone my father said he'd never heard of any link between fis-
tulas and tuberculosis.

"You might say that a fistula is a terminal complaint," said
Alessandro, laughing happily. "There is no connection with TB.
No, wait a minute, seriously, seriously, there is a connection, after
all. It is called hypochondria."

Shame came crawling up, squirming and licking my hand as it
hung down from the arm of a chair. Disgusting truth, it was not
going to win me over so easily. In the summer Rosemary came
back on leave from Baghdad and visited a friend in Oxford where
she met Dyson, who was talking about the Wains, how she had
gone off with a man and he had decided in revenge to go off with
someone too.

It was beautiful weather, and I'd decided to postpone my holiday for a less crowded and busy time, because there was nowhere I

particularly wanted to visit and no one I wished to go with. London in August then was dusty and sleepy. Some of my friends went swimming and took me along: where on earth did we go? Rosemary's brother Mark Boxer, who was very young, said he was in love with me one day, and recanted the next. My own brother, who was at the end of his military service as a medical officer in the navy, married and set up house near Portsmouth. My father and mother took me to see a film at the Academy Cinema in Oxford that was taken from a story of Neil Gunn's about two little boys in Nova Scotia who kidnap a baby because they want a pet and are forbidden a dog. The two little boys were enchanting and so of course was the baby. When the lights went up the audience sat with tears running like a lot of freshets after a thunderstorm, and I felt, not for the first time, the depth of a related passion.

And John McCormick suddenly rang me one day in the office from his modest hotel in the West End. He had gone from the Salzburg Seminar to the Technical University of Berlin, where he'd been appointed a lecturer, and was now on his way home to America to look for a job, as I'd learned from our correspondence. His wife was working as a librarian in the American Information Service and his little boy was at boarding school in England. I felt sorry for the three of them. He was too good-looking to be forlorn. He invited me out to dinner, and afterward we walked along the river late at night, on that part of the Embankment that runs between old Somerset House and the water, where in the old days barges and wherries used to row up and discharge their passengers in the lower portals. The stark functional London of the fifties had no such graces. It was a metropolis in a bankrupt country and nothing more. The benches along the pavement were the merest of gestures toward leisure and convenience. There was nowhere to go for a drink. Perhaps because of that unkindness we felt drawn to each other, and later he invited me to drive in his wife's car down to Cornwall with the little boy. We stayed in a cob cottage for bed and breakfast near the south shore, and swam from the beaches, picnicked in the fields, and afterward crossed the Severn on a flatbed ferry for Chepstow in south Wales; this was the old way north from the West Country before the building of the modern bridge across the Severn, the way Wordsworth and his sister Dorothy took, past Tintern Abbey, toward the end of the eighteenth century, after their stay with Coleridge at Nether Stowey in Devon. From there we drove along the Welsh Marches to Chester, where John's wife was working. John met her to discuss the details of various arrangements, including now their divorce, while I had a bath in the great old railway hotel—a bath big enough for a pony, in a bathroom the size of a small house. I was struck by the ease of the relationship between man and wife. Once they had agreed to separate, once the disagreements and rancor were in the past, they appeared free to make the simplest of arrangements for a final break and for the care of the boy. I thought it would be beautiful to have an openness like that in a relationship with a man. Life with him would offer comfort and space and scope. We would all thrive in it, the man, the boy, I myself, the mysterious, bravely independent wife. Chiefly, he and I would get on, two equal partners, understanding each other's drive and will. Even during our Cornish vacation, he had gone up to London to be interviewed at the BBC for a job as a talks producer in its North American program. With a job like that we could go on living as we were in my flat in Kensington Church Street.

Though what had gone wrong with his marriage? And he had singled me out with alarming speed. There was a great deal that I did not know about him. On the other hand, there would be several months before a divorce came through, enough time to get to know him better.

"I am getting married," I told Clarissa, the coffee lady in the office.

"And who are you marrying, my duck?"

"Well, his name is John, and he's an American. . . ."

Clarissa was hooting with laughter: "Oo, miss, an American! Oo, miss!"

And I remembered the Americans who took us Wrens home from the dance in Wiltshire and assaulted us in the back of the truck.

"He's not like that, Clarissa."

"Oo, miss! I never would have thought it of you!" And off she went behind the coffee cart to spread the news.

My parents, as expected, were also undone by our announcement. He was a man with a divorce in the works, a Catholic, and the father of a son. Moreover the BBC had turned him down for the job because he would have to be paid in dollars, which the country was short of. So he had no income until he landed derisory employment instructing members of the U.S. forces still in Britain. And what would Aunt Mary say?

I said to my mother, "Aunt Mary was always horrible to you. Why do you care a fig for Aunt Mary?"

How different John's relationships were! And yet his old father in the American Midwest wrote his condemnation of the engagement too. Catholic and of Irish descent, he objected to me as a Protestant and an Englishwoman. My mother wanted diamond rings for me, hothouse flowers, and the means to pay for them. Since they were lacking, following her instincts and testing him out, she began instinctively to flirt. So that was fun. He flirted back. Bit by bit my father and mother grew very fond of John. The fondness came first, and then the reconciliation to our future plans. They must have known we were living together, even while they went along with the pretense that John was staying with a friend in Soho. My mother called to see us one afternoon and found him underneath a car in the lane changing the oil. "John looks nice even in his work clothes," she said. It was most unlike her to admire a man covered in oil and in rags, but I don't think she could help it, any more than I could. By that time he had canceled his passage to New York and put his dog in quarantine and cluttered my tiny flat with his possessions, which filled me with pride and alarm.

"I am going to get married," said Alessandro.

"I'm going to get married too," I said.

"Not to—"

"No."

"He was not enough for you, I said so, didn't I? And this other one, is he enough for you?"

"You really can't ask people questions like that."

"I like to ask such questions."

"I know you do. Is it in the best of taste? I wouldn't dream of asking you a question like that."

"No one expects you to ask a question like that, but they may expect me to do so. I wonder if I could call myself an expert in such matters. Yes, I think so. Rosemary is getting married too, I expect you know."

"She told me."

"Of course she would."

Years afterward, Alessandro took John and me out to dinner in Soho, and later came to stay a night with us in New Jersey. He was much the same, but the exhaustion of years was catching up with him and showed in his face, the noble Etruscan face that looked as if it had come into the world imprinted with a lifetime's experience. By then he had achieved eminence, and his habit of falling asleep the moment he relaxed into a chair was well understood. I never got to know his wife, but she must have been a remarkable woman. All his children went into medicine and did well.

PART TWO

THE HEART OF IT

"Realism" is the only completely vague word.
"Satire" is the technical word for writing
of people as they are; "romantic" the other
extreme of people as they are to themselves
—but both of these are the truth.

—DAWN POWELL, *Diaries*

HOW MY MARRIAGE BEGAN

In a continuum anywhere begun
What's an occasion?

When two people take to each other, that good writer David Thomson has written, they start to uncover each other's past, not in layers like archaeologists, but always seeing the whole person who contains that past, with the present always obvious and clear, made up of the past. It is part of the great joy of marriage that you uncover the motor energy of the self continually, without a break. One of the first oddities I discovered about my husband was that he was without the common feeling for a particular place where you grew up, where you are deeply familiar with the ground you walk on, its grittiness, the soil and the plants and trees that grow in it, the color of its stones, the look of the people of the place and their houses and gardens, the animals and birds that share their habitat, as well as the composition of the roads and their smoothness or roughness and straightness or curves, the kinds of fence and wall, the habitual shape of the clouds, the width and depth and strength of rivers and streams, the direction of the prevailing winds, the position of the stars at night, the views. That is home in the narrowest sense and the most meaningful. It gives shape to the past and a place in the future, as it goes on giving shape to our awareness of surroundings and a direction to further knowledge of the world. This home isn't primarily a political concept, nor even a patriotic one. For millions, even in this present age where flag-waving demands instant response, their nation is the street of the village where they lived as a child. Not so for John.

This was not upsetting, of course. In fact it was reassuring. Women don't marry their brothers, men don't marry their sisters, they marry strangers, and John's choice of me may have had something to do with my unacknowledged rootedness, and mine of him something to do with his unattached openness. It was not as though he was unpatriotic. He loved America, his native land, and its laws and customs, and took them as a measure of difference, and this was interesting, because we were near enough in other ways—sharing half a common Celtic stock, for example—to make allegiances a matter of curiosity that could be usefully remarked on. But America here is an idea, or collection of ideas. There was no place that he acknowledged as home, and not having a home, he didn't miss one, or recognize the knowledge of one in other people's lives. Instead, he was a little like the stars in the beautiful gloss Coleridge attached to a stanza in *The Rime of the Ancient Mariner*, "that still sojourn, yet still move onward; and every where the blue sky belongs to them, and is their appointed rest, and their native country and their own natural homes, which they enter unannounced, as lords that are certainly expected and yet there is a silent joy at their arrival."

He had therefore no wish as to where he wanted to be, or what to do and how to live when we married, although he had been married before. When he gave me a ring I had cried at the threat of the marriage house that goes with most proposals, that imprisons a woman and demands cleaning, dusting, ordering, side by side with other houses for mile upon mile, containing people as dull as uniformity could make them. Hadn't comedies always ended with a wedding, as if the jokes were over and the serious business began, with money, sex, and family establishing themselves like bailiffs downstairs? John had no such thoughts. You lived where you wanted to live, with friends you chose, and as you wished. He simply didn't recognize the threat. So it subsided, in the face of more important issues. This was the London of early 1954, when things couldn't have been more difficult for us.

When the BBC had to refuse him the job of talks producer in their North American department, he gave courses in American literature at the City of London Institute, until he was forbidden there too. The laws protecting native workers from foreign nationals prevented him from finding a job in an English university or, as it turned out, anywhere else in the United Kingdom. (The tide that later brought many Americans to work in British universities had not advanced, to bring some amendment to the regulations.) Then, to my dismay, two months after marriage I became pregnant. The National Health scheme provided maternity leave for working women and paid a benefit—forty pounds in my case— when the baby was born, a considerable sum in those days: the idea was to encourage women to keep their jobs. I'd always loathed the thought of being "kept" by a husband. Nevertheless I hadn't the self-confidence to work till the last moment before the baby was born, as other women did. I couldn't swagger into my office, big and admired, as was perfectly possible. There was nothing to prevent me but a crippling sense of modesty. (My colleagues would in fact have applauded and been kind.) Nor were there shops with pretty clothes for pregnant women then, which would have made pregnancy more fun and an occasion for parading my new form. My mother, too, was surprisingly unhelpful, moved perhaps by a wish not to interfere. Moreover those were the days when the male ego was considered as delicate as porcelain, and women who threatened it were considered battle-axes, ball breakers, and worse. It seemed imperative to lean on John, so he should appear manly and I should appear womanly. The nonsense of these assumptions was perfectly apparent even while I embraced them. Of the options, though, the one concerning good wifeliness was the easiest, and matched the feminine ideal of my parents' generation. There was no one to advise me not to be a fool and see that my income, however small, was necessary for survival. My parents held their tongues. So when I was five months pregnant I resigned from the advertising agency and relied, insouciantly, on the blessedness of the pregnant woman. Without a job or hope of a job in the United Kingdom, in debt and paying child support for his young son that pushed him even further into debt, and with a new wife pregnant, John was more realistic. One morning he woke with a headache so severe he vomited. The headache lasted several days. He spoke to a neurologist. It cleared up.

Our situation went on, however, with its curious mixture of hope and despair, until in summer quite by chance an angel appeared, in the shape of a German professor called Bogislav Lindheim.

Professor Lindheim was a tall awkward man of about fifty, very thin and frail and stiff of manner, a man of honor clearly, without guile. He and John had met during John's year teaching at the Berlin Technical University. Now, he said, the chair of American Studies was falling vacant at the Free University. Would John be interested in returning to Berlin, to become a full professor and director of the Amerika Institut? How about me, would I like to live in Berlin? Would we like to go to Berlin at the start of the next academic year?

The news was a huge relief. We rented my little flat to two young women, one a nurse and the other a doctor, thinking we could perhaps come back in the summers. John wrote to friends and borrowed enough money to keep us going. The Free University advanced some more for our move. We had a little time to get to know each other in this respite from the frantic anxiety of the recent past, and the long explanation of marriages began, with its grace that has so much to do with endurance, the knowledge that the most dreadful storm subsides and becomes barely noticeable in the continuum. One may compare avalanche patterns, or those of stock market crashes, or outbreaks of war, or rainbows, or building booms, which reveal themselves to mathematicians and can be plotted. The lack of a sense of home in any one particular place allowed John to live anywhere with the same constant amount of hope and disappointment.

I longed to find the whys and wherefores in his history.

He had been born in a tiny settlement in northern Minnesota, on the Canadian border. When he was still a babe in arms, his mother became pregnant again, and the little family went on a visit to her parents in Wisconsin Rapids, where the young parents caught the Spanish influenza and John's mother died, five months pregnant with his brother, who died with her. His father recovered. What to do with the boy? He left him with the grandparents and went off to earn his living. John barely saw him again till he was twelve.

Not long after the death of the young woman, the grandmother died too, destroyed by her bereavement. So it was the grandfather, born Herman Beauchemin, a skilled cabinetmaker, who took charge of the toddler with the help of his other children, John's uncles and aunts, some of whom were married and had children of their own, all in the little town of Wisconsin Rapids, where the main source of income was from the paper mill and from the nearby cranberry bogs. These industries were attractions that enticed the Beauchemins from the province of Quebec in the second half of the nineteenth century. When they arrived, they changed their name to Smith, but Herman and his wife, Marie Antoinette Germond, still spoke Canadian French at home (John was *le petit crapaud,* their little toad). They had settled down so well that their children lost not only their French but also the knowledge of their parents' past, and here again there's a hint that place doesn't matter and isn't memorable.

"Where in France did your father come from?" I asked John's aunt Elizabeth on a visit to Wisconsin Rapids years later.

"Paris? Yes, I think it was Paris."

"No, no," said Aunt Gabrielle. "It was Lille."

"Lille. That sounds right," conceded Aunt Elizabeth.

The Beauchemins and the Germonds had in fact lived in the province of Quebec for more than two hundred years. A descendant of the next generation has discovered that. The earlier generation discarded the history that ours is out to recover.

On that visit of ours to Wisconsin Rapids, Aunt Elizabeth drove John and me and our small son to visit his mother's grave. The cemetery gates were drawn back and the car took us right up to the tall gravestone: *Marie Antoinette wife of Owen McCormick, dearly beloved daughter of Herman and Marie Antoinette Smith,* and the date of her death, 1920.

"I saved a few dollars and arranged for it to be put up," Aunt Elizabeth said.

Not John's father. John's father was a wretch. He didn't send money for his son's support. His visits were years apart. We drove out of the cemetery in silence, the dead woman's sister, her son, her son's wife, her grandson, nearly forty years after her death.

Marie Antoinette, John's mother, was the youngest child and the favorite, a very pretty girl to judge from her high school photographs, the cleverest and the best, as the dead tend to be. She was working as a bookkeeper when she met Owen McCormick, also a Catholic, from Campbellford, a tiny settlement in Ontario.

Owen's father, Hugh, had been brought from Ireland as a child of two to escape the Great Famine following the potato blight of the 1840s. The immigrants were granted land to farm, and when Hugh grew up, he married a girl born on a farm nearby, called Catherine. The land was poor, the family was large, the only hope of betterment lay in further migration, and Hugh and Catherine's fifth child, Owen, in due time moved to work in a tie factory in upper New York State, and afterward, because he was afraid of the tuberculosis liable to follow breathing the dusty air of the cutting floor, he went west and became a locomotive engineer for the sake of the outdoor life. And then, unfortunately, because schooling had not taken him as far as he thought, he decided to become a salesman in the property boom of the rapidly expanding economy. The salesman and the bookkeeper met and married and set up house in Thief River Falls, where John was born.

As he grew up, first in the grandfather's house and then, when the grandfather grew too old, in the houses of aunts, passed from one to the other, John saw that he was in effect on his own. He went to Catholic primary school and did so well that a future in the priesthood was predicted for him. When the Depression took hold, however, he passed from one public high school to another as he found work in one town or another in the Midwest; he baked bread for a YMCA, washed up in a restaurant, waited on table, was a fry cook, then a roustabout in a traveling carnival; he even dug ditches: all while attending school. His best job, the one that influenced him most, was as a deckhand on a freighter sailing out of New Orleans to the Mediterranean. At the outbreak of war in Europe he was a student in the University of Minnesota, where hand supported head in the same way, the possessor of hand and head often suffering great hardships. After Pearl Harbor, John joined the navy, and spent more than four years commanding escort vessels or acting as navigator on larger ships on the Atlantic or Pacific. On demobilization he entered Harvard Graduate School on the GI Bill, to study comparative literature. He was already married, and had a child, Jonathan. The family went to Salzburg as soon as his thesis was accepted.

I liked these stories of death, deprivation, and endeavor. I liked the America that could throw up a decided, hardworking man who longed to understand and to master ideas, who'd gone out and got his own education: not always the best education because constantly interrupted by the need to earn and hindered by lack of quiet and books, but an education that carried him out of narrow

circumstances, making use of the best America had to offer, coming up the hard way in the classical tradition, coming up every
day of his life. He always evoked kindness. When he turned up at
school in the Minnesotan winter half dead with cold because he
had no coat, his teacher went out and bought him one. It was still
in his possession when I married him, a reversed leather deerskin
coat, brown, with a good lining of navy woolen cloth. For years it
stayed with us, revered, with other coats now, easily keeping its
primacy because it was a really good coat. I liked that. And all
those severances, awful as they were, had not chilled him. He was
a warmhearted man, he was passionate, he was loving, he was
good to be with, in bed and at table and in the street. And with all
these delightful qualities, all was generality, he could settle anywhere, flowers were called *flower,* bushes were called *bush,* birds
were *robins* or *jays* or, rather oddly, *canaries,* and when we were
passing through the Dordogne on our roundabout way to Berlin
and I said how nice it would be to live in one of the caves that dot
that region, he said he'd speak to the farmer about it. A cave, a
summer home for us, as good a house as any.

That lack of a sense of a dear familiar place, and that indifference toward discussing the details of differences, which I used to
enjoy, and which now met with disbelief that I could be bothered,
where had such characteristics come from, and were they keys to
his history? And what about his depressions? His jealousies? His
preference for traveling alone? His irritability? His preference for
books over people (so tidy, so understandable, "the precious life-
blood of a master spirit," carefully distilled, not the confusion of
the everyday spirit I like so much)? These properties also surfaced
from time to time, and I felt I had to account for them, but not to
him, it was too intrusive, too unmanly, though I could never understand why. It was the stuff of life itself to find out about people, it seemed to me, and so it still seems, as witness these words
in the account of my life. Must I blunt my understanding, even
now, out of consideration for him and for our old marriage?

John and I drove into Berlin in early September 1954, arriving with a kitten a new friend had given us en route. We'd journeyed through France and slept out in the fields or, when it rained, in the back of our former window cleaner's van, the roof laden with our possessions. We'd bought food in the street markets and cooked on a Primus stove. When at last we drove east and north out of France and across the Rhineland, across the North European plain, through the various checkpoints toward Poland, the Russian official at the last border crossing stared at the kitten rather than at our papers.

"What kind of animal is that?"

"It is a little cat."

"A little what?"

"Cat."

"I have never seen such an animal."

"It is a little *Siamese* cat."

"Ah." A nod.

We drove into the city at dawn, our gaze drawn to a huge rusty tank established in the middle of a boulevard on the outskirts. It was a monument, among the drifting brown oak leaves and dry grass on the central alley of the boulevard, to the Russian army that had entered the shelled and defeated city in 1945 to loot and rape, in revenge for the nine million Russian war dead, while the other Allied armies waited outside. Nine years had passed and Berlin was still ruined. Broad boulevards stretched between acres of rubble. Sometimes you'd see people emerging up into this wreckage from invisible cellars where they lived. There were also rebuilt districts with shops and workshops, and well-clad women on the street carrying baskets or pushing babies in prams, and policemen and postmen, and buses and trams, and the overhead railways that stretched into East Berlin without hindrance, not even the hindrance of the Wall that was yet to be built.

So we came with our kitten to the pretty garden district of
Dahlem where our landlady was expecting us, and began our lives
there for a month or two, when we executed the first of many
moves in our early married life, for no reason that I can remember.
Now we were in the district of Grunewald in a pseudo-Scottish
baronial house, renting a ground-floor apartment which we fur-
nished meagerly with furniture bought from John's predecessor at
the Amerika Institut: the barest table and chairs, bed, chest of
drawers, made of the driftwood of the wars, for there was simply
nothing entire to be had from the old days; it had all been destroyed, and the recent Soviet blockade had made the import of
fresh furniture impossible. We had a hard time shopping for such
necessities as china in the depleted economy of the city. So for me
it was like wartime all over again with its shortages and make-do
attitudes, and I felt the irony of being a citizen of the country that
had inflicted the damage from which we were now suffering.

Operatic ruins, therefore. Parks. Sandy floors and pinewoods.
Red squirrels. Not many birds; Berlin not on the flight paths, perhaps. Double-glazed windows in preparation for the icy continen-
tal winters, with plants frequently flourishing between inner and
outer panes—begonias, cyclamen, ferns. The new apartment had a
lovely garden room overlooking the little dark shaggy lake below,
with a lawn running down to it and an old jetty and boathouse.
There was a big drawing room too, and one big bedroom, and a
kitchen, and a bathroom. Our furniture was lost in this ancient
grandeur.

I crossed the city twice a week in our van to reach the British
Military Hospital in Spandau, where I attended a clinic for pregnant wives of army personnel, spies, the British Council, and the
Control Commission. Usually I was the only client. The Allied
occupation forces were being wound down. My obstetrician was a
plump and benign Irishman I'll call Major Sullivan. His midwife
was a tough bird from the Army Nursing Service. The nurses were
German, and so was the physiotherapist, a sweet young woman

who taught the art of relaxation. She was so successful with me that we both fell asleep in our chairs every session.

I went through a natural childbirth, as it was called, when the American establishment was practicing caudal block delivery, in which the woman was paralyzed from the waist down and could not expel the fetus by herself. I liked fending for myself, but found the natural agenda a little unreal. Just before Christmas I found myself there on a roller coaster of pain that dropped me easily downhill, then rose giddily to a height in which I'd be hauled round first slowly, then whippingly, before I was allowed to plunge downward again. Finally I lay on the new, iron-hard delivery table. The German nursing sister had tied back my hair with a ridiculous pink ribbon. The baby left me and everyone cheered. It was six in the morning and I had entered the hospital at midnight. It was a glorious moment: John not there, thank God, he couldn't be nervous for me nor I for him. He arrived at noon after the morning's classes.

"He looks interesting" (peering into the cradle).

"*Interesting?*"

His second son, I told myself.

A stout little Christmas tree had appeared with him, decorated chastely with gold baubles and gold ribbons with a gold bow on top, and yellowy beeswax candles attached to the dark green branches with clips. It was glorious. The nurse Sabine lit the candles for an enchanted moment.

"*Schön,*" said the other nurses.

"*Wie schön!*" exclaimed Ann-Marie the therapist a little later. She had come to hear of the painless delivery.

"Not painless."

"I did not think so, truly."

"It was wonderful, though. Quite wonderful. When the doctor put my baby on my thigh."

"Ach."

"He clutched my finger when I touched his little hand."

"Ach."

"I feel nothing for him. I wonder if I'll ever love him."

She fetched the hard-bitten sister.

"I'm afraid of not loving him," I said.

"Why not?"

"There's his half brother. He's going to be upset."

"Love isn't rationed," said the sister.

I'd had a terrible dream in which young Jonathan stood on the deck of a submarine which I had ordered to crash-dive. I'd woken in terror at the moment of the plunge that would leave young Jonathan in the sea.

"You will love your baby," said the nurse Sabine, delicate and young, with red cheeks and black hair.

That night I woke to hear a baby crying, and got up and peered through glass at the cradles in the nursery. There seemed to be three or four bundles, none of them wailing. It was quiet, and the world was dark and calm. I went back to bed and thought, I do love him, yes.

On Christmas Day there was singing in the distance and the tramp of heavy boots nearer and nearer till a troop of twenty large British soldiers crashed into the hall into which the rooms opened, four of them carrying a hand organ between them. The chaplain sat down to play and the soldiers bellowed "There Is a Green Hill Far Away" and "God Rest You Merry, Gentlemen." Then they picked up the hand organ and tramped off, and the babies, who'd been startled by the rough male voices, were brought wailing to their mothers to be nursed.

The nursing techniques were carefully imparted. Suckling every few hours for a few minutes, then three times a day, then four times a day and for longer. By the time I went home at the end of a week, the wrinkled baby face had filled out. But he was as small and fragile as a teacup.

"Something has been added," said Major Sullivan on the doorstep as he must have said a thousand times over. He waved goodbye with the midwife and the three delightful German nurses and kind Ann-Marie the physiotherapist, all lined up on the doorstep of the entrance to the maternity ward, fluttering their hands. The little Christmas tree rode in the back ready to bring Christmas to our new apartment in the Grunewald. I sat beside John holding the warm woolly bundle of human life smelling of soap and lotion, holding it carefully and correctly and above all tenderly, in the crook of my arm, measuring the lovely weight. There was snow on the ground and the van was cold because few vehicles had heating then. I didn't know cars could have heating. I said to John that I could not tell him how wonderful it had been to bring a child into the world.

"Oh yes?"

It occurs to me that he, too, must have had qualms about Jonathan and the challenge this new life would bring, for there was a special absentia in his answers. Yet he was kinder and more loving than ever, and when I think of it, he had come straight from his classes in the university, which was extremely demanding of him. He was very much the outsider there, the youngest and of a different background, missing the flexibility of American ways of thought. Yet German faculties had the tremendous advantages of governing their own universities. The professional administrators who were to be in John's eyes a brake on enterprise and initiative had not been heard of. The meetings of professors in the Free University were therefore extremely responsible and continued for five or six hours. John would come home reeking of cigar smoke, his head bursting from the confinement and stuffiness of the council chambers, the burden of German locutions, and the climate of thought still struggling to free itself from years of oppression. Or so I thought, as I freewheeled.

Reason enough therefore for him to be preoccupied. And there were an unusual number of petty annoyances. Keys, for example: first there was the business of getting into the building. Two keys necessary, one for the outer door, one for the inner. Then the key necessary for entering the upper floor where the faculty offices were. Then the key to the office. Then the key to the library, always locked. Later came the business of unlocking the students, who tended to crowd into the lecture rooms and sit attentively taking notes but not venturing a question, let alone querying a conclusion, and perhaps (one suspected) not even tackling the texts for themselves. Later still came the business of releasing participation in the small groups John set up to read and discuss their essays. Once, fed up with a lazy answer, John took a hunting knife out of his pocket and stabbed it in the table in front of him so it stayed there quivering, causing the students to jump with terror at this possibly mad professor and creating a legend imparted to me years later. The message was that either you came to learn or you left. There was no middle way. This attitude came to be admired among the better students, who felt cheated by the generality of professors' inattention. It was not admired by the professors, since they were paid by the student head; they crammed their lecture rooms to overflowing and could not tell one student from another.

"Ach, dear Mrs. McCormick, so you've just had a baby. I wish I'd known. Peter. So. Ach. Allow me to say, dear Mrs. McCormick, it is so very un-English, poor young woman, you are so far from home."

"I am very happy," I said. "It is nice of you, but there is no need to be sorry for me."

"*Lieber Kolleger,*" said Professor von Fritz, the professor of Greek, "hearty congratulations."

"Our son is also called Peter," said Louise von Fritz. "When may I come and see the baby?"

They were a handsome old pair and I thought them particularly warm and kind. John, however, disliked at first what he thought was condescension. Later he thawed. I could see what he meant; their distinction was overwhelming.

I used to walk miles with my new baby. He was a healthy, beautiful child who grew and grew and disliked sleeping except when I trundled him along the sandy paths, by the shallow waters of the Grunewaldsee, back over the bridge with vast sphinxes at each end whose nipples the boys painted red, or else over the little wooden footbridge of the Dianasee to our apartment from Berlin's palmy days. Sometimes I wondered at the amount of time I spent pushing the pram when the house needed time and so did my writing, but it was good exercise for me, and as I say, the baby slept. I would meet distinguished people like the elderly gentlefolk next door who drove a beautiful old Mercedes sports coupe, and who had a succession of pretty maids, none of whom lasted more than a month. Or like the butcher, Herr Schuchardt, in his astrakhan-collared coat and homburg hat, and Frau Schuchardt, fur-hatted, fur-coated, who would bow magnificently when we met. And always there'd be other mothers pushing prams like baskets on wheels, the babies in them wrapped like papooses and with stuffed expressions to match. During the walks I'd consider the nature of motherhood while my baby woke up and kicked and laughed, bareheaded and bare-toed: this was the biological reason I existed, to bear the next generation. Was my frustration biological too? What I managed to write got no response, memory tells me, though my work continued to appear in magazines and anthologies at home, and my files contain letters from people who were interested in it. The great event in my life was my baby, not my conclusions about the torn city. When we turned up at Spandau at the British Military Hospital six weeks after his birth, the major called the nurses to witness my Peter, who examined the doctor appreciatively, holding up his head with only a slight wobble.

"More like a six-month-old baby than a six-week-old one," said the major.

But some thought we spoiled our baby. They themselves tethered their infants to their cots and went out for the evening without leaving a baby-sitter. One professor and his wife went away for a weekend with the baby tethered like that in the empty house, a bottle or two of milk thoughtfully provided for sustenance.

On our walks we attracted a good deal of advice, as if negligence was a real threat. The baby should be wearing a woolly hat and woolly bootees and should be covered up, because it was chilly, no, it was snowing, and *gnädige Frau,* should you too not wear a hat, to protect the head? Then the gaze would shift to our dachshunds. Where were their identity disks? Why weren't they on leads? Why was the big one digging up that stone?

Answering at random: He collected stones. His bed was so full of stones he had to sleep on the floor. They didn't need disks, being foreigners' dogs. As for leads, they seldom wore them. The big one liked to romp. I liked him to romp. Once the dog was waiting for me outside Herr Schuchardt the butcher's when a compassionate citizen took him away home to warm him up and give him a second dinner. Meanwhile I had gone home, found he had not returned before me, returned to the butcher's still pushing the pram, the baby wailing for his supper now, and met the kidnapper face-to-face. The dachshund was on a lead, stuffed with food, hot, and only moderately happy to see me. Night had closed in.

"Your dog was cold," said the kidnapper kindly.

"He is a very jolly dog," I said, using the English word. "He's always warm. If he feels cold, he runs up and down."

"The poor dog should wear a coat," said the kidnapper. "And he should have a nice lead, not a piece of string like the one in your hand. He is a beautiful dog." The last was a reproach.

"You are very very kind," I said, undoing the stranger's lead and handing it back to him and stuffing the piece of string back in my pocket before rushing home with the baby and the very warm and jolly dog in a hail of barks.

Was this really enemy country? I'd come to Berlin prepared to be magnanimous, not to be told what to do. I had anticipated hostility and met nothing but consideration. The slave labor camp at Ravensbrück was only thirty-five miles from the city. The inmates there were worked to death, a fact uppermost in my mind." You must understand," said the wife of the porter of our building to me, "that the people who were in the camps must have done something wrong."

"What wrong? Some of them were *children*."

She looked terrified. Of course the persecutions, particularly the persecution of the Jews, were completely beyond reason. But then, logic failed to account for the 1953 uprising in East Berlin (which John had rushed over to observe when he was teaching in the Technical University). Work norms had been arbitrarily raised in the building of the hideous Stalin Allee, the workmen rebelled, and the Soviet occupying forces sent in tanks to confront the parade of workers demanding freedom from the workers' regime and throwing stones at the guns. It was a strange spectacle, too, in Brecht's theater in East Berlin when a chorus line of actor workers marched on the revolving stage carrying red flags, singing revolutionary songs, in a production of Gorki's *Die Mutter*, while the audience of workers sat politely below in their best, not sure whether to clap or boo.

In the heap of contradictions that made up our daily lives, you could sometimes identify two wires ready to short-circuit your idea the moment you connected them. We met Helene Weigel, Brecht's widow, at that same Theater am Schiffbauerdam, a woman with a charming warm voice and manner but severe in appearance—without makeup, graying hair drawn harshly back, drab clothes, flat shoes. Brecht made all his women like that, said Lotte Lenya when we met her later when she came to Berlin to cut a new recording of *Rise and Fall of the City of Mahagonny*, written by Kurt Weill, her late husband. "No matter how glamorous or elegant a

woman when he met her, he'd turn her into a hag in a matter of
weeks."

So there was a belief at work here holding up this terrible drab-
ness as an outward and visible sign of an inward and spiritual
grace. We all want to be decent and self-sacrificing for the common good: we also want to be beautiful and elegant because we
honestly don't believe that ordinary appearances do much for us.
We're better than that. Let us persuade you of it.

Louise von Fritz arrived on foot to view the baby, white hair flying. She spoke excellent English because she'd lived in England
and then America since 1933, when her husband refused to sign
the oath of allegiance to Hitler. Only two other German professors also refused. Kurt von Fritz was eventually appointed professor of Greek at Columbia University in New York. He and his
wife had returned to Germany after the war out of a sense of duty.
America had been good to them. And her son, Peter?

Peter died. She did not like to tell me, but yes, her Peter had
died.

I was so very sorry. In the war, I thought. How ghastly—
imagining a son dying in a fight against your country. "Forgive
me," I said. A hideous situation.

She waved a hand, bent her head toward the baby and admired,
and said the love between mother and child was the perfect love,
since nothing was expected in return. It was absolute love.

She said—and I remember all this with the utmost clarity,
partly because she was so memorable in herself, with her white
hair and her grandeur and her dignity and her having come on
foot to see my Peter and me, and her terrible bereavement, partly
because the mind thinks of nothing but children after a birth—
that American children were different from German children, and
when her grandmother was dying and her mother cried, her son

Peter, aged four, put his arms round her and said, "Don't cry, Oma, don't be sad, I'll be your mama now."

Not an American thing to say, no. Then the kitten Gauloise, almost full-grown, leapt up the back of Louise's chair and started investigating her knot of blowy white hair first with one paw and then with both front paws together, and poor Louise had to beat her off with the back of her hand. So I never was able to ask her about the manner of the young man's death, what with her cries of alarm and her effort to prevent her knot of hair from disintegrating.

She said, however (when Gauloise had been caught and pushed out of the room), that she owed America an immense sum, more than she could ever repay. For that reason she was not going to reapply for the German passport that had been taken away from her in 1933. And yet if she stayed in Germany and did not go back to renew her visa through residence in America, she would lose it, together with her U.S. passport. Then she would become stateless.

I was inexperienced in the ways of passport authorities in those days, and was too busy registering what she said to be properly shocked. Stateless? A woman like Louise?

Apparently her husband felt no qualms in taking up his German nationality again. As for her, she felt unable to do so, because of Peter's service in the American army and his death.

How dreadful, I said, hardly able to understand. I thought I would swallow my pride rather than be stateless. But to be stateless on behalf of your dead child might involve more than simple pride.

Further explanation came obliquely. My informant was the wellborn Prussian wife of a Jewish professor who in the late thirties, before the war, was threatened by the Gestapo with a slave labor camp. The moment his wife got to know of it, she went directly to Goebbels and complained. She came away with an exit

visa for her husband, who left immediately for Turkey. She herself
went to England with their daughters. Louise von Fritz, she said,
was spoiled by her husband. Their Peter, serving in the American
army, killed himself. Yes, he committed suicide because, it was
rumored, he was appalled at what the German army had done in
Czechoslovakia in the last days of the war. No way to behave, said
my informant, refusing your passport like that and being such a
nuisance. Kurt von Fritz was soft; he should be firm with her. The
boy was disturbed. That was why he committed suicide. Louise
was greatly to blame.

"You mean the sins of the children are to be visited on the
mothers?" I asked naively.

"What are you saying? Oh, you are sorry for her."

"I was thinking, how awful to be blamed for your child's
death."

"I did not mean that, of course."

John used to bike to his office every day to teach or meet students
or work in the library of the pleasant white-sided Amerika Institut, given by the Ford Foundation. I was left with the baby in the
flat with its garden room overlooking the garden and the lake,
with the two dachshunds, mother and son, and Gauloise the cat.
The animals played rowdily and the baby was lively and still not
sleeping much. He was a sturdy baby, but his frailty compared
with my strength and John's frightened me. His weight on my
knee, nevertheless. His hand like a starfish on my cheek. The hum
of his love, the blowing of bubbles and crowing through them,
his runny nose, his increasing plumpness, the spasmodic kicks
and waving of arms, the laughter and unreasonable tears. We had
got pretty good at nursing and spent hours every day at it. It
seemed to be the one thing I needed no advice with. The prospect
of weaning was worrying, since there was no one to ask about it
and no baby food to be bought anywhere, and he was advancing

fast, walking at nine months. Soon he would be a toddler and I was unprepared. Though what was this, we were doing fine, if only there was someone to tell, let alone someone to advise me, let alone someone to help me. I had to shop every day, wash the diapers, and hang them in the huge attics under the roof where the breezes soon dried them. John was extraordinary: he had his own work, and yet he helped me with all these things. Occasionally I wept for no particular reason, unless it was for my old life. Frau Dingler had come to clean, a sweet woman about sixty years old. A student came to occupy the maid's room in the attic in exchange for baby-sitting. My novel was published in London and got fair reviews, especially from Olivia Manning. A far cry from Berlin.

So I wrote to John Wain telling him of the baby and what I was writing, only to create a storm in the Wain household. Two letters arrived from it in one day, one addressed to my husband from Mrs. Wain, the other from Mr. Wain telling me to destroy it. I destroyed them both, furious. So much for the republic of letters.

One day a very fat woman with three small children and a pushchair came to the door and introduced herself as Mary Jones from the official British housing down the street. I was delighted and asked them in. Mary and her husband, Alun, had come to Berlin with the British Commission at the end of the war, she to help homeless mothers and children, he as a school inspector, setting up and supervising the new and democratic educational system. Six years on, they were part of the diminishing British presence, fluent German speakers but still using the NAAFI that supplied cheap British food and clothing and books to the British contingent. Mary introduced me there in return for transport of her groceries in the Isetta which had replaced the van. It was a godsend for me to complete the main week's shopping in one swoop.

"She smells," John said.

"It's true, isn't it? Try not to think about it."

"And those kids smell too. They are filthy. Why are their teeth black? Candies, is it? I don't like them near our child."

"They're very nice children. Mary is adopting a little girl from one of the orphanages. The child lost her own mother, then she lost a woman who adopted her and got polio and had to return her to the orphanage."

"Poor little wretch."

"I know."

"I don't think Mary likes me."

"Too clean, I expect. You should see their bathroom. No, perhaps you shouldn't. The fact is, she doesn't like Americans."

"Tough."

The orphan eventually arrives and is brought round to be introduced one morning when John is safely out of the way. The child's name is Johanna, and she is a good-looking, robust child with red cheeks and cropped hair.

"I wanted a dainty little girl!" Mary complains, as Johanna leans possessively against her. "And I get this!" The boys swiftly open a little box and organize several lines of soldiers on the floor. The oldest boy pulls Johanna down to join them in a kindly way, but she jerks her hand away and pouts. "She never had the advantage of that good early training," says Mary.

A joke? Huge dirty Mary. A sturdy little girl in a dirty dress and carpet slippers. Three boys already deep in their game. Johanna leaves Mary's side, kicks the soldiers far and wide. She is torn away from the kicking, hitting heap of children. Smack, smack. As before, thumb in mouth. Everyone quiet. They trail off home.

Frau Dingler bursts into tears one day. I have recommended her to Mary and she goes to Mary's after helping me. By now the Joneses have joined the Berlin school system and Alun is a German inspector of German schools. They have a large official flat some distance away. I do not see the family for weeks and make no effort to do so. "Oh, that Johanna!" weeps Frau Dingler. "The punishments! She is locked in her room for hours! *Mein schönes Kind!*"

Her tears fall on John's newly ironed shirt. I have no idea what to do. Johanna cannot be sent to the orphanage a third time. What happened in the end? There is no one to let me know.

Berlin is of course on the eastern edge of Germany, a few miles from the border with Poland, and it was an island then in the east zone, hard to get out of except by air, which we could not afford. Far away in history as well as far away from London, that Berlin, like a black box chucked into the field of the past. Without its federal government, West Berlin in our day looked provincial, as the city must have seemed when it was the old capital of the kingdom of Prussia, before Bismarck made it the capital of a united Germany. The history of the university reflected the changes, the original Berlin University coming into being in 1810 after the Napoleonic Wars, and becoming the Humboldt University under the Soviets. In 1948 some students peeled away in protest against restrictions the Soviets had imposed on education and crossed over to West Berlin to found an alternative university, with academic freedom in the traditional sense. So the new Amerika Institut in Dahlem was a counterpart of the Amerika Institut over at the Humboldt. The duplication of life in Berlin was a perfectly common local phenomenon: two universities, two opera houses, and so on, one in the East, one in the West. Once, challenging this characteristic, we invited members of the old Amerika Institut in the East to meet members of the new one in the West, and offered them supper.

"Boston baked beans!" murmured Professor Katske of the Humboldt, who'd last sampled them in Massachusetts in the twenties. He was a square man with pronounced Slavic features and pale

blue eyes, who entered the flat dressed like a capitalist businessman on a Communist poster, with a thick plushy black double-
breasted overcoat and a gray homburg hat. His wife came in as a
tightly corseted mattressy figure in a Persian lamb coat to the
floor and hair wild and bobbed like beauties on postcards from the
twenties in sleepy English country towns.

"You must come and see our outfit in the sticks!" said Professor
Katske kindly, in a powerful Boston accent.

Whereon Professor Hübner, John's senior colleague, turned his
back. Professor Hübner said often that English was better taught
in Berlin than at Oxford, and that Shakespeare sounded better in
German than it did in English. He thought Gielgud's version of
Much Ado About Nothing, brought to West Berlin by the British
Council at vast expense, was out-and-out wrong. Nor could he
forgive Professor Katske for refusing to take the post that he himself, as second choice, now occupied in the Free University.

In spite of Professor Hübner, the party was a fair success. I'd
been afraid that the Humboldt people would not speak out. They
had a lot to lose, their housing and stipends being far better than
other East Germans', and they had nowhere else to go in East Germany for the same advantages. They could even get on with their
careers without getting politically entangled. In fact the wife of a
young *Dozent* told me that she had never really thought about pol-
itics until the police came for her own father in the middle of the
night and arrested him without warrant or explanation.

However astonishing her naïveté, there was always the possibility that we in the West had been misinformed about the "Terror" in the East. I said therefore how glad I was that they came to
meet their opposite numbers over here.

Yes, she said, she had been curious.

And to judge from the level of noise and laughter, both sides
had been curious till then and glad to meet. Yet I don't think our
party eased matters. No friendships were made, no books exchanged, no brilliant and stimulating conversations begun, but

everyone went home smugly interested in what had happened, and that was that.

As foreigners with special permits stamped on our passports, John and I often drove past the checkpoints into the eastern sector of the city, down empty Unter den Linden where new lindens were growing tall, past the portentous Russian embassy with its lace curtains, and the elaborate Opera House built at a cost of ten million pounds, and the bomb sites still being cleared by hand, the rubble loaded on little wagons on rails and trundled off pushed by hand. We went to the Brecht theater or the opera or else visited an exhibition like the one in 1955 which showed the paintings from Dresden that the Russians had sequestered ten years earlier and that were now being returned to the German Democratic Republic, or East Germany. A surreal scene, it was, the wind blowing across the vast square where the great center of the city had been.

Through these two mirrors, or holes in the face,
I leap into a land of ice; a lopped cathedral,
an acreage of snow, a plain where stood a palace,
on which men drift like odd black flakes
and melt upon the sticks of far-off scaffolding.
The east wind flares upon a lake of light.
A yellow double-decker bus is a mechanic's puppet sun
that glides behind the stage at the right interval
to signify the space of day; but day and night are lost
behind the eyes, in a scooped skull
where snowbank, cloud-packed, rears.
Men dance all numbed over the glass
paving-stones, past a forlorn saluting base
where a flag drips ice. They fly, flapping coats
like storks descending over rooftrees,
over a canal's breath and a broken bridge,
and fold into a bannered hall.

We hadn't the price of admission in Ostmarks. A man examining our car gave us some. No, he didn't want our Westmarks. He had a son in Manchester who sent him food parcels. He smiled at us.

Inside, shabby drab crowds packed the galleries, giving off a foul smell of unwashed bodies and dirty clothes. They moved mesmerized from one rich painting to another, Giorgione, Rembrandt, Rubens; examining the luxury of clothes and furnishings, the carpets, furniture, the flesh of beautiful women and handsome men, their pearls, their elaborate hair, their white linen, their velvets, their flowers and paradise gardens, their landscapes, their noble architecture, their aspirations, their morality, their velour. A dream, a series of dreams, painted long ago. The present general poverty was undreamt of then, the ennobled shapes of desire still cast a shadow before them. How rich the mind was in those pictures, and how wretched the crowds who shuffled past them, drinking in the delights, the questions and answers, the skies, the flowers, the flesh.

Fragments, oddities, also in that black box: the Marxist scholar who told us that Marx had considered choosing the bourgeoisie as the agents of revolution before he decided on the proletariat. The scholar was a handsome man who often called on us, as he had mislaid his wife. One evening he took us to the Comic Opera in East Berlin to see a performance of *Die Entführung aus dem Serail*. The production was by Felsenstein, the theater itself (small, rococo, rebuilt, with lots of gold paint and carving) was stunning, and the singing and costumes and orchestra glorious, so glorious the tears ran down my face. Also: the bluff professor from the part of Saxony that had become Polish, who maintained that the Poles and the Germans loved each other like brothers. Of course! How could you believe otherwise? And the mechanic brought in for a beer who boasted how he had pushed Jews into trenches and helped bury them alive. The woman who raged that she had not been compensated for her factories, bombed by the Americans.

The people we knew varied from spies, diplomats, newspapermen, and soldiers and civil servants of various nationalities, the faculty of the Free University, to tennis players at the British Club and riders at the equestrian school. But the demands of his position and our lack of money and the thwarting of his wish to write imaginatively and the separation from his young son Jonathan often pushed John into depression. As far as his professional career went, there was no outward cause. He was a full professor at an early age, and Longmans was bringing out his excellent book on the novel called *Catastrophe and Imagination*. But rubbish accumulated in the black box bore on his sense of being in the wrong place: the way Berliners drove, their gross eating habits, the stink of bodies on the bus, public pushiness, the American military, the British military, the mediocrity of others, their fatness, their vulgarity.

The depressions lasted a week or more. I noticed that when I became suicidal at his depression, it lifted. I was afraid to leave him in case he killed himself, and yet I myself might be the cause of his depression so I should think of departure. He often spoke of suicide, though as a refined and aesthetic and even witty act, as Stendhal might write of it. There was a hallucinatory dimension to our lives that both encouraged the wish to be yourself and trashed it, and if I had not taken it as a calamity, John's talk of suicide might have seemed ridiculous. Then an alcoholic friend of his in Boston shot himself and, getting used to the news, we went out into the snow one bitterly cold night with a good friend, David Binder, the journalist, and the men threw snowballs at streetlights and broke a couple of them. So it was true, even friends killed themselves, though it made no sense to me. In the effort to understand, I put myself in his skin—became him, which made matters worse.

By 1957 we had moved again, to a house in Wilmersdorf, and

to consolidate our complicated finances, John's father, whom he supported, joined our household. Owen was in his eighties and crippled with arthritis, a sad old man, wintry and blank, and even when charged with whiskey could recall very little of the past, even the interesting years when he was an engine driver in the Pacific Northwest, and met a bear on the line, and had to stop the train till the bear got up and trundled away. When pressed for pictures from his childhood, he wept and said he hadn't been wanted, and once as a small boy slid off a roof while the others were haymaking, and fell down the well, and struggled there till the haymakers returned and heard him shouting. The episode sounded like a dream, or a memory played over and over till it assumed significance. And what significance was that? A dramatic incident, firmly attached to place, the way my father's memories were to his birthplace on Skye, although my father always was tickled by his hardships: for example, how he'd run miles with a message and been rewarded with a whole penny; or how his eldest brother had thrown him into a deep rock pool so he had to find out how to swim or else drown. Those last were occasions for boasting, not for self-pity. I tried to think up some cogent incident from my own childhood, but it seemed one long mild happiness.

The Christmas after Owen joined us, John was away attending the congress of the American Language Association in Washington, so we were alone, Owen, Peter, and I. I went to a great deal of trouble to make the house festive for the three of us, but told the old man firmly that he was extremely lucky to have been a member of a large family and to have lived on a farm in Ontario.

"Lucky!" he cried. "It was a very poor farm. All the good land went to the Empire Loyalists."

"There is no pleasing you," I said.

"My life is empty," he said, thumping his stick several times and looking at me hard.

"You have John. You have me. You have Peter, and Jonathan. And we have this pink champagne from the Naafi." So we finished it between us and he declared it was the best Christmas ever, which was nice, if obviously untrue.

John returned from America via England where he bought a 1928 Invicta, an early touring car, in which he toured all the way to Berlin. It was long and low with a canvas folding roof and a leather strap over the bonnet. He brought news of my parents, and a load of presents, like Father Christmas, but this latest purchase was a dandy's, like the tailored suits and handmade boots he went in for long before he could afford them, things to curtain off the area of darkness in his mind, in case it spread.

I knew I had a corresponding thrift born of the careful economies of wartime, when nothing was thrown away and there was no frivolity. All the same, I wished I could have gone skiing in the Hartz like our friends instead of trying to get the low green monster to start on cold mornings.

Nine months later Owen went back to Minneapolis, where he could at least follow the football and the baseball games on the radio. Our relief was like a long low release of breath.

In the same season when Peter had his fourth birthday, he and I went to the Marx-Engels Platz again, to attend the fair on Silvesterabend: New Year's Eve, when in the West people put lighted candles in their windows for the prisoners of war still in Soviet hands. It was again very cold. Stalls sold engaging handmade wooden toys and simple sweets, and I'd heard there were roundabouts. I parked the car unobtrusively in a side street and ran with Peter, bursting with excitement, to the fair. It was not packed together, as I remember, like the fairs and markets I knew at home, exuding warmth and color and flickering with acetylene lamps (how cozy the one on Stockton High Street had been, thronged with people, resounding with the cries of hawkers and the bellows of stallholders, joshing, joking, even in rain). No, it was scattered over the huge platz, with hungry bundled-up queues of people in front of the stall selling hot sausages and the stall selling baked potatoes. We bought a few things and then

heard the hoot of a train. It was a very small train, in fact a miniature train, with a huge engine driver in the cabin of the hooting,
smoking little locomotive, behind which trundled a long line of
tiny carriages stuffed with children and their giant parents. Peter
nearly died. He had been a fan of trains since he could acknowl-
edge they existed. The toy shelf at home consisted of wooden
trains, tin trains, lead trains, push trains, clockwork trains. We ran
to the dwarf ticket hut and I tried to buy one adult and one child's
ticket. But no, Peter said, I could not go, I was too big. This was
a child's train, and he was a child, he must go alone, it was his
birthday treat, I had promised, he would cry if I so much as tried
to go with him.

But he was just four, too young to go alone.

And I was too old and too big.

Look, though, at all those Vattis and Muttis descending from
the little carriages with their children, of course I must go with
him, I should enjoy it enormously.

No, no, I would spoil everything. Goodbye, goodbye, wait
there, he would be back in a flash.

And he got into one of the carriages and waved. The train filled
up, whistled, and trundled off into the ruined city. I waited and
waited. I must have been insane. He might panic and get off and
run into the ruins and never be seen again. Anything might happen. I'd always consented to other people's nonsense, and look what
messes consent led to. Half an hour passed. And here was the little
train at last, far off over the snowy field of the Marx-Engels Platz,
trailing its plume of fine white smoke, hooting every now and then
in the pure white silence of the New Year. Oh, life was beginning
again all right. Hours went by. At last. Here it was. And here was
Peter, red in the face with joy, running full tilt over the snow as the
adults stiffly piled out and handed their cocoon infants down.

When I told of our adventure, people back in the West could
not believe my foolhardiness. It simply was not safe to go to the
East. It simply was idiotic to let a four-year-old child go by him-

self, by himself, on a miniature train going God knows where through the streets of East Berlin, a city rife with criminal mischief, anything might have happened, you really should have shown more sense.

Well. It had been bliss. A taste of heaven. I'd seen heaven on his face.

I was to go ahead to America in May and find a house, taking Peter with me, and John was to follow at the end of the academic year. We had to find homes for our dogs—the beloved cat Gauloise had died of distemper when she was only nine months old. The big dachshund had got into the habit of nipping and jostling his little mother, so they split up, the mother going to a little girl who had always loved her. When we called to see how the dog had settled down, she was lying at ease in a pink padded dog basket with her name on the hood: ANNA. The big dachshund, her son, tried to join her and received a smart nip on the nose. He himself went to a dentist and his wife, who had a little baby. The dog soon loved the baby to distraction, as appeared in a photo they sent us in which the dog sits by a carry cot with his ears back and a look of calm and boastful ownership on his face.

"It would be best if you and Peter took the Invicta to England, visited your parents, and then put it on the ship for New York at Portsmouth," John said.

The idea did not appeal to me. The Invicta gave me no pleasure, I disliked it on principle, and it was unreliable. Why didn't John keep it himself?

"No, no, you have it. It will be great fun to have in New Jersey."

"Not my idea of fun," I said, or dull words to that effect, ground out with a difficulty that John in his enthusiasm did not even notice. A traditional woman would have refused point-blank, wept, and lain on the ground, or else clapped her hands for joy and thrown her arms round her husband. My philosophy of allowing people their head was indistinguishable from cowardice. It wasn't enough that a friend was alarmed for me. "You're not making her drive that thing through the Russian zone?" Whatever the answer, it changed nothing. I am weak like my father, I thought. "Push, and I give," I said to my incredulous friend.

At dawn after a nightlong party, I crawled in beside Peter in front of the luggage, revved the enormous motor, squeezed the horn, and edged off into the early summer morning, past the monumental tank in the middle of the boulevard, the sandy floors, the pines, the checkpoint.

Out on the autobahn a man in a white Mercedes buzzed us, passing at speed and then slowing so I had to pass him, accelerator pressed to the floor, the gallant old car thundering along at sixty miles an hour. Once he'd had a good look at us—woman driver, small boy, mountain of luggage—the Mercedes drove to within an inch of our back number plate and hung there tailgating for miles. The Invicta resented the drag and slowed by itself, and I let it slow further, down to fifty, then forty-five, then forty, till the Mercedes swung out and again shot past and slowed in front of us. He continued the game till we reached the exit from the Russian zone. Peter and I went into the control point with our passports and permits, and an official asked me if we were part of the circus. A picture flashed in front of me: pantechnicons of caged elephants and tigers, trailers containing the big top, the clowns, the ponies, the trapeze artists, led by the Invicta. No, sorry. Just private people driving to the ferry at Rotterdam in a damned antique with a crash gearbox and a ludicrous upper speed limit.

Outside the control barrier the Mercedes had pulled up and was watching. Under the Invicta, as he indicated with jabbing forefinger, was a pool of oil. I explained to the man at the filling station nearby, and he crawled underneath the car and peered up. There was a hole, he said, in the oil line.

"True."

He went off to confer, and presently returned with a man who explained that he'd been in panzers in the war, and knew a trick that would help. He crawled under the car with a piece of soap and plugged the hole as he'd done in the North African desert. The plug was still intact after I picked up the car in Hoboken four weeks later.

The first night away from Berlin we stayed at an inn on the Dutch border where the wall behind the bar was hung with a big chipped aircraft propeller. It belonged to the plane piloted by the son of the house, who'd been shot down during the war over his home territory and died in the wreckage. The barman informed me of this, and I felt, as I often had in Berlin, that if I cried tears of blood, it wouldn't be enough to express my grief, merely altruistic as it was.

Your return to your own country is usually an emotional moment, and I was surprised to be accosted by immigration officers at Harwich who wanted to know why I was entering Britain. It was like being asked why I was me.

I was coming home, I said finally.

And what was I bringing with me? What, no presents?

Berlin had nothing much to offer, I said.

Didn't I have gifts of chocolate, that sort of thing?

Well, no. My parents didn't eat chocolate.

So what was in my luggage?

In my luggage? Well, clothes. A few books. Writing materials. A typewriter.

Toys, said Peter.

When the two large well-spoken men let me go, I felt annoyed at the false figure I must have cut driving the flashy old car, and then I was annoyed to feel annoyed, for what did it matter? And I was remorseful that I wasn't coming home laden with presents for my parents, who'd always been good to me.

FEVER

My brother was anxious not to be conned.

"You're always talking about Berlin," he said.

"Well, that's where we've been living, after all," I said, amazed. My brother grew stranger and stranger. Surely he was not jealous of our life in foreign parts? Or was he tired of traveler's tales, so tedious from a sister? Berlin was far from glamorous, as I have tried to show. Its merit for him may have been simply that it wasn't Maidenhead, where he now practiced, in the tame Thames Valley with its little snobberies and its sameness. At any rate, he would not tell me, and I found myself attacking him for his efforts to dominate me.

If John and I had had no children, we might have stayed in Berlin. Peter had started going to kindergarten and thrived there. He'd suddenly became bilingual, a useful asset in later life. On the other hand, he was an American, and needed a sense of himself in an American society on American soil. Nor was Berlin the real Germany: it was an invention, precariously kept alive as a political entity, and our sense of isolation, John's and mine, increased year by year. Foreignness has its price. Foreigners dislike the interpretative gaze that is turned on them, so often wrong, or inadequate. There were great rewards to living in Berlin, but in the end I couldn't think straight. The language alone was a brake on spontaneity, and though one of our student baby-sitters had told me that I was a free spirit, I felt imprisoned or, if not imprisoned, on probation. Jokes, allusions, repartee were lost. I found myself

laughing emotionally at very ordinary conversations in English because they involved the play of words and took things for granted
that conversations in German couldn't. Then it became clear to
me from the first horrid moments of applying to the American
Consul in Berlin for a visa to live in the United States that I was
holding my birthright up to the light and no one cared. Had I
been a Communist or a Nazi? Had I a venereal disease? And eventually, wasn't I glad to see the Statue of Liberty so I could be free
at last? A gulf opened between what I felt I was and what I was
assessed to be. I was to ride on John's coattails, the spouse of an
American citizen, allowed in on privilege.

"It would be nice if you found the right house immediately,
wouldn't it," my mother said the moment Peter and I arrived in
Windsor, with that very English way of softening a statement
with a question that queried it. "It's time you had a place of your
own, isn't it. This moving from one place to another, I couldn't
put up with it myself, and it's hard on Peter. Now you'll be able to
have your own things in your own house, and Peter will settle
down and make friends. You really need more stability. I just wish
you wouldn't be so far away."

My parents were now living in a house they had built themselves. It was a pretty house on a quiet leafy street. Outside sat the
extraordinary Invicta, often with a passerby peering at the dash-
board. Inside, in a hall no longer tidy, our luggage was being re-
packed into a trunk to be sent ahead to the ship at Southampton.
My mother tried not to be critical. It had been dreadful for her
when the landlord of my little London flat had complained to her
of our two tenants, not the doctor and nurse they had pretended
to be but a couple of prostitutes, visited by a procession of men
night and day. The women had gone off with knives and forks
and a little William and Mary chest of drawers that I was particularly fond of. We had made a bad judgment, hadn't we, said my
mother. The new tenants, the ones she'd chosen, were charming.

She was a singer. He . . . he? Women had become more interesting than men. My mother particularly liked pretty women, with nice legs and flair.

After this indictment, my mother became circumspect. My clothes were nothing but rags, and the sales were beginning this week. I could run into town tomorrow and have a look round for some decent things. Here, take this money. She and Daddy would look after little Peter. This was our sixth move in five years, wasn't it. Such an expense. Mercy, how happy they would be for us if we kept to one address.

I wished with all my heart we could oblige her. Moves usually looked wise before we made them: the three different addresses in Berlin, one for an intervening year in Bennington, Vermont, another in Berlin again when we returned, and now an address in Princeton. But on and on we moved. When the lease of the little house we rented in Princeton ran out after nine months, someone offered us a rent-controlled apartment on West Twenty-third Street in the Chelsea area of Manhattan. We spent the summer in Maine, where as if by accident we bought a house and rented it out, as I shall tell later, but it was the apartment in Chelsea that lured us. Who wouldn't want to live in Manhattan? Yet it, too, was a disappointment. The New York lycée didn't suit Peter. John wrote a novel that couldn't find a publisher. The commute to Rutgers, where he was now professor of comparative literature, proved exhausting. The anthology on censorship I was compiling with a commentary—censorship in the West was disintegrating year by year—was hard to complete without desk or files or space to organize my papers. Blizzards that winter blocked the streets of the city, delayed trains, trapped the school bus on the cross streets. And the apartment, at first so charming in its nineteenth-century brownstone building, proved awkward for a family of three used to more than two rooms. Worst of all, we simply couldn't afford to live in Manhattan on the low academic salary of those days, even though we'd sold the Invicta handsomely to a wealthy Princeton undergraduate.

We were no more than keeping our heads above water when John came home one day and asked if I'd like to go to Mexico City for a year. He'd been offered a Smith-Mundt Fellowship to teach at the university there with the glorious name of Universidad Nacional Autónoma de México. A wise move professionally, we nodded. A clever move, we'd learn Spanish. A liberating move: Peter would go to the little English school some friend told us of and get the grounding in reading and writing and arithmetic that the lycée had failed to impart. An aesthetic move, toward the great unknown beauties of Mexico. An interesting move, an escape from the drag of society that ground you in the grit of the undertow. And in the afterglow of the news I thought to myself that we'd be free, as travelers are, we'd be simply foreign objects (as I wasn't really in America—no British people were really foreign). Conveniently forgetting my previous feelings about Berlin, I thought that something in the state of real foreignness disembodied a person in a delightful way. You became free to be a pair of eyes or ears, and let your intelligence float. And gazing around me, I at least wouldn't be able to patronize things, the way I did at home or in America, identifying this and that and making odious comparison. I'd be like a child, to whom all things are new. The ordinary self, the *moi,* even Baudelaire's *pauvre moi,* would disappear in a shower of exclamation marks. When I was thoroughly entertained, I forgot myself, I was taken out of myself, and with any luck, that would happen in Mexico.

However, ironically, this realignment happened far more profoundly to John than to me. With his locus in idea, he was to find in Mexico a more honest version of himself, more heroic, purer, in a classical tradition.

We therefore left New York with renewed hopefulness, borne along on a mistake, a secondhand English Ford prone to mechan-

ical failure ("English electrics are no good," Jonathan was to remark truly). Our journey was to take us over a fortnight, because
we went to Mexico via the Midwest, in order to see Jonathan and
Owen. Unfortunate that we didn't choose one of the huge bound-
ing mattress cars common in 1961 America. We despised them
for their chrome and fins and great plushy seats and unnecessarily
large engines. Here again taste got in the way of practicality.
We'd have been far more cool and comfortable in a big secondhand American Ford with air-conditioning. But there we were,
full of stylish prejudice, sweltering.

Jonathan was now midway through high school, a great tall
boy yet to fill out, sweetly courtly, growing his secret self under
the carapace. He would join us in Mexico City at Christmas. And
there was Owen, even stiffer with arthritis, who would join our
household on our return. Peter put up with the long hot drive
with remarkable bravery. He was not yet seven. There were
rewards—among them the enormous beach on the inland water-
way near Mustang Island, in Texas, where he flew his first kite in
the offshore breezes—but the scenery that increasingly absorbed us
had no interest for him. It was as though he could not see the ashy
colors of the increasingly arid land, the rocks, the cactus raising
their arms for us to halt, the sky burning white as we drove south
from the border from Brownsville. Young children glance out of
the windows once, the way guide dogs assess traffic, and that is
enough. The chief reward of the journey occurred in a small dusty
town a few hours over the border with a half-built white concrete
hotel where we found a room for the night. From the bedroom
window we could see a fairground in the central square. As darkness fell, flares sprang into being, a mariachi band began to play,
the brass instruments bamming and blasting not quite in time
with each other, and a ramshackle Ferris wheel began to shud-
der round, worked by two small men cranking twin iron wheels
at the hub. In a pause Peter and John entered one of the cars, un-
American and unsafe, and were swayed up. Most of the other cars

were occupied by serious single men with drooping mustaches or girl couples. The cars swung dangerously in the light of the lamps and candles in the square below, and Peter's face assumed the ecstatic look he'd worn in Berlin two and a half years previously when he sat in the miniature train.

We went back to the half-finished hotel in a stupor of satisfaction and exhaustion, upstairs turned right instead of left, and found ourselves gazing over an abyss where the corridor had been left unfinished, suspended in midair over the lobby.

We settled on an apartment in a modern section of Mexico City, in a concrete block of flats run by a Frenchman. By the time I left Mexico City I wished we'd lived in a traditional thick-walled stone house roofed in pantiles and floored in ceramic tiles, built round a courtyard hung with bougainvillea. However, the block on the Calle Liverpool was convenient and new. It leaned over the street because an earthquake had recently left it in that position, and when Peter dropped an egg out of the living room window, it broke in the middle of the sidewalk. This temporary quality extended to most material objects. The roadway was in good repair except for a manhole in the center of the crossroads that had lost its lid. Wheels crashed in and out of the manhole day after day, week after week, month after month, and often the impact split tires and bent axles so traffic was held up while the disabled vehicle was helped to one side.

What had happened to the manhole cover, I asked the porter at his desk downstairs.

"Someone has taken it, señora," said the porter, to show he was no fool.

"What for?"

"*Quién sabe,* señora?"

Who knew, indeed. A useful phrase, peculiar to Mexico.

The elevator to our fifth-floor apartment twice fell out of control when I was in it and hit the giant spring at the bottom of the shaft. A cry to the porter then brought me up to the ground floor. However, I never felt vulnerable there, except when I shut my key inside our apartment and the French owner commanded the porter to climb from corridor window to our kitchen window, both windows opening over the ventilation area and a five-story drop. He duly did so, all the while wearing his smart peaked cap, and appeared grinning inside at the front door while I trembled outside it. Why did he grin, I wondered, why didn't he shake his head at me. *Quién sabe?*

The splendor of the university was equally flawed. The university library was housed in a tower decorated on the exterior with a wondrous mural of colored tiles designed by Juan O'Gorman, but the tiles kept falling off and anyway the library was shut and had been for years, waiting for funding or cataloging or staff or shelving, air-conditioning, locks to the doors, tables, chairs, lightbulbs, running water in the cloakrooms, who knows what. The university was open to any Mexican who wished to attend, and among the teeming thousands who took advantage of the privilege were some interesting and aspiring students who enrolled in John's courses. Unfortunately they balked at reading lists because the library wouldn't let them in and they couldn't afford to buy books for themselves and they had never done much reading anyway, and certainly no writing of essays in either English or Spanish, they had never heard of such a thing, for what was there to say? That left only lecturing and classroom discussion as tools of higher learning. Presently a students' strike came along and the lecture rooms were picketed. So John was left to get on with his own concerns.

Meanwhile Peter had settled happily into his new school. He had liked it from the first, when we attended the prize-giving in July to get a notion of what the school was like.

"Where's my prize?" he whispered to me.

"You're not even a pupil here yet," I explained. "You won't get

a prize till you've been in the school for a year and been very hardworking and brilliant."

"But I *am* hardworking and brilliant. I think I deserve a prize."

"Perhaps when you've been at the school a bit they'll give you
one."

"I think I need one now."

The breakdown of reason was to become familiar in Mexico.
Driving out on some errand once, early in our stay, we were
stopped by a policeman on a motorbike. He said I'd gone through
a red light. I said I hadn't. He looked at my driving license and
handed it back. He addressed me at length and I didn't understand. I remembered terrible stories of how the Mexican police
put you in prison first and asked questions afterward, imposed
huge fines, confiscated your car. The policeman spoke on and on,
grinning a little now and then. Finally he shrugged and waved me
to proceed. When I told the story I learned the correct etiquette,
the money folded and handed over with the driving license, the
motorist released, guilty of traffic violation or not, and nothing in
any case said.

The bullfight of course was also in the idiom of the country. For
our first corrida John secured us good seats in the Plaza de México,
which seats fifty thousand people and on that occasion was full.
The air across the O of the arena flickered and teemed with ani-
mation, and color shot brightly at us as through a mesh of light,
and then the raucous brass of the band broke out to stuff the
cracks with sound at slightly differing tempi, and the big gates to
the arena swung open to the sound of a single trumpet and let
through the *alguacil* in black with a black hat with a feather, on
a black horse. Then the costumed heroes strutted out—toreros
and their ring servants—and the pikemen on their quilted nags.
When they doffed their caps and made their bow to the president,
the sand was cleared again, a different gate lifted in another part of
the encircling wooden protective wall in order to release the bull,
and the magnificent dark animal charged blindly out from his

confinement into the sunlight, questing, tossing his horns, and in answer fifty thousand human beings bellowed their joy. And then the ritual of testing and tempering the bull began. I turned to John with a question. He was sweating and shouting, carried out of himself.

It wasn't really surprising therefore when, after attending a few corridas, John decided to write a textbook for English-speaking readers on the subject, in collaboration with a journalist who had once been a torero, one Mario Sevilla, who was introduced to us through a painter, friend of another painter whom we'd met in New York. The bullfighting world exists in a web of common devotion to its cause. One of Mario's assets was his ignorance of English and all the clichés and prejudices regarding the bullfight in the English-speaking world. Besides, he was truly an old hand both at fighting bulls and at writing about it. That said, he drove me mad with his complacency: he was brave, no doubt, and principled, in fact full of both bravery and principles that he inclined to brandish in one's face. He had many theories to impart, which could be recast freshly in the other language and tested by John's experience.

So a new pattern established itself. Instead of preparing and meeting classes, John met Mario every day early in the park at Chapultepec, not far from the Calle Liverpool in the heart of the city, and with other aficionados practiced the passes by which a matador would subdue and finally kill the fighting bull. Then the two came back to breakfast and engaged in discussion. In other words, Mario talked and John took notes. By this time I'd put Peter on the brown bus that took him to the English school in care of the gentle bus driver and his wife who looked after the child passengers. I'd enter our apartment again to see the two men by the window. They smiled and waved at me usually, and I didn't linger. Once Mario caught my attention with a fluttered hand and I had to stop. It was then I felt I didn't really care for Mario, who had too fine a sense of himself to bother with me although he sat in my home, with my husband. Yet when he interrupted his discourse in recognition of my presence I still disliked him for what was coming and for what I took as a belated manifestation of good manners. I felt he'd make me accountable, and even establish some authority for himself in my eyes, though he was shorter than I, and plump, with small hands and feet, whereas I was tall and fairly thin, with big hands and feet, not the kind of woman who Latins admire: *altissima,* men breathed after me in the street. It must have been clear to Mario that I wasn't an enthusiast, inasmuch as not being for him, I was against him. So did I feel excluded, was I hostile, was I jealous? "Tell me, Maria," he asked me in his grandee fashion as I stood in the doorway and he sat in his easy chair opposite John: "What do you think of John's *afición?*"

My Spanish was definitely improving. Mario tended to repeat himself, which helped. "His instruction is like the training in courtesy and arms undertaken by the knights of old," I said piously.

"Oh, bravo, señora, how marvelous."

"You bet," I said in English.

Mario stared at me to make sure I was not making fun of him and then turned back to John. The usual words began to pop up in his exegesis: *síntesis* (the uniformity of the matador's art); *garbo* (gracefulness); *cortesía* (courtesy, or respect—for the public, the art, the bull); *vulgaridad* (cheap tricks). I tiptoed out.

I was determined to see as much of Mexico as I could, so presently put my name down at the British Council as an English instructor and found work teaching a large company of engineers. The shape of life changed a little. I left the house every morning at seven and made my way to the parking lot where the attendant greeted me with cries that I was his rose, his life, and rushed to hold the car door open for me. Then he ran into the traffic and made it stop. An hour and ten minutes later I was back. Again the madman rushed into the traffic and halted it by waving his arms in the middle of the road. *"Mi rosa! Mi vida!"* he screamed as I drove into the parking lot. It sounds less dramatic in Spanish, but I got some curious looks.

Later I taught a rich and silly girl, a young businessman, another group of engineers. Wads of exhausted money were pressed into my hands. I thought of trips as far south as Yucatán. One night I got terribly lost driving home in rain and found myself in darkness on a muddy road where great puddles masked the usual potholes and there were no streetlights, only the outlines of shanties that were even then building up on the outskirts of the giant city as peasants came to the capital in search of work. I did not see how I could survive this fearful place. Eventually an old man in white peasant clothes and a big sombrero walked by and I asked him in my primitive Spanish if he could tell me the way to the center of town, and he did so, concerned for me, very gentle and soft-spoken in spite of the walrus mustaches that hung down on either side of his mouth.

After Mario had left, John and I went to Spanish classes. We were at home by twelve, when Peter returned. Then, if I wasn't teaching, we swam at the French club, or played tennis, had the late lunch of the Hispanic world, rested, and returned Peter to school for the late afternoon session.

We brought from New York an introduction to a coffee exporter called Henry and his wife, Soledad, who duly asked us to a party. Henry's family was originally Austrian and Jewish. He was then about forty, a thin tall fierce man, very intense. Soledad was slight and gentle and elegant rather than pretty; she came from Madrid, where she had attended the lycée.

We were engaged instantly in a kind of catechism for visitors. Where was Peter going to school? Henry and Soledad's children were going to Mexican schools because they were Mexicans. Not to the English school or the lycée or the German gymnasium. The

Mexican schools were bad, but they would ensure that the children kept their Mexican souls. Did we know that over half of Mexican territory had been snatched by foreigners, in particular by the United States? And that over half of Mexican natural resources were owned by Americans? Americans drained away the wealth and strength of Mexico. They bought Mexican cattle, corn, fruit, and vegetables when there were not enough for Mexicans.

Why were they permitted to buy Mexican produce, then?

Because they bribed the Mexican officials.

Oh.

Henry said: "The Americans are very rich and the Mexican officials are very poor. The Americans can afford to be incorrupt. As it is, they take advantage of the corruption and make it worse. They should know better."

Henry's brother-in-law Roberto had just spent a year teaching at the University of Chicago.

"They insult us with their visas and paper and fingerprints," said Roberto.

"I know what you mean," I said.

"We do not like Chicago," said his wife.

At the frontier they had passed off their maid as Roberto the professor, a trick that pleased them enormously. I wondered to myself how well the presence of a servant went down with the immigration officials of the great republic.

Mexico had always suffered from foreigners, Henry went on. The Spaniards brought olive trees and the grapevine to Mexico in colonial days. They did so well that in time the Spaniards ordered the plants to be destroyed, because they threatened to undercut the home economy in Spain itself. And look at the Valley of Mexico, a desert: when Cortés came, he found it a garden. The Spaniards destroyed it, they were always bad husbandmen: look at Andalusia, in the time of the Moors a place of great fruitfulness thanks to an intricate system of irrigation. At the Reconquest the Spaniards destroyed the system and in a year or two the land was barren.

Soledad smiled sadly.

"Come and take a look at Henry's paintings," said his sister Madeleine. She led us down a corridor and from one room to another. The walls were covered in paintings of owls—berserk, blind, hunting, sleepy, livid, horned. Then there was a crucifixion, with Henry as the Christ. And there was a portrait of a woman in the style of Soutine: razzle-dazzle, with cropped hair, slipped breasts, and a tarty smirk. "It's Soledad," said Madeleine.

"But Soledad is beautiful," John said.

"It's quite like her," said Madeleine.

"Very like her," said Henry.

After supper a man with long floppy hair sat at the piano and smiled at us, and gradually chairs were found and all the guests came into the room and sat down and waited for him to begin to play.

"How long have you lived in Mexico?" I asked the woman next to me, who was wearing black silk and pearls and had trouble getting me in focus.

"Five bloody years." I caught her bag as it slid off her lap. "Lived in New York thirty years, born though in Texas. Going to Texas tomorrow. Good ole Texas. You'll love Mexico. It's wonderful."

"But you hate it?"

"I loathe it." She began to cry, then hiccuped and dabbed her eyes dry. She nodded at the pianist and he began to play, fortissimo. His hair flopped over the keys.

"*Precioso,*" murmured the lady in black silk. Her bag fell to the floor and disgorged the usual things—lipstick, comb, coins, pen, hairpins, a paper clip, tickets, a small diary, a small gold screw-top pencil with a loop at one end, two elastic bands, one blue, one green, and a house key. The pianist was marvelous and we forgot everything to hear him play.

Toward Christmas, when we were well settled, I telephoned Henry and Soledad to invite them to a meal, and Soledad answered. Henry was away, she said, but she would love to see us, and half an hour later she came round in a cab. Her appearance was a shock: old and shabby, her hair limp. We had a moment or two together while John was uncorking the wine, and I told her of John's passion for the bullfight.

"That's *afición*. A kind of madness. He is enjoying himself. You can do nothing." She nodded and smiled.

"And Henry?" I expected some robust news about imbecile American ways, and was surprised to hear that she didn't know how Henry was. He had gone to New York on business with his sister and her husband and had collapsed in someone's office and been taken to hospital. He had pneumonia in both lungs, then pleurisy. Henry was not strong. He had rheumatic fever in Paris as a young man and his heart was not normal. He was on the critical list. Since then she had heard nothing.

"You must call the doctor," we said. "You must call Madeleine or Roberto."

She had called the doctor repeatedly, she said, but he never called back. Madeleine and Roberto were always out, and, like the doctor, they didn't return calls.

"You must go to New York yourself."

"You forget," said Soledad, "that I have five children. The youngest is only two, and I have no one reliable to leave them with."

Besides, she had to take care of Henry's business. There was another difficulty. She had no money. She'd had to sell the car, and she'd put the apartment up for sale. We offered our money, she shook her head. Could she borrow money from the bank? Oh no, impossible in Mexico.

This was worse than living with a man besotted with the bull-fight. *Afición:* "A kind of madness. He is enjoying himself. You can do nothing." I thought of her words often. They explained an existence the opposite of hers, which was calm, frugal, and well rooted in her own traditions. I thought of them when Mario arranged for us to visit a ranch where fighting bulls were bred, on a particular day when heifers were to be tested in the ring for the bravery and stamina they might pass on to their offspring. John would take part by practicing some of the passes he had learned in the park at Chapultepec, and he and I and Peter would have a day in the country, a picnic, and a lot of fun, with Mario, his wife, Amparo, and their three children.

Mario had declared an early start essential, so we drove to his house at eight in the morning as arranged. It was shut and barred. Our knocking and shouting having no effect, a passerby threw a handful of stones at an upper window, which produced Mario, hastily buttoning his shirt, and presently the three children, smiling sleepily, followed by Amparo, a small fat woman who rattled as much as Mario did. We were to go to a bar to pick up Mario's friend Diego, who desired to come too. Diego was not at the bar, so we drove to his house, to be told he was at the bar. We left Mario at the house in case Diego returned, drove back to the bar, picked up Diego, and returned to his house for Mario. At the stoplight nearby Diego got out and hurried ahead, to be met at the corner by Mario, who had tired of waiting. They crashed into each other, got up, dusted each other down, and squeezed into the car. Thus laden with nine souls and a trunk of swords and capes, our small car crawled into a countryside of huge boulders and the cactuses with arms that signaled us to stop.

Some little black cattle stood under a tree.

Amparo jumped, displacing the child on her lap. *"Cuidado! Toros bravos!"*

"*Ai, toro!*" screamed the displaced child.

"Why are they so small?" I asked.

"It is the altitude," said Mario. "We are all small in Mexico."

"And you don't drink milk. The calves clearly do not drink milk." The last sentence came out in English.

"You are absurd," said John.

Had they tried artificial insemination?

Mario explained that the cow of this noble breed had to have her pleasure of the bull.

Whose hands had we fallen into, I wondered. The altitude affected size. The cow had to have her pleasure to conceive.

It was noon by the time we arrived at the little plaza where the cows were to be tested. The ring had a smooth earth floor and a perimeter wall of adobe, within which was a ring of heavy wooden walls, or *burladeros*, to provide the toreros with refuge from the charging bull. A small roofed stand for spectators was built over the entrance. Peter and I sat on the *burladero* and watched the men whirling their capes and the boys charging, pointing their forefingers like horns. At last the breeder shouted for silence, the ring emptied, and a little fawn calf darted into the sunlight, about the size of a Great Dane. You could see her little udders high on her belly and her neat little cream horns as she dashed round the ring, hooked at the cape that Mario's elder boy held out; followed it, lost it, found it again, and followed it round the boy's body as he swirled it. Then John emerged and extended the cape gracefully, and the little heifer left the boy and charged him. A more substantial target than the boy, and less sure, but again she failed to hit the body. At last Mario ran out, planted himself in front of the calf, which eyed him severely and then charged him. Mario executed a large slow movement of the cape to the right, all round his fat belly. The calf followed the cape, hooking. Her charge finished with a swirling of the cape. Mario twisted it, trailed it, and marched off, calling "*Un síntesis!*" The calf stood and looked up, bewildered and blown. We clapped madly.

About an hour later two huge American cars with Mexican plates jolted to a stop beside the ranch house, and a party of young men and women jumped out. The women were slim and wore jeans and silk shirts and fine boots of reversed leather with two-inch heels, and their long hair was tied back with colored scarves. The men wore jeans and checked shirts or the *traje corto,* a costume where the trousers are turned up below the knee and worn with the same reversed leather boots as the women's on that occasion; the jacket is short too, and worn with a flat brimmed hat of gray or black felt called the *Cordovese.* After them came a third car, even bigger, from which the massive worldly figure of a man in *traje corto* stepped out.

"The minister of agriculture!" whispered Amparo.

A little boy in the same getup followed him, the minister miniaturized.

Our party retreated, and the minister of agriculture took up a position in the shade. The little boy strutted about the ring followed by other little boys more plainly dressed. Young men practiced passes. A group of men in embroidered black suits and frilly shirts, huge sombreros, mustaches, and deadly expressions appeared on the roof over the stand, received brass instruments and stools from below, gave a toot or two, and launched into the deafening blasts of mariachi. Some servers set up a counter for food and drink, a bucket of pulque was set on it, and a procession of handsome, beautifully turned-out guests strolled from a set of cars at the back to the stand or to the perimeter wall, where they sat and dangled their heels.

Behind the stand two men were setting up a butcher's scale and hooks and a trestle table laid with an array of cleavers and knives. The calves beside them, each in a stall, lifted up shiny gray muzzles to examine me and moo. The mariachis suddenly stopped, and I went back to Amparo and the children on the perimeter wall and watched an elegant young man below in the ring passing his cape in front of a small bull calf that the minister was to kill. The minister waited at the *burladero,* big, burly, and middle-aged. Next came the placing of the *banderillas* in the calf's hump, behind his little horns, while he charged: this was to make the animal lower his head so he could be killed more easily. One of the *banderilleros* wore glasses. "*Olé!*" called the girls on the wall. At last the minister advanced with his *muleta,* which he waved in front of the calf, and the calf obediently charged time and again, and the band blew several deafening blasts to congratulate the matador. "*Olé!*" cried the spectators.

The calf, being a calf, was soon exhausted, and the minister received his killing sword and lined him up to be dispatched. When his front hooves were together and his head was lowered for a final charge, the minister crouched to get him in view (because the calf was so small), looked along the sword to the narrow opening between his vertebrae where the sword could penetrate the aorta and the vena cava, and plunged it in. The sword struck bone and sprang out, again and again and again. Blood streamed over the calf's withers. At the fourth attempt the minister sliced the flank behind the hump and blood spouted over one side of the animal's body and ran down his legs. Two young men, acting the part of *peónes,* flicked their capes under the calf's nose to arrange him for the matador again, but the punctures went on till the little beast was as full of holes as a sponge. Finally he walked over to the gate from which he had first emerged, as if to go back to his stall. The minister pursued him with the dagger used to sever the spinal cord, and with the young men jabbing the calf's nose to keep the head low, he stabbed away behind the horns until by a stroke of luck he succeeded in killing him.

The next calf received over thirty punctures, each meant to kill, before he died.

After each death the band bammed, the people waved handkerchiefs, and the minister's little boy ran out to dip his hand in the blood. The *ganadero* cut off an ear and offered it to the matador and they toured the ring gaily, holding the ear up together.

Behind the stand the exquisitely trousered señoritas and señoritos walked up and down while the butchers flayed and disemboweled the two carcasses, which they hung on the hooks previously set up. Lumps of bone and gristle lay in the dust beneath, covered in flies. The calves' testicles were hissing on a spit over a fire of roots and thorns, and presently these were served, cut up, beside a bowl of sauce for dipping each piece in.

My engineers expected me to put English in their heads like a transplanted organ, or as Zeus implanted the embryo of Athena in his own head to let her grow there till his head should be split with an ax and she should spring out, fully armed and uttering a war cry. They turned up for the early morning class and spoke English. Then they went away and forgot what they had learned till the next day, when they learned it again. One morning I had planned some extempore conversation and had hardly begun "Are you going to Washington, Mr. Chavez?" when our third floor shifted under my feet. Then my book slid off the table and one of the men crossed himself. Back in our apartment John witnessed how the water in our lavatory sloshed out on the floor. When the earthquake was over, our apartment leaned even farther out over the Calle Liverpool, as Peter found when he dropped yet another egg from the window of our apartment and it landed on a passing car.

The engineers laughed at my fright and suddenly released little spurts of English.

"Señora, you like Mexico? You travel, yes?"

"Mexico City—is nothing. Acapulco—is nothing. Cuernavaca—is nothing. But Chiapas!"

We had been to Oaxaca for the weekend, and I now spoke admiringly of the beautiful town, its archaeological sites, its fine black pottery.

"Señora, in Michoacán is much fine pottery, very good. Yes, in many parts is much good pottery."

"*Qué maravilla,* good boy, *brava!*" cried the others.

I had been struck during the drive to Oaxaca by the country people on the roads carrying burdens on their heads. I'd wondered to John why they did not use carts and donkeys, or even wheelbarrows or bicycles. The answer, I know now, is that the roads to the villages were too rough for wheeled traffic, and country people could use wheels only on the main roads. Could it be, I said unwisely to my class, now regarding me brightly and with apparent affection, that the wheel brought by the Spaniards hadn't made much difference to village people?

At this there was an uproar and an imploring clasping of hands in my direction. "Dear teacher, Mexico is not *primitivo* now."

"How long you are here, teacher? Dear teacher, in village now we have school, we have plumbing, we have tractor."

"In Puebla province we build hydroelectric dam," said Chávez, the managing director. "Also in Sonora." He pointed to the map on the wall. "Here we have dam. Here we have dam. Here we have dam. In 1970 we give power to many many village who have no power now."

"That was not my point," I said. "I was talking about simple country people, not about grand sophisticates like you, not about engineers. Of course you know about wheels. . . ."

No one was listening.

"In Mexico we look forward," said Chávez. "One day we are industrialize too."

"We learn English for this," said González.

I gave up. Thoreau was unimaginable in Mexico.

The next morning González was waiting for me outside the engineers' offices in order to invite John and me to visit the Puebla dam with him and his wife over the weekend. He was a big swart teddy bear of a man, now with wounded feelings. Nevertheless he spoke with solicitude and even touched my arm, as if he cared for the state of my ignorance.

"We have to go," I told John. "They don't like the idea of tourists looking only at archaeological sites and bullfights, they want to show their modern, up-to-date side, and the least we can do is to go and appreciate it."

"I like bullfights," John said.

"You must admit that dams are important too."

"Why?"

"It would be dull of us not to go. I long to see other parts of the country."

"We might miss the bullfight on Sunday. Then there's Peter."

"He's staying with his friend Pablo."

At four in the morning, when it was still dark, the Gonzálezes were waiting in their Opel in Calle Liverpool, he in a thick sweater knitted in Aztec designs, she in a camel-hair coat, a silk dress, pearls, earrings, silver bracelets, charms, and several rings on her pretty manicured fingers. John wore khakis and a linen jacket, I wore a dress of local cotton and sandals. There was barely room for us in the back of the tiny car. González drove like a madman up into the sunrise to where Popocatepetl and Iztaccihuatl loomed, twin volcanoes, vast in the gaseous air. As we plunged down into the plain, other huge clean cones presented themselves—Orizaba and Malinche—and we became aware of two other Opels darting behind us, which González said contained the rest of my English class. The speed of the car was too great to talk, but the señora fondled the ears and neck of her husband, and only the biggest potholes in the road bounced her hand away.

After many hours we left the plain and descended sharply into deep jungly vegetation. Suddenly González jammed on the brakes and made us get out, agonized as we were with cramp, and hob-

ble into the choking noises of the forest. Far below, a white concrete crescent was holding back a milky pool. A huge tunnel was
being cut through the rock on its farther side. The water in the
pool would eventually drain down and pour under the mountain
through this tunnel, entering great pipes that ran steeply down
the hill face about half a mile. At the bottom the force of the
water would turn turbines and produce electricity through gener-
ators. All this González explained to John, ignoring me, though I
stood as close to him as I could, examining his fat cheeks and
black eyes, and nodding as if I understood every word. It occurred
to me that I should have stayed in the car with Señora González,
but she had made no effort to detain me. When we got back to the
car, I spoke eloquently in English of the mysterious and beautiful
dam in the jungle, the engineers' pride, and she listened and
smiled, not understanding a word.

Her husband took us to the headquarters of the site and loaded
us into a jeep, which he drove about at breakneck speed. I thought
my head would burst with hunger and fatigue, but it was three in
the afternoon before he mentioned lunch. First, though, we had to
view the face of the dam. We walked out on the top of the graceful narrow curve of that enormous structure, with rising water on
one side and on the other a muddy bowl where men and bulldoz-
ers were scraping the sides and bottom clean. I peered down the
smooth curve of the dam curtain and a workman in ragged overalls and straw hat glanced back up. He was daubing the finished
concrete with a trowel, holding half a bucket of cement mixture
in the other hand, and held up by a mere rope at the waist and
kept away from the wall by the thrust of his bare feet.

González at last addressed me. "We lost a man here yesterday."

"I'm not surprised," I said. "Do you lose many?"

"About twelve a month."

Twelve a month? It seemed obvious why, but I asked the reason
anyway.

"Imprudencia," said González. He scowled at me. I wished I knew the Spanish for "proper equipment," "block and tackle," "basic training."

John began taking photographs out of politeness. With his eye pressed to the camera and retreating to get the best angle, he nearly fell down an unrailed manhole that opened onto the muddy bowl hundreds of feet below. He went white. González frowned. I murmured to John, *"Imprudencia!"*

Now at last it was lunchtime. The engineers were waiting for us at a footbridge suspended from a couple of cables over the chasm, and suggested I lead the way along the narrow planks, taking care not to fall between them or lose my balance, when presumably I'd join the statistics of the imprudent. It was a terrifying experience, though the engineers followed me without complaint and down below, very far away, workmen like ants waved. I imagined Señora González tottering after me in her high heels. If she could, so could I. But as we reached the other side of the chasm, we found her waiting for us, politely waving. She had come round by car, driven by her husband.

"Have you visited the United States?"

"Please?"

I gave up. "It is nice and cool here," I said.

Señora González indicated the swimming pool of the engineers' club. Once blue and white, it was gray and cracked and devoid of water. The diving board was shattered and the ladders had rungs missing. We sat with a glass of lemonade in the wild garden, she cool and white-skinned and tidy, I dirty and sticky and pink. The men had abandoned us. No one but John had spoken a word to me for hours, and I'd given up my comments and intelligent questions because the responses were directed to John alone. If someone was forced to talk to me, he looked at my forehead as if a label there said, "Here's a woman who thinks Mexicans are a bunch of peasants carrying bundles on their heads," and he'd drop his eyes out of embarrassment.

Suddenly the men returned, laughing and wiping their mouths. As soon as they saw us, they became grave. We trooped into the dining room.

John said: "They behaved like human beings in the bar."

"And they have always been friendly to me up to now, in the classroom. What on earth has happened? What have I done?"

"You haven't done anything. With any luck we'll be back home by nightfall."

But González came up the moment the last mouthful was swallowed to announce that we were going to the sea at Veracruz to eat shrimp. Veracruz was supposed to be *alegre,* compared with Mexico City, which was *triste,* and I looked forward to smiles and sweetness, yet the most rigid solemnity prevailed among the shrimp and the drinks of warm Coca-Cola, even after we'd bathed in the tepid water of the Gulf, and the engineers had played decorously with a large beach ball, until, well into the night, John turned up a waiter who provided long cool drinks of rum, fresh lime, ice, soda water. We sat in a kind of beach pavilion on canvas chairs, and Martínez and Pinilla came drifting up to join us, and then Rubio and Guzmán, and soon it didn't matter what language we spoke, decidedly *alegre* as we were, and so we stayed till we fell into bed in our rooms in one of the complexes by the beach.

The next day the atmosphere had reverted to being *triste.*

When it was time to go home, González whipped the Opel out of the motel yard at the head of the stampede and remarked: "Of course in the United States you are always in a hurry."

"Never like this," John said. "We would die."

"You are joking, of course." González glanced at us in the rear mirror.

During the long bolt home we stopped only once, at a roadside hut, in a place of long grass, from where we could appreciate the enormous sky and the simple cone of the volcano Malinche, named

after the native princess who became the mistress of Cortés and be-
trayed her own people to the Spanish invaders. Rubio told us the
story as we sipped our Coca-Cola.

González broke in. "We do not care about history. The future is
more interesting." He was senior to Rubio, who raised his eyebrows.

The next morning the class and I were somber with fatigue. I
was careful to say how much we had enjoyed ourselves and how
touched we had been by González and his efforts to introduce us
to the real Mexico.

Only one thing puzzled me, I told the engineer Camino, who
asked for a lift back to the center. He rarely came to my English
classes because his English was far superior to his colleagues'. He
had been trained in Germany and had lived in Europe several
years. No one would talk to me all weekend, I said. All their
friendliness vanished. They behaved like strangers. It was a frightful shock. I didn't know what to make of it, and my husband was
amazed.

"Oh, those people!" He bent his blue eyes on me and gathered
his eloquence together in order to explain once and for all. "They
are ignorant. They have no culture. They do not know how to behave in front of a woman. They leave their own wives behind."

"They are married?"

"Of course. Martínez has ten children, Mola has four, Rubio has
two or three. But when the weekend comes, they all go off together just as when they were students. They have no respect for
women, so their wives never leave home. When your husband was
there, they addressed him because they do not want to make him
jealous by addressing you."

It was a pity that Camino spoiled the explanation by going on
to boast how easily he seduced American girls, English girls,
French girls, German girls, any foreign girl he fancied.

Shortly afterward Martínez, who drove an MG, let slip the
information that he owned a small garage, a *taller*. When our

wretched Ford needed a new clutch plate, I asked González for advice on where to take it, and he referred me to Martínez. Nice of him. Nice of Martínez to take me round to the *taller* and arrange things. When the car was fixed, I drove it away gratefully and the clutch no longer slipped. Instead, it made a noise like a major accident each time I put the car in gear.

I referred it to Martínez, who assured me that in time the grinding roar would lessen as the new clutch plate wore itself in. Days passed and it did not. If anything it got worse. Other motorists pointed helpfully to my engine as I drove by.

"The noise is very bad," I said in front of the class. "The job has been botched. Do you know the word *botched*? It means the job has been badly done."

"It will get better in time." Martínez shrugged. I had always rather liked him. He seemed a little more polished than the other engineers. But now the rest of the class began to catcall. Chávez, the managing director, spoke quickly and quietly.

"*Mande?*" I said, but it wasn't necessary. The *taller* took the car back and the noise was eliminated.

In class the next morning Martínez gazed at the ceiling through the dark glasses that he always wore. "You know what MG mean?" he asked me. "It mean 'Morris Garage.'"

"Fancy," I said. "I never knew that. I know, however, that you are a cheat."

"*Mande?*"

"Perfidious."

"Oh, señora!" He looked round the room and laughed, and the barracking began again, and González spoke fiercely through the din.

Martínez shrugged. "He, Señor González, marry my sister. Eh, *negro*? He my . . ."

". . . brother-in-law."

"And he is very black." Martínez himself was pale, like his sister.

"Let us open the book at page thirty," I said, and the episode was over.

John had shaved his beard, and wearing a borrowed suit of lights and with the *montera* rammed over his eyes, he closely resembled Manolete. Mario posed him on the flat roof of our apartment building on the Calle Liverpool. He looked in various directions. He walked. He demonstrated a pass to the bull. Diego's camera clicked and clicked. (The photographs show a young, serious man, pale, thin, and ill.) The maids who lived in the square white concrete cabins on the roof came out to stare. The families they had gathered round them—parents, grandparents, cousins, children— came out to stare too. There was quite a throng. I had no idea how so many people managed to squeeze together on the roof, in the simple cabins among the clotheslines and the aerials.

Finally Diego turned his camera on me too, and then on Peter.

"He was being polite," I told Peter. "So we wouldn't feel out of it."

"Out of what? Is Father going to fight a bull?"

"That's the idea. The photos are for publicity."

"How can he? He's not a real bullfighter."

"Mario has fixed it."

Things were getting out of hand. That of course was the consequence of *afición*. Fit though he surely was, John was forty-two and slow on his feet. Bullfighting demands slim wiry bodies and lightning reflexes in addition to the mysticism.

John explained that if he were to write about bullfighting, he had to fight a bull. Not just a calf but a *novillo,* a bull up to three years old.

"You'll be killed," I said.

"You don't think I can, do you?"

"Frankly, no."

"Well, you're wrong, understand?"

He produced the first piece of publicity, a long yellow strip of advertisement printed out by Mario's newspaper office in record time, showing the rooftop photograph of John as Manolete and announcing the debut of the North American Phenomenon in Diego's village in Michoacán.

"I wish you wouldn't go," I said.

"Oh, come on. I've never wanted anything so much in my life. You want us to do everything together, that's it, isn't it? You want me to stay home and rot. You don't even like the *ambiente*."

The *ambiente* had come round to our apartment for drinks and a little dancing and in the morning half of John's ties were missing.

"You hate me," John said.

"I don't share your opinions, that's all."

"You despise me."

"No I don't."

"Well, I'm not going to stay home and rot."

I tried persuasion once more, one dulcet evening, drank too much of the gin that was meant to give me courage, and was ignominiously sick.

Mario was late. Diego went to look for him. While he was gone, Mario turned up, found Diego had gone to look for him, and went to look for Diego. Diego returned without Mario. Finally, with a bump, they met at the corner as before, two aging sports, utterly predictable. John sat in the driver's seat of our car, fretting. The back was piled with capes, sword cases, and suitcases. Mario and John sat in front, Diego and Mario's two boys behind them. My refusal to go with them had barely been noted. I wondered aloud who would drive the car back were John wounded by the bull, and no one chose to reply. Hands waved from the car and it started with a lurch. Peter and I returned to the apartment. As we went by, the porter impudently raised his eyes to heaven and giggled.

It was Saturday, and sunny, so we went to the French Club—

quiet, mercifully unfashionable—and swam in the delicious pool with lots of other children and their parents. Then we kicked a football in the pelota courts, and swam again, and had lunch. Later we went to see *Ben-Hur,* with Charlton Heston, a very long and exciting movie.

The next day, the day of the bullfight in Michoacán, we went to the French Club again, swam, kicked the football, swam again, and had lunch. I thought that Peter might have a party here at the end of the school year in a month's time, and we ordered a cake and arranged for a clown. He would invite everyone in his class, and so repay all the kind invitations he'd had. The sun was going down when I paid the taxi that had taken us home to the Calle Liverpool. The bullfight would be drawing to a close in Michoacán.

"Look, there's Father!"

The car drew up beside us. He was not wounded in any way, of course not. Here he was, in the car, serious, with Mario beside him yakking as usual and oblivious of his surroundings. I hadn't expected them till very late, or even the next day.

It must have been painful to say what had happened. The heavy truck containing the bulls for the corrida had fallen into a ditch as it drove from the *ganadería* to Diego's village. No rescue equipment could negotiate the usual washed-out goat track to crank the truck back up on its wheels. The bulls, encased in large crates on the truck, couldn't be got out either. They spent Saturday night imprisoned on their sides, and the corrida was canceled.

I told Peter of these uncouth events, and he shrieked with laughter, and after the shock of hearing him, and seeing him doubled up, I laughed too, perceiving that he was right, he'd recognized fiasco; nervous, though, in case John should hear our screams of laughter and be wounded, or angry. It was clear that we had to get out or be drawn irrevocably into the romantic miasma.

My mother had been ill with congestive heart failure for months. She had given up writing to me. For the first time in years no letters had arrived addressed in her smooth cursive, well-formed, and characteristic script, a couple of pages long describing quiet days, what they'd had for lunch, what repairs they'd undertaken in the house they'd built, what flowers were out, who'd come to play cards, what my brother and his wife and little boy had been up to. My father wrote instead. He wrote warning letters saying how sick she was, encouraging letters welcoming my news of Peter, letters expressing terror at John's activities. Now I rang up Peter's school explaining that he and I had to go to England. I sent a cable to my parents that Peter and I would be with them in a week's time. John would drive back north alone and meet me in Boston in a month's time.

"Promise me you won't fight any more bulls."

"Oh, all right."

"Promise."

"I promise."

The promise meant nothing to him. The *ambiente* bought two *novillos,* two-year-olds, each three hundred pounds in weight, for him to fight in a private bullring in Mexico City, which he duly did. The book he wrote on the bullfight over the next two years was called *The Complete Aficionado* and has become a classic.

We forgot about Peter's party. Luckily we had not yet invited the guests, but the cake we'd ordered was delivered on the date we'd chosen. The French Club called John about it and he ordered it to be distributed to members of the staff.

I said goodbye to the engineers and my other pupils, who understood instantly why I had to go to England and expressed their sorrow for me. Mothers are sacred in Mexico.

As for our friend Soledad, I had no chance to say goodbye and we were left in ignorance of what happened to her and to Henry. Three years later, however, John was walking through a square in Toledo, in Spain, on his way to El Greco's house, when he saw visitors from New York, the friends who had introduced us to Henry and Soledad. The New York friends were delightful people, José and Rosie Guerrero and their dear children. José was a superb painter who now has a gallery dedicated to his work in Granada, his native city. It was lovely for John to see them again. I wish I'd been there. After they'd sat down together, John heard that Henry had indeed returned to Soledad in Mexico City and was leading a normal life with his children and working as a coffee broker. As to why Soledad had been stranded, they were nonplussed. What nonsense, it wasn't she who had been stranded, it was he.

Then why no word from him? Why had Soledad been left without news when Henry was in hospital? Why had she had to sell the car and put the apartment up for sale? Why her terrible distress?

Oh, in Mexico the mailman throws letters into the river when he is tired, or slips a cable under the wrong door. Mexico is a wonderful country where anything can happen, so unlike the United States where you can bring things to fruition if you work hard enough and there's far less room for fate. And they all laugh for joy in the lovely square in beautiful Toledo where they're on holiday.

MAST LANDING

. . . admirable, and gratis to the point of tears

"There she is," said my father, peering through the small window in the door of my mother's room in the Brompton Hospital. He withdrew and I peered in turn. He was right with his warnings of how she'd changed. I saw an ancient woman asleep in an armchair, her mouth open, and the Wimbledon semifinals on the television screen in front of her. Three years ago, when Peter and I had last stayed with them, my parents had looked much the same age, and though the fiction of her being ten years younger than he was seemed harmless, her cardiologist had made jokes to his houseman about it, so my father said bitterly, and it was clear to me that the whole careful edifice of their lives was crumbling, starting with the exposé of her true age and going on to her efforts to disguise it with fluffed-out hair, pretty clothes, and discreet makeup, and I thought the end could not be far off, for her, and for him too, for what would he do without her and her fictions? But as Peter climbed up on her high hospital bed and instantly fell asleep, exhausted by the long flight, she cried out passionately, "O what a beautiful child! Iain was beautiful too! Just like that!" And we spent an unbearably poignant time looking at the sleeping child.

The next day I was visiting her again when a young houseman in a white coat blew in with the nurse and announced they'd be doing basic metabolism tests tomorrow. My mother didn't understand.

183

"Basic Metabolism Tests!" He leered at the nurse. "Making sure your progress is maintained. Not to worry, dear." He raised his eyebrows at the nurse and smirked.

"Who was that?" I asked my mother as he left.

"Puss in Boots," said my mother.

She came home the next day to a house that had lost the sense of masculine purpose that she had always managed to impart to the places where they lived, with the implication that this was his rather than hers. In the new dispensation, books and papers might not lie about. The lamplight was too faint to read by, the bedside light put on too low a table. I couldn't cook a decent meal because she dreaded dirtying pots and pans and the spotless counters. Her empty hands, which had busied themselves making and mending all her life, twitched in her lap. Her gentle blue-gray eyes, her family's most famous feature, the eyes of a Burne-Jones heroine, moved over the polished furniture and the silver candlesticks and photo frames and the Dresden plate hung on the wall, and she'd ask me again about something I'd already told her.

"Maine is where? You'll be happy there, will you? And Peter? And how far is it from John's work at Rutgers?"

"Six or seven hours' drive. Four hundred miles. Madness."

"And then back again."

"He's going to find an apartment near Rutgers to live in during the week, and his father's going to live there with him."

"John's father is not going to live with you, I hope?"

"No, I told you, he'll be in New Jersey with John."

"Does it make sense to live in Maine?" asked my father.

"Of course not," I said. "I am married to a madman. He falls in love with a house, so we have to buy it."

There was a pause.

"I thought you'd liked the house," said my father. "That's why we sent you the money for the down payment."

"I like the house," I said. "I don't want to live where it is. It's miles from anything, miles from Rutgers, miles from a theater, miles from friends. I want to live in Chicago or Philadelphia or Washington or even New York again, on principle. But as I say, I like the house."

There was another pause.

"We went to a great deal of trouble to find you the money for the down payment," my father said. "Your brother was furious."

"Iain is very jealous of you," my mother said.

"Perhaps he should have married John," I said. "Then he mightn't be jealous."

"So what is the house like, again?"

And I told her again, thinking as I did so (persuaded by my own words) that there was indeed something beautiful in John's desire for it: it had been built for the agent who bought masts for the Royal Navy before the American Revolution. Enormous spars were cut from the ancient forests of white pine that once covered Maine, and were dragged here to the tidal stream beside the house and floated from the landing to sailing vessels in the bay to be floated to harbors and fitted as masts. You could still see the remains of piles driven into the bank where boats took on cargo two centuries earlier. Downstream, seventy acres that went with the house were covered with scrub and young maple and oak and alder and all manner of other small trees—sumac, lichened apple trees from a forgotten orchard, fir—and among them were the decayed stocks of those once mighty white pines. There was a marsh farther on where the bay opened out, the home of wild ducks, beaver, moose.

The house itself nested like a lamp in a hollow of grass and roses by the tidal stream, a big plain old white clapboard house, without the trumpery of mock-classical pillars and pediment, without porches and turrets and flights of steps or widow's walk, no neat low hooped railings and box hedges, as you'd find in Castine or Kennebunkport, the homes of wealthy sea captains a century ago; just a cube and hipped roof with massive brick chimneys at either hip, tall paned windows in perfect symmetry, and a central door between simple pilasters, with a beautiful fanlight over it. Inside, the house had eight lovely rooms, one in each corner on two floors set round a hall and staircase, all very plain and symmetrical, with a pretty fireplace each. The floors were of wide pine boards. There were broad cellars and an attic. Someone had put in central heating and a bathroom. A kitchen connected the house to a huge barn painted the oxblood red of tradition.

John had said, "I simply can't understand your not wanting this house."

It was certainly very different from the sort of house I'd dreaded growing old in, in dreary conformity with a thousand other houses. It was very different from the house my parents now lived in.

Peter said to my mother, "I can have a dog there. I'd call him John."

"John is your father's name!"

"How about Douglas? Or Tom?"

"Tom is a nice name."

"I'll call him Tom."

"It is a pity Iain is so jealous," my mother said for the fiftieth time.

I solved that difficulty by doing a few sums. Our parents had provided him with a down payment on his mortgage, a car, and a quantity of furniture. They had also financed his public school and Oxford and the years of medical study, while in my case they'd done no more than top up a scholarship to school and government grants to the university, and pay for my first year at Oxford. They were now paying for the schooling of Iain's little son.

"It is difficult to please everybody," said my mother, literally wringing her hands.

"If you didn't want to live in Maine, you should have said so," my father pointed out.

"But I did say so. I was overruled." In fact John had not overruled me. I wasn't quite sure what he had done. My parents would have had as much trouble following the argument as I had.

John had said: "You don't want to live here in this beautiful house, so where do you want to live?"

Me: "New Jersey."

"You hate New Jersey."

"That's insane, I don't hate New Jersey. It was you who hated New Jersey and grumbled and grumbled . . ."

"I don't understand what goes on in your head. You don't want to live in New Jersey, you made it plain, but when we find a beautiful house that we can afford in Maine, you say you don't want it. What for God's sake do you want?"

"I didn't say I disliked New Jersey. . . ."

"I give up."

Petruchio employed similar tactics to tame Katherina the shrew, but I was not a shrew. More of a mouse, a good gray mouse. That's why I wrote away to my parents so they might help buy the beautiful house in Maine that I did not want. Looking back, I could not believe how foolishly I had behaved. Even now I am astonished. Something had occurred in Mexico which enabled John, a scholar, a writer, a thoughtful man, a middle-aged man, to start fighting animals and killing them and glorifying the business of doing so in the name of art. And here he was now pursuing his luck with the same masculinity, not to say bullying, in the matter of the house. He was no better than the engineers who went on behaving like students, leaving their wives and children and sporting themselves in the jungle and on the beaches of Veracruz. At this rate he might get himself a mistress or two and I would go on washing his socks because if I didn't do so he might get depressed. I would send the mistress flowers, I would pass on messages, and if one didn't work out, I would pimp for him and find another even more attractive. It wasn't an unknown role. And yet after all America was a woman's country, so they said, and it should be possible to live in equal partnership in Maine, whatever the logistics of houses and cars and schools and jobs where we were concerned.

"We're ordering a Land Rover," I told my parents, and they brightened. A Land Rover is a more sensible vehicle than an Invicta.

I was torn. If ever I'd thought of staying on in England in my parents' house, nursing my mother, I knew I would suffocate. If my parents had not sunk money in the house at Mast Landing, I might have asked for their support, however, stayed on near them, got a job, put Peter in an English school, and somehow or other established myself on an independent footing. It would be delightful to be independent. Of course my parents would have been deeply disappointed and disturbed, and they had enough troubles already without my adding myself to them. In Maine, alone most of the time, with husband four hundred miles away and Peter in school, and with the job I had been angling for at a small women's college in Portland, I would be leading a pretty independent life, though in circumstances I had not chosen. Moreover I would not stifle. I'd have time to expand and write and make friends. I would go on being part of a marriage. The exertions imposed by John's personality were after all legitimate up to a point, appalling though they were. "It will be fun being married to him," Rosemary had said long ago, and of course it was, up to a point. If my initial assumption was mistaken that through him I would escape the traditional role of the married woman, it was partly my own fault. I should have roared like a lion and refused to be compliant. Neither of us referred openly to the traditional wifely role to which I'd been brought up. If I had, I might have been in a stronger position. "You can't expect me to do that," I'd have said. And "You promised to honor me, not treat me like a piece of dirt." Or "I'm not used to being treated like a skivvy." All those proud defensive phrases: I couldn't get them out of my mouth, because they sounded so silly. In any case, I had lost my dream. The question was really how was I going to make sense of my intolerable situation without, on the one hand, throwing it over and returning to the place I'd started from; or, on the other, pretending it was all great fun.

When I consider now my then dilemma, and go over again why John had bothered to get married to me, I'd hazard a guess that he liked my solidarity, my steadiness, the plonkish steadfastness with which I hewed to the line of my inward and circular vision, if I may dress it up as that. He forced me to live, I said to myself, even as he dismissed my withdrawn quality, my shyness, even as he went on with his linear undertakings—fighting animals, buying houses miles from anywhere, trying to rejoin the Merchant Marine (as he did in Boston on my first visit to America); expanding effortlessly as I was compressed. His energy made him a marvelous companion: he was the modern man before the term was coined, and cooked and cleaned house as well as he cleaned out gutters or unclogged drains or painted rooms and mended sagging doors and broken windowpanes, and of course practiced his calling as professor of literature and writer of books of criticism. The trouble was, I said to myself, I didn't fight back, I didn't deploy the usual woman's weapons apart from a little sulking now and then, not right royal black sulks, considering such tactics revolting without replacing them with more up-to-date ploys. So I liberated him, but he didn't liberate me. However, I thought, Peter needed him as a father, and I put this consideration at the end of the argument because finally it lies a little apart from the central issue. So his tonic effect brought Peter and me to Heathrow and another farewell to England.

On my mother's side, so complete, so unsentimental was her state of quittance that when the month's visit was over—Peter choking under the restrictions of an invalid's regime—there was no usual last bone-cracking hug or wet eye or craned neck, only a quiet look from her as she sat on a bench at the airport and the escalator bore Peter and me away. As usual, it was my father who cried.

At Mast Landing you were always conscious of the sea. As far as the eye could measure there was solid land, and the stream at one time used to float masts had shrunk and now was only a few yards across, but twice in every twenty-four hours it would swell to the top of its banks, and at the high tides of autumn seep onto the flats on the far bank, encouraging a crimson plant to spread over them. Whether it was a freshwater or seawater plant I never knew, just as I never learnt its real name. Local people called it "fireweed," and detoured just to look at it, as it was a new phenomenon caused by the engineering of a strong new iron bridge to replace the old one made of planks. At these high tides you could smell the marine smell—coarse, seaweedy, half rotten—even though the sea itself was a mile or so distant. I was always amazed how wedded this salty seaweedy quality was to the alien forests hanging over the stream, the oaks hanging over rocks, the firs and alders that didn't seem to belong so close to the ocean. And yet seagulls came upstream just as herons went down, and in due season shoals of shad came upstream to spawn in fresh water, and were caught in great quantity by hordes of local people standing in the water with shrimping nets, and gutted and carried home to freeze, the largesse of the sea that lay out of sight.

On our side of the stream there was a path down to the estuary, and it followed the gracious and unnecessary curves and runs of the stream through its woods, past a point where rocks above the bank shelved and formed shallow caves. The former owner of the house, a biology teacher in the local high school, had taken us to see them. The caves were too low to live in, but they had been used for storage by local native tribes before the Europeans came, for grain, dried fish, furs, hooks, poles (so one imagined). Local people still hunted over the ground and used the path to do so. It faded at a marsh. At the summit of the point there was an old house, a weathered clapboard cottage of the sort called a saltbox, with a single long roof sloping to the ground like a lid. It belonged to an old woman called Milly Pettingell, said the biology teacher. She used to live there with her brother, who in his last years used to wander the woods at night and one morning was found in them dead. Their father had been a sea captain, and had built the house himself in South Freeport, over the water. At one time he quarreled with his neighbors and jacked the house on to a raft and sailed it over the estuary and winched it up to its present position. The old garden dated from then: its lilacs, its vast rose hedges, its apple trees, the giant pear trees. Beyond lay the wide shining water of the estuary.

In comparison, our house at Mast Landing was the next best thing. Milly Pettingell's cottage brought a lump to my throat. I didn't understand why, but I suppose John felt that way about the house we actually bought, and once I grew familiar with Milly Pettingell's, I grew more at ease with myself.

This sense of belonging and the satisfaction that went with it may have stemmed from a sense of the unpretentious, used-up landscape, at odds with itself, torn up and neglected and still beautiful. It was far from the terrain round Norton in appearance, being rougher and wilder, but it didn't exclude me any more than that did. In fact, when the yellow school bus bore Peter away to his first day at school in South Freeport, and John set forth on the long drive south in an old green Chevy—as reliable as the Invicta and English Ford had proved capricious—it was as though a maroon had thumped in the distance, such as warns of rocks and fogs, or a factory hooter had gone off saying it was time to start work. So I bought some plain Belgian linen and made curtains and sewed rings on them and hung them on brass poles over the beautiful symmetrical windows, laid fires, arranged my papers, and generally settled in, aided by the neatness of summer's end in

North America, when leaves turn color, clouds string out, geese pass southward miles overhead, night air turns chilly, all in a matter of days. In the middle of repetitive tasks that prompted their rhythms, lines came unbidden to be worked into poems.

People called. First, Milly Pettingell. She wore sneakers and baggy black stockings, an old tweed skirt and a cardigan fastened with a safety pin, and a man's hat on her head. Born in the saltbox eighty-three years before. Attended high school. Learned Latin and Greek, always liked them. Had for company a goose and a dog (the leaping black and white cur that waited for her outside). Now Brother was dead, she had no more worries. And had I seen the moose. Reclusive creatures. Yawp, uh-huh. She sat attentively by my fireside and accepted a cup of tea.

Then, Mary Ellen. The school principal and his wife had left an apple pie on the porch to welcome us. Months earlier, from Mexico City indeed, I'd applied to him for a job, before the women's college in Portland had finally offered me a couple of courses instead, beginning in two weeks. I'd let the principal know, but the pie arrived anyway, and as Peter and I ate it—it was extremely good—I felt more than ever that we were back in the nineteenth century where young women learned Greek, their spiritual food, not useful but life-enhancing, and neighbors welcomed you with apple pie. Unfortunately, in a day or two they asked for the pie dish back and I had ruefully to return it with a note of thanks that did not seem adequate.

"You should have returned the dish containing a pie you'd made yourself," explained Mary Ellen, who was calling on me. She was the mother of Peter's best friend at school so far, and very pretty, with bottle-blond hair, good teeth, and a small perfect figure.

"That could go on forever," I said. "Pie exchanged for pie. But I wish I'd known the custom."

I told Mary Ellen about the geese. I'd bought five Chinese goslings to keep the grass down. They wheeled decorously round the house when they weren't swimming on our pond, and indeed nibbled the grass, before unfortunately crossing the road in front of a car, when two were killed outright and a third had a webbed foot run over. The vet stitched the foot up and his wife tried to feed it milk as a postoperative supplement. I told the vet's wife that geese weren't mammals and would not take milk, and in answer she thrust the gosling sharply into my arms. I took it home with me in the Land Rover, seating it comfortably in my lap. We always were especially fond of each other after that, the gosling and I, though it always took several seconds to recognize me, geese not being clever creatures, and would advance with its two friends to attack me until the very last moment, when it would reel back, ashamed presumably.

Mary Ellen and I looked together at the goose droppings everywhere that made the grass ugly and unpleasant to walk on.

I thought that I had a great deal to learn.

"Oh well," said Mary Ellen, and burst out laughing. She was like me, an outsider, like most of the community at South Freeport where she lived. Freeport itself was not the chic town it became after the revolt against formality and deference that took place in the late sixties and seventies and the rise of L. L. Bean, the outdoorsman's mail-order business, which was a fairly modest affair when we lived at Mast Landing. Then it was a rough plain boot town a few yards off the highway north, with its three factories, and its tough old community, made up partly of French Canadians, partly of very old native and impoverished and often alcoholic stock. South Freeport was a pretty place with a harbor and a sailing club. The geese put me in the outsiders' community.

So what brought us here to Maine? She'd heard my husband was Mexican, was that right?

I explained.

Oh. But I was English?

Mary Ellen had never been out of the country, she told me. She was a homegrown product who'd married young and never had a chance. She'd been homecoming queen, though! She explained what that meant. "Hey, we have a young Scotsman sailing with my husband's crew! You must meet."

Why, I wondered. Luckily I did not have to refuse. The men were too busy fitting out the schooner in South Freeport to be sociable. Mary Ellen's husband was sailing to the Windward Islands to ply for hire during the winter season. What fun!

"So why do men go to sea?" asked Mary Ellen, examining the furniture we had bought at auction.

I told her how John would have renewed his master's ticket, the one he'd acquired in 1949 through his service in the navy during the war, were not the age of shipping drawing to a close. There weren't many freighters left, and so he gave up the idea. Bullfighting had to suffice. However, the sea called to him.

Mary Ellen examined me in wonderment. "Yeah? Is that right? The sea calls to him? What did you think when he tried to get his master's ticket renewed? He was thinking of going to sea again, right?"

"I wondered why he'd bothered getting married," I said.

"Yeah. That's what I wonder."

"Of course I pretended to think it was a good idea."

"I do too. I pretend I'm glad."

She peered into our bedroom with its brass bed, beautified with knobs on posts at each corner. "So you'll be all alone, except for your great little guy there, your Peter. Jonathan and he are real good friends already. Yeah, once Cheever's gone, I'll be alone too, except for Jonathan and his sisters, and of course the entire population of southern Maine."

We must have gone downstairs again and looked out of the old parlor into the back garden, because Mary Ellen took to identifying the birds on the old rosebushes outside the window: pine grosbeak, purple finch, chickadee. "So your husband is commuting to New Jersey, hey, how about that? Four hundred miles, is that right. Eight hundred round-trip. Gee."

Before she left she gave me a plant with red berries in a tiny glass-stoppered jar. A bayberry, she said it was, out of the woods. I hadn't seen one before and was touched.

Through the leaves and across the marsh, appearing out of the water itself, was a huge horned head moving its jaws and big soft lips as it chewed, the upper lip so big as to overlap the lower, the rest of the body hidden deep below the surface. The animal fled the moment I moved, leaping through water with prodigious splashy bounds into the shadow of trees and bushes, the great rack of horn carried high as a dresser on a strong man's shoulders, and instantly blending with branches.

Thoreau calls moose "God's own horses, poor, timid creatures, that will run fast enough as soon as they smell you, though they are nine feet high." He was horrified by the way his companion removed the hide for moccasins, cut a steak from the haunches, and left the huge carcass to rot. That was in 1846. The felling of the ancient pine forests and the massacre of moose were proceeding at a fast clip simultaneously. More than a century later our seventy acres were bare and scrubby, but that one moose of mine lay outside history. Yet I had to keep the knowledge of it to myself because I was alone, and that lifted me outside time, too, in a moment of great fulfillment and regret.

In the harbor of South Freeport as I drove by to return Mary Ellen's visit were lobster boats and some small sailing craft and power boats and the single schooner that by its size must have been the *Windfall,* where Cheever, Mary Ellen's husband, and Ollin the Scots lad were working with three others to prepare her for the voyage south. The scene was so peaceful and idyllic and clean as to have little in common with the usual grimy litter-strewn waterfronts elsewhere in Maine. This was sailing-club country, where people understood why we'd come to Maine better than I did myself. I could tell from casual conversations with Peter's teacher and the people who ran the general store and the people from whom we'd bought the house at Mast Landing that they took us to be like themselves, refugees from big-time America, violence in the cities, pornography, stampede to judgment, working wives, godless children, costly household appliances. In their own mind they thought they were returning to the land, the nineteenth century, the church, homegrown food, handicrafts, the practice of social equality.

Mary Ellen's house was full of children, Peter among them. He used to go to Mary Ellen's straight after school. Other people's families are far more interesting than one's own. Besides the noise of the children, there was the noise of the television, the radio, the dishwasher, a parrot on a perch, and engine roars from the attached barn where someone was tuning a car. By degrees these were muted or switched off, and Mary Ellen indicated the barn. "Ted, there, he expects to . . . I said, nothing doing."

Ted was a salesman of DDT, the salesman of catastrophe. So he wasn't lucky with Mary Ellen either. And she didn't deceive him, at least not after an initial fling. If I were as frank, I thought, I might be much more capable of honest thought, though I was not besieged with lovers, as she must be. And if I were besieged with lovers, I might be flattered, as she clearly was not. I don't think I would tell anyone much about it, the way she was telling me. "Know what?" she said. "Cheever sold group insurance, he sold pots and pans, he sold vacuum cleaners. He couldn't sleep. The shame appalled him. So he gets this chance last year to hire himself out with this boat. Seems like at last he finds himself. So I get to stay in the village. Me and Bonny. Her husband is a painter." She turned to me openly, as a door opens into a house. "Do you flirt?"

"What?"

"Last year, when Cheever was going on this first cruise, I'd flirt. Like at parties when he was there? When he went, that was it, I stopped." She added, "He really suffers when he's working at some job he despises."

"Most jobs are—"

"Shit, right? Cheever wanted to know if he could sail those waters, in the Caribbean? They're a challenge, right?"

"Most jobs are just hard work," I said, and thought of John, and bullfighting, and his professorship at Rutgers that he'd gone back to, and the slog of housework, and the teaching job I was about to begin, which scared me. I never wished to teach.

"But you see, we tried to think things over. We tried to rationalize," said Mary Ellen with her almost idiotic innocence.

"You mean that you tried to be reasonable? Or that you tried to justify what you were doing?"

She considered carefully. "Well, to tell the truth, in the end he just went. We never made a decision."

Older, better educated, more articulate, possibly more sophisticated, I was again jolted that she saw her predicament much more clearly than I saw mine. Moreover she ran over it as if briefing me, or as if she'd been over it a hundred times and become more and more practiced in describing its impossibility. "Other women have said to me, I wouldn't let him go. They'd say to their husbands, fine, but I won't be here when you come back."

"Oh dear," I said.

"I didn't want to live with a man full of 'quiet desperation,'" said Mary Ellen.

"Of course not," I said, wondering about my own brand of quiet desperation and its possible effect.

"I'm not jealous of Cheever," Mary Ellen said. "I can do without Cheever. I found that out long ago. I used to be resentful when we first married and he went off sailing, leaving me with the baby, but it did me no good. Cheever says that women have taken over the dominant role in marriage."

"Poor old Cheever," I said. "You don't think that marriage is a proving ground? That if someone you love wants to do something very badly, you must clear his path to do it?" I was trying to prove a theory of my own. Mary Ellen took not the slightest notice.

"Now look at the schooner," she said. "It's Cheever's because a woman in Virginia responded to him by giving him eleven thousand dollars. And you've met Bonny? Bonny and George have starved for years. He wouldn't let her out of the house because they'd only rags to wear. He refused all jobs because they would take time away from his painting. But he's going with Cheever because it is something honorable to do, and he hopes to earn a bit of money to see them through the winter. He's never sold a painting yet."

"But it's OK to go away on a schooner and not paint?"

"Like I say, that's an honorable thing to do."

"And to keep your family in rags and imprisoned at home is not dishonorable?"

We walked up and down the lane outside her house in the half-light of evening and the children played in and out of the doors and her would-be lover once more tuned her car in the barn.

"You'd be surprised how much he influences people," Mary Ellen said as the lane darkened. "The men came in the moment they knew he was going and they'd say, 'I can't stand it!' How about that? One said, 'I'm thirty years old, and I've done nothing.' Cheever never replies. He just stands there and they fall apart."

I met Cheever one evening when the mothers were waiting for the children to return from some school expedition. Of course it was a terrible disappointment. It was dark and the air was peppery with the smell of rotten leaves. I'd been sitting in my car in the dark at the assembly point in the village when Mary Ellen appeared at my window with her husband beside her holding her hand, a small dark good-looking man with a silly fringe of beard round his jaw and a pipe clenched in his teeth. I remember that he made himself agreeable by removing the pipe to smile and nod, but I don't think he spoke. Then the bus came, with its horde of excited youngsters. The next morning at dawn the *Windfall* moved out of the little harbor of South Freeport on its long journey south to the Caribbean.

John was then coming home to Mast Landing every second weekend. He had taken a small apartment down south in New Brunswick, near the university, to house himself and his old father; a down-at-heel place near the railroad, where in spite of the intensely urban surroundings I once saw a deer in the scrub along the embankment, looking for woods and the cover of tangle along the parks and golf courses that was the nearest thing to the wild in that part of New Jersey. With such odd reminders of elsewhere, it must have been an affirmation and relief to escape the squalor of the welfare town for the sandy tracks and pinewoods and rocky coastal fringes of southern Maine. When he arrived at Mast Landing John had to spend a night or two retrieving his other self, the imaginative writing self, or the craftsman self, and recovering Peter and me. He'd made a table out of driftwood planks with branch legs, and bound it with brass. We both stuffed insulation under the roof. There were plenty of jobs to do. The weather was brilliant in the days after the departure of the *Windfall*, promising an endless summer, the leaves turning yellow and the air puffing sultry suffocating breaths. Hurricane weather, John said, leaving early on the Monday morning because it was going to blow and rain hard.

About then, when I was alone in the house, I was looking dreamily out of the bathroom window which faced the woods at the back when I saw a huge creature come sauntering through the yard below making for the river, noble and oblivious and gigantic, with two smaller versions a short way behind. At first I couldn't think what animal it was, because it didn't have those characteristic horns, two feet high and as much as six across, that the bull moose sport. A horse, then, a shire horse? And then no, it was bigger than any horse I ever saw, it could only be a moose, and I shouted for joy at the clear sight of the amazing creature, alone in the empty house though I was, so keen to share the pleasure that I rang a friend who promptly drove over, by which time of course the moose and her calves had vanished. But he understood, that friend. And again I'd had the uncanny sense of standing outside time and place and observing the nameless, unparticularized, melancholy and giant creature making its way through its life and brushing slightly against mine, to my infinite enrichment because I had never really taken it into account as I should have done.

"So John's not here," said David, our friend, "we must tell him," and he looked at me as if he'd only just seen me.

I said unwisely, "No, he's in New Brunswick, shacked up with a blonde," not thinking David would take me seriously, pleased to try out the phrase, wanting David to go and leave me alone, unable to see why he took his time. For months after that, I later learned, I was an object of pity, invited to dinner to meet a possible partner, and included in parties so I wouldn't grieve, so well did shacking up with a blonde explain John's rationale in establishing Peter and me in Maine far from his work.

Presently David left, and I went back to considering the house. The air was beginning to stir violently when I heard on the radio that the storm was veering out into the ocean west of Cape Hatteras in North Carolina. I didn't even think of Cheever and his schooner until Mary Ellen rang up.

The *Windfall* was reported missing, she said, and when I had understood, she said that it had been missing last year too, and had turned up safe and sound.

Well, good, I thought, not upset in any way.

She kept telling them not to worry: her mother, the children, her friends. The *Windfall* had been missing for two weeks last year. His radio had broken down, that was all. It broke down all the time. It had a hand transmitter (what was that, and why not replace it with something sturdier?). The Coast Guard had been out looking for him last year, same as now. She told them not to worry, and he eventually turned up. He was a very very experienced sailor.

The man from the Portland newspaper had been at the house. "You know," she said, "I say not to worry and I don't believe in giving up hope." Giving up hope, my poor Mary Ellen? "So he looks at the parrot. 'Gee, what a cute bird,' he says. 'Is that a parrot? Does it speak? What sort of parrot you call that?' 'To hell with the parrot,' I says. 'You're not here to interview a parrot.'" The telephone screeched with her laughter. "I called the Coast Guard," she went on, ignoring the little I had to say. "They're going to call me back tonight." She'd had a call from the mother of Ollin Baird, the young Scot. She'd had a service for Ollin in the village church in Nairn.

Already, my poor Mary Ellen?

She wanted Mary Ellen and Bonny and their children to go and stay with her in Scotland, but Mary Ellen hadn't given up hope.

"I dreamt of him Wednesday," she said. "I dreamt I was sitting with him on the deck at South Freeport watching a green sailboat go out of the harbor and suddenly a storm came up, and a man came running along the dock, and he called out to Cheever to come and help him save the sailboat. We could see she was in danger, and I knew he'd go, and I started crying and said, "If you go this time I will leave you, I will divorce you." So he turns to me and he says, 'You know I have to go.' The next day, Thursday, I read in the paper the *Windfall* was missing."

There was no news for two or three days. Turgid winds came and bucked at the roof. Mary Ellen rang to say that another schooner, the *Belle,* had met the *Windfall* in Newport, Rhode Island, on the fifteenth, the day before her dream. They were to have sailed south together. The day the newspapers reported the *Windfall* was missing, the *Belle* foundered off the Bermudas, without loss of life. They reported they had run into violent storms, in which they lost sight of the *Windfall* when she hauled away from them in a friendly race.

Then a Belgian freighter sent signals picked up by the Coast Guard to the effect that she was 250 miles off Cape Hatteras standing by five men clinging to wreckage in waves thirty feet high driven by winds at hurricane force. The holds of the freighter were empty, and she was bobbing on the waves, finding it hard to keep her bows into the wind. Nevertheless she shot lifelines over the men in the sea, until it was clear that the wind and the waves were too great, and the lines drifted away. She'd come across them at one-thirty in the afternoon, and at nightfall she was still there, when her calls for help were at last answered by two naval vessels and a Coast Guard plane, so "she looked to her own safety and departed" (which I thought cavalier, because how could the men in the sea be found except by her presence?). The navy was silent on what happened after that.

Days later the Coast Guard recovered a wheelhouse two hundred miles off Cape Hatteras. Mary Ellen went down to Cape May alone to identify it, and brought the wheel back, and hung it on the outside wall of her cottage.

By then the little church at South Freeport had held a memorial service for the drowned men and afterward the congregation walked down to the harbor and threw wreaths on the water. Mary Ellen and Bonny did not attend.

How were they going to live, I wondered, these young widows with five young children between them? Of course Cheever Rogers and George wouldn't have insured their own lives, they hadn't the money, they hadn't the foresight, and Herman Melville's Ishmael wouldn't have taken out life insurance when he went whaling, so they wouldn't, either. The township put the widows on relief, and the two young women went to the official food store and got supplies of butter, flour, beans, and so on. Middle-class girls as they were, they found their charitable status a joke, and laughed themselves silly, and then cried, according to Mary Ellen, who in spite of herself was enjoying the drama. That bright snowy day just after Thanksgiving when she told me the state of affairs, we stood in her kitchen with the packets bought with food stamps displayed on the table. They'd been out driving the previous day, she and Bonny, just driving the sandy lanes together, talking, "having fun" while the children were in school, and I

thought that they'd reverted to adolescence and girlish friendships and confidences. Peter and I were going to take young Jonathan to walk along the beach a dozen miles away in the state park.
The boy looked white in the face but resolute as we passed the
empty kiosk at the entrance to the park, and parked, and walked
over the glittering dunes. Our boots cracked the ice on the edge of
the sea, and the boys picked up ice plates and skimmed them over
the water. The rocks and isles in the bay were snowy and the wind
cut our faces. When we came to a huge driftwood pine trunk on
the shore, Jonathan sat on it and looked out to sea in an attitude of
grief conventional and noble and appalling. Would Peter have sat
like that? Would John have died like Cheever? "He's thinking of
his father," Peter said to me as we watched. It was bitter cold, so
we soon went back to Mary Ellen's warm kitchen. Other visitors
were making their way in, a married couple.

"I brought you a gun, Mary Ellen," said the man. "To protect
yourself? You should have a gun. In case you get nervous."

"But you might shoot someone," I said naively, and everyone
laughed, especially the children.

"They say I should have a gun," Mary Ellen said, aiming the
gun at the fireplace.

"You can give me twenty for it if you like," the man said.

Mary Ellen raised her eyebrows at me. "Twenty? Oh, all right.
OK."

The man said to me, "You should have a gun too, alone as much
as you are." I said I'd rather be raped than kill someone, and he
laughed and said he might come round later, and his wife laughed
too. They seemed to be enjoying the situation as much as anyone,
and that gave me the idea of writing Mary Ellen's story for the
local newspaper. I put it to her and she said, why not. Why not,
said the editor, he was always on the lookout for freelance material. So that night I wrote about the loss of the schooner in the
hurricane and how the widows and children coped with their loss,
and how Ollin Baird's mother coped. In the morning I drove to

Brunswick and dropped the article off at the newspaper office, and on the way home saw Mary Ellen coming out of a store in Freeport, and on an impulse offered her the carbon.

So far as I was concerned, that completed the sad business. Death was the end. Five young men had thrown their lives away. John had been critical, though I thought it strange that he didn't equate his bullfighting with Cheever's venture. Supposing John had been gored or even killed in the final weeks in Mexico after Peter and I had gone to England? I'd have had to face a sequence of decisions to do with fear, anxiety, incapacity, earnings, insurance, hospitals, medical care, even mourning. And suppose I'd decided to stay in England? My teaching in the small women's college in Portland was a defeat. A character in one of Iris Murdoch's novels says that in America everyone is a professor, which may be why so many people I met were keen on edifying others, draped in their brief authority. Never had I felt so artificial as when instructing the young women who faced me in those still-orthodox times, fresh from their bad high schools and bookless homes. They were nice girls, but they knew so little and had so few ideas that I wondered how they'd survived, and spent most of my preparation for class in making my material simple and interesting and, where possible, shocking, so they might waken from their complacency.

I returned from a class on *Measure for Measure* and a fierce discussion on the value of virginity when Mary Ellen rang.

She'd had the usual crowd of callers the previous evening, she said, among them an art teacher who'd been affected deeply by Cheever's death.

I'd met him, hadn't I, she said, he was one of the eleven best etchers in the country.

Why eleven, I asked, who were the others?

She didn't answer that, but said he'd picked up the carbon on the kitchen counter and started reading it. Then he asked if she'd really said all that. Sure she had. So he went on reading. Then he broke out and said she could not possibly let that be printed. But why not, she'd said it, after all. She meant it too.

But it was a revelation of her life with Cheever and how he was filled with quiet desperation.

Well?

Cheever's reputation would be ruined.

What reputation?

What he stood for in the art teacher's mind.

She'd said simply what he meant to her, to her as Cheever's wife.

The typescript suggested that she was putting Cheever down.

Putting him down? Never.

But that business of flirting with others?

It happened!

She liked what I wrote, Mary Ellen told me humbly, and I replied that I did not understand why she was calling me. Because, Mary Ellen said, the art teacher declared to her that he was Cheever's oldest friend and had her interests at heart, and was terribly upset, and said she was killing Cheever all over again. So she grabbed the typescript and read the article through and found nothing there in the least sensational, even in the bit about flirting and how she could live without Cheever and how she had to let him go: it was perfectly right and proper.

So the art teacher read out the part he found offensive, and the other people in the room listened, including Bonny, who was not as open as Mary Ellen, and who was shocked and said it should not be published. Close to midnight the art teacher drove over to Brunswick and met the editor, saying he was keen to safeguard Cheever's reputation and protect his wife and children. Mary Ellen pointed out to me that he was an artist and very sensitive. When he'd come back, she'd asked him what she should tell me, and he said that I was a woman of the world and would understand.

I was angry, and the editor was of my turn of mind. He came to

Mast Landing to explain that the art teacher had shaken his re-
solve by crying over the presses when he refused to stop them. Not
only was the art teacher's peace of mind in danger, but also the vi-
brancy of some imaginative drawings he'd made of the loss of the
Windfall. He said he owed Cheever things he could not repay.

"He was in love with him," said the editor briskly. "So I killed
your piece. But I also said to him, look, what come over your
friend Cheever to run down that coast in November? I said to
him, look, I was a commercial fisherman running out of Montauk
for five years, and I know you don't sail a schooner down there in
November, you use the inland waterways. Sure it's slow and expensive, but you don't drown. I bet he didn't have charts, I said.

"Some of these fellows," said the editor to me, "they don't
bother with charts, nor a radio because the skippers a hundred
years ago didn't use radios, and they get lost and they drown. That
Cheever was missing for two weeks last year. You'd think he'd
look after himself a bit better this time—but no, he loses his crew
and his boat and his own life. And what about his wife, huh? Did
he think of being a little bit considerate of her before he sailed
into the eye of a hurricane, because that's what he did. And the
freighter? And the navy and the Coast Guard? And his kids?
Right, so he's a hero, great, and he had a big effect on your artist.
So I killed your piece.

"Hey, listen, there were hurricane reports long before he left.
You don't catch Mainers going out in those conditions. He knew
what it was going to be like. That's what he wanted, you figure?
He wasn't a Maine man, of course, though he talked like one.
Yawp, uh-huh. His father was a doctor on Long Island for years, in
the Hamptons. He turned his back on all that. You get plenty of
them down east. Out to be a living legend, right? These guys,
they read Thoreau in high school, and bam, they've had it."

Bam.

All my life, I told the editor, I'd wanted to live in a horse-drawn caravan and drive my horse slowly from place to place, stopping where I felt like it, washing my clothes in rivers, gathering firewood, picking blackberries, buying milk from farms, living out summers (not Maine winters), close to the weather and the landscape I journeyed through. (I still think of the horse's broad back swaying in front of me, because it would have to be a strong Welsh cob, or a Morgan. The reins lie along its broad back, gathered into my hand as I sit on the stoop of the caravan, overlooking the hedges and the land as we plod past.)

"Of course it's just a dream," I told the editor, who listened carefully as he always did, slightly cocking his head and looking up asquint. "Though one day . . . when I'm old . . . when I'm Robinson Crusoed by death and disaster. . . . I mean, I understand why men want to go to sea. As Johnson said, 'Every man thinks meanly of himself for not having been a soldier or not to have been at sea.' But what about me? I can only dream of the equivalent, and so can Mary Ellen and Bonny. We think meanly of ourselves, left behind as we are."

The editor was amused by my eloquence. Why didn't I write another article, expressing my point of view about going to sea?

Not on your life, I said. People would be turning up in their dozens to pull such an article from the presses, yelling that I was a ball breaker or a sweet winsome dreamer. To begin with, I couldn't write longingly about the sea, because I got seasick, and as for the equivalent, a horse and caravan, people wouldn't begin to understand what I meant.

"It would be youth," the editor said, "it would be freedom. It would be adventure."

"Oh la la," I said. "Have you noticed," I went on, "how people sail round the world single-handed, or climb huge mountains, or walk into the wilderness stark naked, or bicycle to India, and manage to survive, and thrive on the books they put out afterward describing their experience, and somehow suggest that they have turned out to be true to themselves, whatever they did before, and so they have honored the estate to which God called them? Do you think," I asked, "that this was true of Thoreau's Walden?"

"I don't doubt it," said the editor, brightening. "He was a phony, though not a mean phony. Remember, he refused to pay taxes because the taxes would go to the upholders of slavery. The whole idea of civil disobedience comes from Thoreau. Mind you, the simple life's extremely hard on women. Write that piece, about not going to sea."

"No," I said. "I will one day, but certainly not now."

I don't know if the editor heard. He simply took off, embracing me first. An interesting man, in love with Maine as so many are, a man of ideas as so many are in Maine, as captivated by the simple, basic life Maine called for as John was and Henry David Thoreau was, and poor Cheever Rogers. Live simply, says Thoreau. Don't waste time on niceties. Your needs are few. Abandon drudgery. Bam.

Peter was going through a trying time. No sooner had he settled down happily in the South Freeport school befriended by Jonathan and encouraged by an unusually enlightened teacher than the school boundaries were redrawn and he was sent to the Freeport school, an altogether more dismal place. The building was gloomy and the intake mixed, which would have been healthy if the teacher had been worth her salt. Maine schools are the worst in the country.

"Peter don't know his phonics," the teacher told me when I attended one of his classes.

"But he reads very well."

"He don't know his phonics!"

"Then I don't know what phonics are," I said. She didn't try to explain, so I went to the back of the class while she strummed a guitar and sang "The Streets of Laredo" and the children fidgeted

and looked back at me. Presently a senior teacher came in and
asked for the names of those entitled to a free lunch. The boy beside me raised his hand.

"Jason?"

"Yes, ma'am." While she ticked his name on her list, Jason said
to me, "My dad, he sits and don't do nothing. He drinks a lot,
though, my ma says." And he laughed.

"I expect he knows what he is doing," I said.

"No, I don't think he do know."

"Well, you have a good lunch, Jason," I said.

I was thinking of him the next day when the principal rang up
and asked if I permitted Peter to give away his pocket money.

"Of course," I said.

"Peter has given it to Jason. Jason gave it to me. I thought I
had better ask you." So modesty also had its pride. Peter had done
well. Yet when I thought of the useless teacher of phonics and
her guitar, and how much Peter had suffered from our constant
moves, it was clear Jason did not have the power to keep him. As
it happened, I had only to tell of these events to an experienced
colleague at the college where I taught for her to ring up the head-
master of the excellent private school in Portland, and for him
to give Peter a scholarship. At last his education looked set on
course.

Winter set in, so violently that the cylinder block froze in the
Land Rover. It had to be towed away and the block replaced. The
old house was not insulated, and I wore boots and overcoat at my
desk in front of the kitchen fire. Load after load of logs sent their
warmth up the vast chimney. The furnace roared all night to very
little avail. The geese tired of their frozen pond and took to the air
a few feet over the snow and flew out of sight downriver. After
several hours I went in search of them, floundering through several feet of snow along the bank, past the Indian caves, and almost
up to the marsh, where I found them sitting on the snowbound
frozen stream. They greeted me with honks, and I grabbed the

two females, tucking first one under my left arm and then the
other under the right, and set off back, leaving the gander to stag-
ger along in my snowy wake. With an alert goose peering to my
left and right with little round button eyes to the side of proud
knobbed black nib, and falling headlong myself every few yards
because my hands were full and the snow along the path hid pock-
ets like bear traps, I finally reached the goose hut and ushered the
three of them in, bedded them down with fresh straw and plenty
of corn and water, and got myself back into the house as the snow
ploughs roared by, followed by the gritters and the salters through
the pure icy landscape, creating a beautiful band of clear road.

The deed must have been witnessed. In the ensuing thaw,
William Coffin the carpenter, our neighbor, came to the door with
Milly Pettingell's gray goose under his arm. It was a huge bedrag-
gled stupid-looking creature compared with my small elegant Chinese geese. "Let's see," William Coffin said, and walked through
the kitchen and set the gray goose on the snowy muddy grass,
where my own geese rushed up and attacked it, nipping and hissing and wafting their wings. Coffin scooped up the gray goose and
shut it in our barn, saying they'd settle down together.

I asked what had happened to Milly.

She'd gone, said William Coffin. She'd given up her house that
very day and gone to live with cousins on Sebago Lake. The carpenter burst into laughter and a froth formed on his lips, which
he wiped away with the back of his hand. He was hard to com-
prehend because he wasn't wearing his teeth. I gathered that old
women got too fond of creatures. Milly Pettingell's mongrel had
met a porcupine in the woods and got its nose full of quills, and
the vet put it down. He, William Coffin, had offered her a beagle
pup and she had refused. He burst out at this again, in an explosion of mirth and ridicule which again covered his lips with spit,
and which again he wiped away.

I found it hard to believe that the loss of her dislikable and disobedient mongrel would force her to leave her beautiful cottage, but a few days later a note from Sebago Lake came though the door:

Dear Friend,
I am sorry I did not stop to say goodbye but after she died it was more than I could stand to go on living alone, missing her so much where she and I were so happy.
Your friend,
M. Pettingell

I saw her only once more, seated in the back of an old car driven by her cousins, peering out attentively. She had come to negotiate the sale of her cottage to a wealthy Philadelphian who ran a nearby farm of Aberdeen Angus cattle, grass-fed in an early shot at organic farming. Rumor soon had it that the rich man was going to build a motel on the point, which of course didn't happen. Paranoia is rife in Maine. In any case, I was glad the car did not stop, for then I would have had to confess that her goose was dead, savaged by my geese when I wasn't watching and then shot by John out of pity. Presently the windows of the cottage were boarded up, to protect them against vandals. The yard was kept mown, but the garden gradually became overgrown, and in the spring no one planted scarlet runner beans over the front door as Milly Pettingell had done or tied back the roses or trimmed the lilacs after they'd flowered.

Mary Ellen and Bonny, widowed young, pretty, and brave, attracted the usual tributes from men, married and unmarried. Mary Ellen made no secret of her own desires. She came to lunch with John and me and couldn't stop gazing at him. He was wearing corduroys and a thick gray turtleneck sweater he'd had for years.

"Oh, you're lovely," whispered Mary Ellen, examining him from close up. To me she said, "He's lovely, isn't he?" and laughed at her own brass. "I shouldn't say it, but he's lovely."

John was not particularly embarrassed. He gave her an encouraging kiss, and we had lunch.

Within the year she and Bonny had married again, Mary Ellen to a reporter who had interviewed her when the *Windfall* was lost. I don't know whether it was the same reporter who had been struck by the presence of the parrot in her kitchen, but it wouldn't surprise me. The man showed a candid interest in the unusual, and it would not have taken long for him to have transferred his interest from the parrot to Mary Ellen. I never met Bonny's new husband, either, but she told me that she had found someone whom she called "another good man." She was a beautiful young woman, as Mary Ellen was. It seemed strange that they'd been married and left, and then bereaved, for no compelling reason other than their beauty and youth and vulnerability, which might appear like deer that hunters felt forced to bring down. It was tempting to see some pattern in the sequence of their lives that I could apply to my own, though I was not beautiful, and in my late thirties. John, too, was adventurous. Did marriage inspire men to be foolhardy (its boredom, its restriction, the challenge of women driving them out)? Or was marriage a launching pad for them, the wives waving from the doorstep, child in arms, as they set forth? I could see the beauty of it from the man's point of view. What I couldn't see was the man's unwillingness to put himself in the woman's shoes and to recognize that his longing must be the woman's too, in egalitarian America. Nor was my blindness due to extravagant desires for equality. It was clear that as many women were adventurous as men. I was as venturesome as John, to speak plain, but had more sense and the child to look after, and therefore had to stay behind, when a chance came to go climbing up a creek in Vermont once, or skiing in Germany, or going off to

Spain every year as was to happen. But make no mistake, I did not like it.

I supposed, seeing around me the usual instances of infidelity and adultery, that I was in fact pretty lucky. The latter self views with horror the things that went wrong. Without errors, no experience. Without experience, no truth. Yes, and nothing venture, nothing gain, and so on. Shouldn't I write about these things? Everything's simplified in the telling. Everything is also codified according to the codes in fashion. I may have failed to convey the devotion that carried us through, as I questioned it repeatedly, as I'm sure others did. What game were we playing?

"I think we should have a daughter," John said.

PART THREE

AFTER ALL . . .

. . . in an aftermath, when principle
turned awkward, and the air hazed with rebellion

WHY YOU?

"Why you?" asked Jeannie the mailwoman as she stood at the door with our mail in her hand.

"Because I have a degree from Oxford in English, perhaps. . . ."

"They have women at Oxford?"

"For a hundred years, now."

"Did you finish?"

"Did I finish? Heavens. You mean it doesn't show?" I made a face.

She made one in return, then went grimly on. "So why you?"

Some simple and convincing statement about myself was called for. So I examined my conscience and told her I'd studied the language from its origins, and knew some Latin, and French, and German, and Spanish, and had published a couple of books and, with John, compiled an anthology on censorship that was published a year ago. All that would be useful. In my heart I knew I hadn't said the right thing. We were still standing at the door. "I shouldn't be saying this, should I?"

"Someone has to."

The bluntness was not meant to disarm. With my usual vile wish to please, I added that John had recommended me for the job, and she smiled at last. She was the clever wife of a poor farmer; they were Quakers and had dropped out of Swarthmore together, to get away from what they called the "rat race." She illicitly read our magazines and reviews before she delivered them to us, and told us which the interesting articles were, and then sighed and raised her eyebrows and said "Hm." She was obviously annoyed with herself for being so irresistibly drawn to ideas, and annoyed with us for our worldliness. She certainly hadn't escaped from the world's great snare, for all her formal renunciation of it. And who could blame her? Their farm was evidence that they weren't coping with the demands of a more spiritual life (if that's what it was), with its broken gates and fences and filth in the yard and dirty milking herd and overflowing midden.

Why you, indeed. Why me, why lucky me. We weren't exactly good at managing our affairs. Such talents as we had were grossly overextended in the service of our whims, and even more than other people we were always short of money, and were ready to work harder and for longer hours to justify the absurd expenditure on the two establishments, the one in New Jersey and the one in Maine, and the two cars. The ethic has become familiar, but then it seemed strange. John was soon to double his salary, and as for me, even then women made up a third of the workforce, and in 1963 the Equal Pay Act passed through Congress, acknowledging their importance. In Maine, decent jobs were hard to find. Hence the lure of the job at Rutgers, which I could manage at home with periodic visits south. The task for which I was hired was to compile a dictionary of the various uses of words used in the study of alcohol and alcoholism. It was needed because words such as *tolerance* were used in slightly different senses by different disciplines and even by different people in the same discipline, with bewildering results.

I thought I could run both jobs together until the end of the academic year, when I would drop the teaching.

"Don't take it on if you don't want to," John said.

"I hate not earning my own keep."

"But you do already."

"There's nothing in the bank."

"We'll manage."

It was obvious what to do. Once a month I'd board Peter with one of his teachers in Portland, drive to the airport in Boston, park the Land Rover, and catch the air shuttle to Newark, where John met me and drove me to New Brunswick. That afternoon and the morning of the next day were spent in my senior colleague's office in the Center for Alcohol Studies while he began to read the definitions I'd devised from certain key texts. His remarks soon tailed off into the great adjacent territories he was interested in: his boyhood in the Bronx, his schooling, his first job, his mentor and the mentor's fame, the necessity of language and its unreliability, and the possibilities of nailing it down. He had the pedantry of the self-educated, who don't know how much others know or how far to accept common knowledge, and he was getting old, so in the manner of the old he repeated his anecdotes again and again. One of his habits was to overarticulate, as if he were inventing the language as he went along. Hours went by as he mouthed his way through routine English and ruminated his commonplaces. I don't know why I didn't make it clear to him that he was holding things up, unless he reminded me of another bottleneck whom I'd worked for in advertising. He had a similar embattled view of the world, and yet he was imaginative and clever, a working-class boy with a sharp eye, much sharper than Bottleneck II's. Yet some of the answers to my questions would undoubtedly crop up by default, and the other colleagues were far more open and forthcoming, especially the physiologist and one of the social scientists, who had actually imitated alcoholic behavior for months, landed up on the Bowery in New York, was rescued, taken home, restored to health, and there wrote analytically of his experiences. Others of the staff appeared to have succumbed to the disease they were studying and were being carried along on the tide of grants and fellowships from Washington. Down in the basement were rows of caged mice and rats and rabbits being fed alcohol; there were even some cages of sad monkeys with electrodes in the brain that were kept topped up with alcohol over long periods of time. The morality of such procedures was questioned now and then, but largely taken for granted, just as the alcoholics on the staff were taken for granted until one drove into a tree on the way home from lunch. Even the National Institutes of Health now and then lost their bearings, as when they financed a study of delirium tremens by feeding some men in hospital large quantities of alcohol daily over three months and then withdrawing it. Delirium tremens resulted in all subjects. Thus it could be inferred that delirium tremens was a withdrawal phenomenon.

Hold on, though, someone said, suppose the men had *died*?

Hey, they were alcoholics, weren't they, said the investigator. They were warned of the dangers in advance. They had to sign a form declaring they understood.

But they were *alcoholics,* someone said. *Alcoholics* cannot resist *alcohol.* An *alcoholic* will do anything to get hold of *alcohol,* even subscribe to an immoral experiment.

The alarming aspects of the job made it all the more interesting. Above all, it was clear what needed to be done.

After the day's work at the office in New Brunswick I'd go to the apartment John shared with his father, we'd have supper together, sleep together in connubial bliss, and after lunch on the second day John would run me to the airport and I'd fly back to Boston.

Back home in Mast Landing I pushed ahead with definitions and quotations, using the general method of the great *Oxford English Dictionary,* taking examples of usage from relevant texts and forming a definition through each one. This method was superior to Bottleneck's formulations based on what he thought should be understood and his own didactic rules. Working with words in the new sphere of the sciences was interesting, the pay was good, and a twelvemonth should see the job completed in draft form, even on the nine-month academic teaching schedule they allowed me, with its spacious vacations.

On one particular visit from Maine the plane was bucked by tremendous turbulence over the oil refineries and industries of New Jersey. I was pregnant and the plane's antics as we came low over Newark frightened me out of my wits. What if panic lost me my baby? Was this way of life worthwhile? On my return to Boston, snow and freezing rain were falling in the wintry evening. The Land Rover in the crowded parking lot at Logan Airport started up without trouble, the good creature, and I drove along in the throng of vehicles that crept through the dark snowy suburbs. And then the Land Rover began to speed up of its own accord. I very gently put my foot on the brake and very gently we slid sideways. I lifted my foot and we started to gain on the man ahead as if someone else were driving. Nothing much could happen—we were hemmed in left and right, ahead and behind, by slow vehicles in the same plight of darkness and softly falling snow and freezing rain and ungritted roads. The preposterous heating system sent a jet of heat against one leg while the other one froze, but in spite of the cold I burst into a sweat. I kept braking slightly and skidding slightly till the army of cars thinned out as we passed through the dark northern outskirts of the city, gradually accelerating in spite of my efforts till we were going along at a good whack. Once out into the country—over the spit of New Hampshire and into Maine—I burst into the forecourt of a motel and found a room there, avoiding the chummy owner, loathing the prospect of asking him for help. In the night I worked out that the accelerator had frozen. In the morning the fog had lifted and the sky was blue and the accelerator pedal was loose and obedient. I left at six and got to my morning class in Portland in time to discuss the current news that the students would later write about, marshaling the arguments: *on the one hand, and on the other, it must be said that, there are three points to be made, contrary to these views, some people believe.*

It was the time of the Freedom Riders, when principled people, mostly young, took buses to Alabama and other points south to register black voters and were received with bricks and sticks by conservative whites. James Meredith, a black man, enrolled in a university and state troopers had to escort him to his classes through baying white mobs. Latterly a poor old black woman had been put on a bus north, her fare paid, so when she stumbled off in Boston with no idea of where she was or why, conservative whites in Alabama were heard congratulating themselves. My class in Portland was indignant.

"What she doing? She don't belong here."

"Just so."

"Poor woman, she didn't know what was going on. She was made to get on the bus and go north. She had no idea. . . ."

"She ought to be ashamed."

"It was cruel."

"Yes. Yes?"

"No, but I mean, why don't people like her leave us Americans alone?"

"*Us Americans?*" I repeated in amazement.

"We Americans? Leave we Americans alone?"

"No, no. That poor black woman is from Alabama. She is American. And it was not her fault she came north, as most of you appreciate. Some cruel whites put her on the bus as a point of retaliation."

"Retaliation?"

"Look it up. My point is, it was not her fault."

I felt sanity fleeing before me like a beast in the glare of my headlights. My first classes had included several girls in convulsions of homesickness. Some had gone home, some had recovered, but all were vulnerable at the advanced age of seventeen and eighteen. I had already got into trouble with the president of the college over the lewd parts of *Measure for Measure*. Even with editing, the girls had trouble with the obscenities.

"Bawdy is not a family word," explained the oldish woman who allowed me to share her office.

"Can't you cut that stuff right out?" asked the president.

"It is essential to our understanding of the purity and chastity of the heroine, Isabella, that we keep the bawdy scenes," I told him. "Shakespeare places the pure and chaste heroine in scenes of sexual corruption that she understands, as the girls should. Shakespeare is addressed to us all. You can't be said to be educated if you don't know a single play, as our students usually don't."

"We don't claim to have a drama department," said the president.

"He must be read, then. These girls are grown up, they are going out into the world."

"The world of retailing, catering, business offices. . . ."

"You can't send them out in a state of ignorance!"

"If you insist," said the president.

"I am amazed," I said to my office colleague, "how prim and conventional America is. Its reputation is quite otherwise."

"Maybe you could give us a talk on the subject," she said, and arranged for me to address the student body on the matter of America's reputation abroad. I gave my talk, mentioning among other things the reputation of American soldiers when I was young. To be seen out with an American soldier, I said, meant you had lost your virginity. This item was met with shocked giggles. Nevertheless, I added cheerfully, I'd married an American.

Afterward the president was furious. He censored the report of my speech that was to appear in the Portland newspaper, for fear it would cast too lurid a light on the little college he headed, where a compromised and possibly tawdry woman was an instructor.

All in all, nevertheless, *quand même,* from the perspective of today, I was reluctant to leave Maine. For one thing, I had got fond of the house at Mast Landing and the bare isolated life Peter and I lived there. In the winter evenings when I'd kissed him good night and he'd nestled down in his big old colonial bed made of heavy maple posts and boards strung with rawhide under the mattress, I'd go down to sit by the fire in my boots with a blanket round my shoulders, no end to the hours ahead, and the poems came, one after the other. I was no longer the pretentious wife swearing to herself that she'd nurse her talent by writing so many words or for so many hours: the poems wrote themselves. Maine led me to take the low road in writing a poem. At Oxford, where I began writing in earnest, words had burst out like paint from a tube, daubing the grandest phrases over grandiose themes. Wallace Stevens checked the process with his wit and dandyism and mock solemnity. By the time we came to Maine I'd learned American poetry's great lesson of ordinariness and simplicity, and with it the notion that the world was made up of common things. Elizabeth Bishop's voice spoke in the night, not Robert Lowell's. He took the stage, she stayed in the wings. He had bravura, she disliked it. Even now, long after his rhetoric has dated, her voice continues to speak its everyday speech. And pregnancy's awareness shone on the everyday like a light. The bare room, the bare life, bare work and routine: as in talk, the clearer issues surface, the quiet lets confusion settle, and intermittently I began to see the physical world with something of the intensity of childhood, the interesting whorls and circles of a paving stone, for example, with chipped margins like a fingernail. I could see faintly the essential life of inorganic things. That life was to be obscured again by the social world, which was regrettable, as it was a useful brake on subjectivity, and a thickener of feeling. That is, the primary understanding of the world was to give way again to social understanding, the pooled understanding of others, and frequently, as before, I could no longer really see or feel for myself, but had to think through others, with others, my mistakes compounded by not having grown up to that society. Yet I still trusted the physical world to back my judgment. This worked in reciprocal fashion, as I understand it. The body was that portion of soul perceived by the five senses, said Blake, and though he was referring to the human body, the same perception of soul extended to the whole of the physical world, helped by the special acuteness of the senses in pregnancy. Years later I saw the same outlook and process depicted in the still lifes of Chardin.

As far as the new poems went, an objective assessment was lacking, more so than usual, and I tried one out on a young art instructor from Bowdoin who called on us one weekend. It concerned a case of chicken pox I'd recently suffered from—not, mysteriously enough, caught from Peter, who stayed pox free— and ended with foreboding:

I see me presently old and sick, a big strong hag
Bellowing from her bedroom of neglect.

The young man obligingly shrieked with laughter and held up his hands toward me as if to warm them at my fire. Nevertheless I was crushed. Surely no self-respecting person would think that was an answer? I'd poured my wits into the poem and he treated me like a clown! No praise would have been enough, of course, and no criticism enough either. I had to wait till the poems were accepted and published in little magazines before I could pretend for one moment they were worthwhile. Meanwhile of course John read them. Yes! No! Or, disconcertingly, Thanks very much!— turning red, believing I was writing about him, reading himself into the plot. A wretched solecism, and from a professor too! More and more I learned to distance myself from him, because he had too much power over me just as I had apparently too much power over him. This push toward doing without a mentor was progress, though a mite sad. There must be something intrinsically unlikely or illogical about the independent and solitary work of a woman, especially of a wife and mother. My parents had asked in regard to my first publications, "Did John Wain write that for you?" Later a faculty wife would ask if my husband had written an essay I published on alcoholism in the novels of the midnineteenth century, not a great likelihood on the face of it. Silly—

but he was the professor, the authority. The woman is the lay figure. Naturally: for where would she find the time, the space, the furious willfulness to write from a heart already engaged to the hilt? And who does she think she is, anyway?

True, in the days when the sheer force of circumstance prevented me from writing, as when Peter was a baby in the isolation of Berlin, I wasn't bursting with ideas to rush and put on paper. On the contrary, I had no ideas at all. The emptier I became, the less I could live my life and the less I had to write about. That was the real crux. So it came down to a matter of control. In Maine my life was pretty much my own. Husband, job, child, house; nothing neglected. The new pregnancy, of course, threatened the balance, but contrarily I rather liked threats of that sort, of richness encroaching on the puritan life.

Another fondness for Maine grew out of the same hankering for plenty: I might become a matriarch. First Owen would leave New Jersey and join us at Mast Landing, and then my father would join us too. My mother had died and he was lonely. I'd have the new baby, and perhaps another, as well as Peter and Jonathan, who might come and stay more often now he was to enter Yale. Ruth who lived across the creek would be glad to become our daily housekeeper, and John and I would come and go as our jobs warranted. We'd play cards, and sing, and laugh, and have the neighbors in . . .

"*Two* old men?" wrote my father.

"You could keep an eye on things," I wrote back.

In the days following my mother's death, when I was with him, he had called me by her name. He used to call her *lover* and I was afraid he'd call me *lover* too, though it never came to that. He begged me to lengthen my visit to Windsor, and I did, though years would not have been enough. Her cloistered life threatened, her old grieving for her lost youth, her fuss over their possessions, the furniture, the silver, her fur coat, her diamond ring. The thought of it made me want to live in the Indian cave along the

river. As matriarch I'd keep things simple: block off some fireplaces, put thick carpets and quilted curtains and Franklin stoves
in every room, buy good skis and skates and toboggans for winter
and in summer grow strawberries and asparagus and plant an orchard, and have a boat and go sailing and fishing.

"It will be idyllic," I wrote.

"When are you expecting Baby?" my father wrote back. "I'm
planning to visit you."

I wrote to John of these things. I wrote that I wished to stay in
Maine, where we were happy and would be happier.

Will it be by the same father, a woman in the village asked me
one day, eyeing Peter. Yes, same old father, I said. I'd always
wanted more. "Did you," she said with glittering eye. "*Did* you
indeed."

Peter was disconcerted at first at the thought of another child
in the family. However, the woman opposite was pregnant too.
Her name was Denise. She was one of those plain, admirable
young women more prevalent in America than elsewhere, literate,
efficient, comforting. She already had two children with her husband, Donald, who sold billiard tables, something well within his
powers, clearly—a sweet, awkward figure, disowned in demeanor,
like an odd child in the playground, all staunch pride and mirth
and shame. Their daughter, Mary, was Peter's age, and I took both
to see a Jerry Lewis movie once. It began with crude scenes of the
actor stuffing himself with food, dribbling it down his front,
smearing it in his hair, squashing it over his ears. The children
laughed so much they fell off their seats to the floor. Anarchy
must have been fun, and it brought them together. Mary said she
looked forward to the new baby. After that Peter said he did too.
He had also a friend at school who had a pregnant mother even
older than I was; he admired the friend's mother, a very pretty
woman. The friend was delighted at the prospect of a new baby in
his family, so Peter came round even more to a pleasanter attitude.
It was a rosy time of my life, in spite of crises in the world outside,

as when John and I went shopping in Brunswick for a new oven in
a big store for domestic appliances, and were wandering the white
sepulchral rows of refrigerators, ovens, freezer chests, washing
machines, dryers, and air conditioners, and were wishing someone
would turn his hand to advising us: the piped music was replaced
by a radio man's voice, overurgent as usual. We half listened. I
began to hear the words: someone was dead, the president had
been shot, in Dallas, he was dead, John Kennedy was dead. A man
came out of the office, we bought an oven and arranged for its delivery and drove home. "Poor bastard, he wanted so much to be
president," John said. He found the Kennedys manipulative and
their glamour spurious. By the time the assassin had been assassi-
nated, and *his* assassin arrested, the falseness of the plot began to
bother us. I returned hastily to the pleasures of pregnancy. Never
had trees looked so treelike, mud so muddy, snow so cold and
white, sea so "cold and calm and absolutely clear." In the background, as in the war, the great historical movements of the time
sounded in our inner ears. The civil rights movement growled
on, student unrest, protests against the Vietnam War, the peace
movement, the second wave of feminism, the repeated return to a
simpler way of life. Maine itself was changing. The modest mail-
order outdoor equipment company of L. L. Bean was becoming
fashionable as a purveyor of egalitarian clothing, even while old
Mr. Bean, in his nineties, presided daily in his office over the store,
a slumped figure in brown who reminded me of Mole in *The Wind
in the Willows*. Bowdoin College, always a haven of the arts, began
to rival Harvard and Yale in popularity, as students looked for an
end to privilege and deference and ancient dug-in institutions.

Meanwhile John went on looking at houses in New Jersey as if
I had never penned a word in opposition. "But of course we've got
to move down there," he said on his next visit when I remon-
strated. "We can't go on like this, four hundred miles apart."

"What's changed?"

"The baby, of course. And your father coming."

"You haven't read my letter."

"Of course I've read your letter. I love your letters."

"You don't take them seriously."

"Of course I take them seriously. They're marvelous letters. The only compensation in being away from you is your letters."

"I'll never write you another as long as I live."

"What are you saying?"

"What's the answer to my letter?"

"I've found a house I think you should look at."

"I told you in my letter that I wanted to stay in Maine. I was trying to persuade you of my point of view, and you think I'm practicing fine writing. Do you think that because a letter is interesting it isn't meant? Do you think only clumsy writing is honest? What must I do to have you listen to me?"

"Why must you be so aggressive? You made it very plain when we first came here that you did not wish to live in Maine. Now that I think we should move, you're all in favor of staying. I really don't understand you."

"I know," I said. "There is very little to understand, though you seem to have difficulty getting there. That was why I wrote you a letter, so you could think about it at your leisure."

"You'll like this house I've just seen. It has a carriage barn next to it that's been made over and is delightful. It would suit your father. He'd be independent while just a few yards from the door, and he could bring over his furniture from England and arrange it just as he wished. The yard covers about four acres, and there's a pond that would suit the geese if you wanted to bring them, and lots of grass, and a little tractor with gang mowers to keep it down, and a walnut tree, and a hut that'll do for my study. Peter's going to love it. On the far side? Fields, nothing but fields. The cat would love roaming and hunting there. Originally the place was a farm. Four bedrooms, two staircases, a fair-sized kitchen, a terrible bathroom with pink tiles. There's a great big cherry tree beside the drive, covered with blossom. . . ."

"It sounds very ordinary," I said. "Terribly practical." I was using John's own prejudices against him. *Ordinary, practical, sensible*: these were words of condemnation.

Years later, in one of those moments of despair when I am driven to divulge a secret to myself, I wrote in a notebook that I hated Maine. Years later still, it was a shock to happen on that entry. The past changes color under scrutiny. It is sad to revisit some old opinions which when fresh made me happy. The discrepancy is due less to the dawning of truth than the gain of the long view, when time is drawn out distortingly from milestone to milestone and all that matters to the mind looking back is the distance covered, with the achievements like bus shelters along the way. In each moment, on the contrary, there is a spaciousness of thought and emotion in which time has a purely spiritual dimension. I lived in these moments. John lived in history. He was usually sad, I was usually happy.

With my gain of the long view, I see now that staying in Maine would have meant a widowhood, not an engagement with life. Physical desire would have been horribly botched, and we'd have been deprived of the incremental emotional attachment which is the flower of marriage. I'd have gone back to the severely restricted life of my first boarding school on the verge of the North York moors, in a landscape of dreamlike beauty. I'd have experienced again the puritan dedication of the war, where everything was directed to one purpose, and I'd have written reams of poetry. It was not John's way. He liked to live well, to eat well and dress well, with style, and carry the style into conversation and good jokes.

At the same time he, too, had a good notion of the earthly paradise that he'd like to create and inhabit. Perhaps the spaciousness of America encourages the idea, or the possibility of redemption in the big loose-knit society that you realize through moving on and establishing your own base again and again. Or it's just a fundamental desire that we all have, from the first treehouse to the willow cabin that gardeners weave for the delights of a single summer, when the withies take root and burst into leaf and form a bower hidden from outsiders, where one's beloved can sit and serve tea and share conversations of great confidentiality and wit. So my grandfather had sailed out to Australia as a lad from the Staffordshire coalfields, eighteen years old though already with wife and child, to build a new life, make a fortune, order an imposing house, keep famous horses, own forty pairs of shoes, and employ a man to polish them. So John had spent his severance pay from the navy on a huge old house in North Reading where he parked Jonathan and Jonathan's mother, while he was a graduate student at Harvard. He removed umpteen layers of wallpaper and unblocked fireplaces, reroofed and rewired the place, pointed the brickwork, painted, plumbed, and generally exhausted himself and his sustenance. Mast Landing was a similar effort. There was to be yet another, in Yorkshire, in retirement, part of another big old house miles from anywhere. It was partly to tune in to the music of these spheres of the earthly paradise that I wished to stay in Maine.

The enemy of these isolating drives is the consolidating unit of marriage in a society. I didn't know whether I could play the part assigned to me in that. I could have done with a mother or a sister as helper, or a cousin or two such as my Scots grandmother pressed into service as she gave birth to her eight children and also performed as telegrapher in the post office, in the hard conditions of the Hebrides in the 1870s and 1880s. The trouble in America was that there was no family to fall back on. We were always beginning again from scratch, perpetual pioneers. I myself was a new beginning. In time I was able to find such a helper, as will appear, and in the meantime I was nosed toward the idea of living in New Jersey, in the house with the cherry tree and the pink bathroom, where the two grandfathers might take up residence with us. We were leaving a lot to chance. Chance, however, should be respected. So often barely distinguishable from carelessness, it can bring greater happiness than plot simply because it is a surprise and a bonus. We were amazingly fortunate. Our neighbors Denise and Donald lived where they did thanks to another of those isolating drives I saw exhibited in John, and not uncommon in Maine. Poor creatures, they weren't so lucky.

When my daughter and her little brother were toddlers, three or four years later, our family returned to Maine for a seaside holiday, and broke our journey north in a house near Mast Landing that belonged to the daughter of a friend I'd made at the little college in Portland. Our old house had been turned into an antique business with a sign outside to identify it, and there were an old sleigh and a couple of horse-drawn carriages outside the barn to catch the passing eye. For some time I couldn't make out to whom the house where we were staying had belonged in our day, until it dawned on me it was Denise and Donald's. Our host told the story. Denise hadn't liked the usual childbirth procedures with her previous children, and chose to be delivered at the local homeopathic hospital a few weeks after we'd left the district, and there after kidney failure she and her baby died. Left alone with Mary and her little brother, Donald began to drink heavily. Relatives took the children away. He lost his job, and though neighbors did what they could for him, he passed his days in the way I'd seen described over and over in the textbooks at the Center, till he was found dead of malnutrition and alcohol poisoning in his own front room.

As for Denise herself, I knew that women still died in childbirth, but never expected to have known them. The old burial grounds of Maine are full of young women's graves, sometimes three or four to a man's, as a man remarried and begot more children and the new wife died in her turn of childbearing. Never again would I find them simply a sad feature of bygone times, poor Denise.

———————

Days before she was born, my daughter turned round in the womb, poking her elbows and her knees against the tent of my belly as she wriggled, so she came into the world bottom first. All the same it was an easy labor. She was born at one in the afternoon on 3 July 1964 as my father's plane touched down in Boston. John met him and they drove north immediately to the hospital at Brunswick. There was a scuffle at the door of my room, where my father, naturally proceeding first, remembered himself and gave way to his son-in-law, who was equally determined to come second.

"Ah," said my father, who had delivered more than three thousand babies in his lifetime, some of them the babies of his babies. He put on his glasses and held up his descendant in the soft lacy white shawl from Shetland that he had brought her. "She will be a great beauty, I can tell." And he was right, she's always been beautiful. He loved all babies. If he'd had the money he'd have become an obstetrician. I have before me the splendid bronze William Hunter medal for obstetrics that he won as a medical student at Glasgow in the summer of 1912. "Why didn't your doctor turn the baby round?" he inquired in due course.

"Why didn't you turn the baby round?" I asked my doctor.

"I should have done that," he said humbly.

By that time champagne was on hand.

"A forty-five-degree angle," advised my father, and the cork emerged with decorum and the champagne filled the tooth glasses and the doctor and nurses drank with us all, and very soon I was allowed home with our daughter, to Mast Landing, where John ran the show, and my father was there too, and Peter, and Jonathan. My father, that well-rooted man, was anxious to understand this foreign place. How did a combined harvester work? Who paid for the poor when they were ill? Why did people need those enormous chest freezers? He mistook an oven for a television set, and worked the knobs to change channels before I could cover for him. We had a party and John cooked and served. My father drank too much and fell asleep on his bed with his clothes on. In a week they all went off to New York and Washington to see the sights, leaving me with the baby, who woke several times in the night and cried with hunger and vitality. Then they came back. They had visited the house we were buying in New Jersey. "It is a much better house for you than this one," my father said one evening when we sat together in the backyard watching the geese sail on the pond. He described John's visit to him in England, the September after my mother's death in June, on his return from the Continent, where he'd been on academic business. John had stood out against the backdrop of Windsor society my father had introduced him to. How tame they seemed, how snug, how narrow, how complacent, in comparison to that vigorous and entertaining man, my husband! My father implied that Maine would be dull like Windsor if we stayed, and we would be dull too. "I must try and entertain him better when he comes to visit me at the end of August. We could go to the theater. I could take him out to dinner. Would he like that?"

"If he didn't, you could invite me instead," I said. "No, I am teasing, of course he would like it. I wish I didn't have to be left behind. Why can't I visit you too?"

A look of stern surprise alit on his face. "Where would I put you all?"

"Only joking," I said. "I was just thinking, it doesn't seem fair, does it, for him to visit you and not me."

"No, it's not fair. Of course not. Whoever said anything about fairness? Certainly I didn't. He has to leave you, I suppose. University business again, I understand."

"So I believe. I forget."

"Very wise."

"I'll manage."

"Of course you will."

"How nice this is. Why couldn't we talk like this before? Why did we have to wait till I was nearly forty? You were always so busy, and then you and Mummy were a unit, and units are hard to talk to, and what would I have said anyway? It takes practice to talk."

"You're like me."

"Now, if you come and live with us in New Jersey, we can talk every day. If you could bear it. You'd have your own house and be quite independent. Owen will be with us, next door, of course."

"Owen is a very decent sort."

"You may be bored."

"I'm never bored, you know that."

"It's very cold in winter compared to England."

"I'll order a new topcoat."

"And the house?"

"I'll see what it's worth. I'll put it on the market in the spring. Now what are you paying for the house in New Jersey?"

Oh, the masculine curiosity and outwardness of men! It gave me pleasure to think of John and my father together in Windsor, going to the pub, eating out.

We took Peter and our baby girl with us to Boston to see the old man off. It was raining in the heat of August when he walked into the darkness across the tarmac apron where the plane was waiting to carry him to Heathrow, looking back at us for the last time and waving and crying so much he couldn't see where he was going. He staggered. An attendant caught his arm. He blundered toward the plane.

We arrived at the new house six weeks after our daughter's birth, and were signing papers at the attorney's office at Flemington, the nearest town, when the movers rang to say they heard a cat mewing in the depths of the huge furniture van that had brought our goods down from Mast Landing. It was Polly, who had disappeared on the eve of our departure from Mast Landing and stayed missing in spite of a massive search by a dozen of us including John and Peter, the Coffins, Ruth and her family, Donald. Opinion was that the cat liked Mast Landing and rather than leave it had hidden in the woods. This was pure sentiment. It turned out that she had got into a bottom drawer with one of the pillows as our bed was dismantled, to be borne south over two days without food or water. When we returned from the attorney's to Springtown Road and our new house, the movers had shifted most of the furniture out of the van and on to the lawn, so it looked as though a big barn sale was taking place among the plum trees and lilacs, and there in the recesses of the van stood the last item, the Regency press in shining mahogany that my parents had given us. One of the men opened the big bottom drawer and Polly the cat sprang out, rushed into the house, accepted a little cupboard space that I found her in what was to be the main bedroom, and purring loudly, gave birth to three kittens. A pleasant omen: Polly was always the best of cats, a little light seal-point Siamese who lived to be over twenty, always gentle and given to sweet gestures like patting my face with a paw when I picked her up, or creeping under my chin when I slept as if she couldn't get enough of me. She was fond of the baby too, and liked to curl up at her feet, purring even at the baby's explosive gestures when she might be kicked or thrust violently to one side with a baby fist. If I walked in the big fields behind the house she'd come along, or I'd sight her catching up in leaps and bounds like a dolphin over the sea of the crop till she arrived, suddenly dignified, stalking me on her long black legs, or, when I turned for home, bolting ahead in a long thin streak of fawn, gray, and black fur.

Polly arrived at Springtown Road as our only animal. Her mate had gone off to be king of a Maine cattery, the geese had gone to decorate a farm, the rabbit who'd grown up with the cats had run off into the woods at Mast Landing never to be seen again. The three kittens that were born on our arrival gave the new house a positive quality, reinforced by Owen in his wheelchair on the terrace, the baby asleep under the pear tree, Peter riding his bike up the dirt road or fishing in the pond or trapping turtles. People came by with a show of indifference, very different from the neighbors at Mast Landing; none of them native, all middle class except the people in the mobile home that was said to be a long-time disgrace. It was a small community of some twenty people, five miles from the nearest village, ten from a town. The arable was largely abandoned and scrub beginning to take over. There was talk of development in the near future, but no one knew the details. We were fifteen miles from the university at New Brunswick, not close, but well away from the refineries and industries that lie between Newark and Princeton. From this place and situation John departed in a couple of weeks for Europe.

I spent the days unpacking, sorting, moving things from one place to another, while cooking and laundering and cleaning up, all during the intervals of nursing my baby. Peter went off to school on the yellow school bus to yet another set of strangers. The late summer heat was tremendous and built in spells till it exploded in thunder and torrential rain and a brief calm of coolness and freshness. Several times a day I bathed the baby in a few inches of tepid water to cool her off. Fans whirred upstairs and down. The water began to run pink and smelly from the taps as if the earth were bleeding into the well. They expected me back at the Center for Alcohol Studies in a few weeks, a world away. The pitch of my anxiety grew. The baby was always hungry and I hadn't enough milk for her, and made the mistake of giving her a supplement of artificial milk instead of eating more and persevering with the nursing. I had nursed Peter for nine months and he'd been wonderfully healthy and the experience had been magical. There had been support, however, in Berlin: a health visitor, a babies' clinic. In Springtown Road, every day, instead of more milk, I produced less, and felt I'd failed to give my daughter her due, especially at night when she woke up after brief naps and took a long time to settle down. Often, when it was still cool, I'd stroll in the darkness of the unfamiliar garden and look at a certain small tree which bore a small yellow fruit the size of a damson, and bite into its delicious sharp flesh till teeth met the stone and once were chipped: another misfortune.

Did I have help in the house? I don't remember it. If the refrigerator was empty, I had to drive several miles to the shops with the baby in the heat, a major undertaking that would have been nothing at other times. Letters came from John in Paris. He had met James Jones the novelist and his wife, and Ralph Manheim the great translator, and our old friends Joe and Marguerite Frank. Joe was writing the life of Dostoevsky, Guigitte was a mathematician. They went to Paris every summer together with their children in model fashion. John had adventures trying to read something in the Bibliothèque Nationale, something to do with the lack of catalogs, indexing, ordering. About then, that night perhaps, wandering in the garden and failing as usual to identify the clusters of stars, I wondered which was Cassiopeia, and remembered a line of mine from my old overwriting days: "Cassiopeia leans down to chant her song." I felt I wouldn't be averse to a grand line, good enough to rival Paris, and imagined myself John, not the complaining, weeping, accusing wife who was me at heart, tiresomely flouncing and ridiculous: no, I was John himself, Jupiter Tonans as John, with the constellation of Cassiopeia hanging over him. And a poem began itself immediately. It is much easier to write as a man than as a woman. A man's writing is anonymous. A woman feels obliged to declare herself. The vast reservoir of emotion that had been building up now ran sweetly over the dam as I fooled with the poem for a day or two and then sent it off to Paris. In the poem the narrator, I-as-John, dealt with me-as-woman, ravening force of nature, before she turned into the muse herself, a divine figure, telling him to call down the lambs (her poems, her children, her ideas) from the hills, and they'd crowd up to him and he'd ask in bewilderment, What is it that you want? Is it this? Or this?

I called the poem "I Object, Said the Object" since as a man I could clearly see myself playing the role I so much objected to.

How splendid, John wrote from Paris, what a good poem.

Idiot, I thought, disappointed. He didn't take the poem to heart, he just read for once as if it had no relevance to him. No solecism here. He'd become the pure reader, who read with a pure and disinterested heart. Damn. Surely there was a middle way? Couldn't he ask about it? I let subsequent letters accumulate unopened. What did anything matter anyway? I was far too busy and exhausted to read letters. Next, my father telephoned from Windsor, where John was visiting him on the last leg of his journey home. How was I? They hadn't heard, they were worried, was all well?

Champion, I said. (A northern word, from my childhood, that I never used.)

What?

Dandy. (One of John's words.)

I thought, he has even taken over my father, I have nothing of my own left, I am completely consumed by Jupiter Tonans. Then John came back and things fell into place, the books on shelves, china in cupboards, clothes in closets. I thought: a lot of my life has no point, and that is the point. In spite of the baby, that is, and in spite of Peter, adorable children. And in spite of the house and its garden and the thousands of books and tools that have nothing to do with me and that keep us poor, and the multitude of our effects scattered throughout, and in spite of Polly the cat who pats my face with her velvet paw, and though I love and am loved, yes, my life has no point, and that is the point. At home my life was mostly slog and domestic drudgery, not unlike my mother's. Yes, I had machines to wash clothes and dishes for me, but she had two maids and an odd-job boy, and a nanny when my brother and I were small. My job was interesting and useful and I liked it, whether I worked in the office or at home when the children were in bed. That was my chief advantage over her. I was no better off financially, as what I earned was spent on domestic help and the extra car. It is possible, though hard, to be a wife and the mother of young children and to have a job. It is impossible to practice an art too; there is no time for it and no leisure. That is well understood. It is also well understood that not being able to practice your art is painful. I can vouch for it. Who cares? No one. As in a headache, the pain is invisible and you may be a hypochondriac. What is less clear is that the practice of art—or simply the struggle to gain mastery over the material—creates intolerable tensions. Most arts threaten the social order and work against the calm and stability in which families thrive. The tantrums of art are simply not worth the space they demand within the family, or the tolerance, or the congratulation demanded of the family, who, after all, are concerned with their own individual comfort, usages, and protection, not someone else's higher thoughts. So it is better for a mother not to struggle to write poetry, irrespective of her talent. I used to keep a notebook, though: *Memorials of a Quiet Life* was the name I used to identify it to myself, after a favorite book by Augustus Hare, a Victorian clergyman, and I often used to throw my notebook against the wall to counter its platitudes and high-souled intent not to sacrifice my children to my soggy floppy intolerable art.

For years after the poem called "I Object, Said the Object" I therefore wrote little. There was no point. And yet pointlessness was in a sense created by that failure to write. A poem is a laboratory where experiments are made and the nature of things is discovered. So we get away from always damnable subjectivity, the moans of me, the shrieks of beauty. So it is as far as I am concerned. Yet this is a simplification.

The fact that my husband wrote as part of his profession in the secondary sphere of criticism, and successfully wrote book after book, bothered us both. It couldn't fail to. There is a natural war between critics and poets (even poets *croyant, pas pratiquant,* like me). When poets were given places on the faculty of universities, they lost their independence, and were patronized, but critics were always in their element. John was hurt at the lack of honor I gave to critics: as when I pointed out how willfully obscure R. P. Blackmur was. "You can talk about life, but you can only talk round literature," Isaac Rosenberg says, and there seemed an immense circumnavigation of literature, and no putting into port, when university colleagues came to dinner. I suppose this is a well-worn complaint. I repeat it here to back my dismay at not being given room to make a fool of myself in those years when criticism with its fringe benefit of scholarship was all that mattered.

As he advanced further into the philosophy of art, John left me further and further behind. He was wounded by my indifference, as it seemed to him, or by my distinct focus, as it appeared to me. When we lived in Maine, this mattered less. Maine had been like an art itself in its rigor. It didn't much matter if you weren't good at it, because you were engaged by it. You had to face up to it and learn from it; at the very least you had to cope. Some kind of truth emerged from the confrontation. In New Jersey that truth sank into obscurity. We remained divided by our preferences, even those preferences that were thrust upon us, as John's were by his profession. The differences were to be muddled by our concerns such as the social, worldly ones I have already mentioned, but they were fundamental, even provoking me to question the usefulness of theory in literary study, and thus the usefulness of studying literature at all. For me criticism was a tool. Do you study tools? They are secondary. Abstraction is easier than the world of things, as well as more prone to error. For the habit of collecting such tools I had no time at all. Literature was immediate and physical like sticks and stones, and, where poetry was concerned, disinterested, as sticks and stones were disinterested. Trying to write a poem meant trying to be honest. So it was hard to live a lie and write a poem.

I could have shut up altogether. I was very quiet, anyway. "Silence is the virtue of fools," says Francis Bacon, and I was an incoherent fool, shouting now and then but quiet on the whole, with physical desire well matched by emotional attachment, and yet without the words to bring them a proper balance.

ABSENCES

When my daughter was sixteen months old, my last baby was born, a son named Fergus, after the Irish prince who with his brothers founded a kingdom in Scotland in the fifth century. He was a beautiful child, as his sister was. He had reddish curly hair, hers was fair and curly. When I looked at them sometimes I thought I had never seen any more beautiful creatures in my whole life. Peter grew up to be a handsome man, but as a child he was no more than good-looking. All amazed me, though: unmerited, unearned claps of fortune, bonuses.

My father died when Fergus was just six weeks old. We flew the Atlantic together, leaving Peter and the baby Antoinette with John. It was January, which made a cold homecoming. The central heating in the Windsor house was not working and the man who came to fix it said that it had not run for years. My father was oblivious of the cold, and in any case found central heating wickedly expensive. I found an electric blanket and laid my child on it well wrapped up and kept the window open so the air was fresh.

A clergyman came to tell of long talks he'd had with my father. I was dumbfounded. My father had not been in a church for forty years. He was not throwing himself into the arms of the church, however; he was preparing to meet his Maker.

"'There's many a good Christian never goes to church, Doctor,' I said."

I murmured thankfulness.

"And your mother: he feared hellfire."

"Dear God." My mother not only never went to church, she

also detested the clergy and considered them hypocrites. The question in my father's mind surely concerned her faith: she didn't have any.

"There's many a good Christian never goes to church," repeated the clergyman. "'God is merciful,' I said to your father. 'There is no question of hellfire.'"

"*Of course not,*" I cried, and felt bound to explain. "He was very strictly brought up, as an extreme Calvinist. Do you know that he didn't believe in evolution till I sold it to him? He believed that the universe came into being in 4004 B.C. What about the fossils, I said. And the dinosaurs. The layers and layers of deposits that far outdated 4004 B.C."

"You sold it to him," said the clergyman in a kindly manner.

"And he was a doctor! You'd think, wouldn't you, that he'd think the matter through."

"We're all a mass of contradictions," observed the clergyman, benign.

"One push from me, and the doctrines crumble. I was only a girl. No scientific training to speak of. He was quite relieved when I insisted. He used to say himself that his parents were ignorant people. But they were devout, and he was dutiful. He used to read the Bible every day, in Gaelic, until my mother protested. She thought the Calvinists were a bad influence on him. She said they were narrow-minded." I choked back the other things she said.

The clergyman put up with my intemperance. He said mildly, "You know, he was reading the Bible in Gaelic every day again recently."

"I don't think she kept him from it, mind you," I lied. I thought of him reading, totally removed from his surroundings, his lips moving, living the Word, and my mother's irritation. "My mother was a force of nature," I said, surprising myself and thinking of her as a river rejoicing as it burst its banks and poured through villages and fields, drowning sheep as it went. How could

I convey the essence of my mother in acceptable fashion? How could I tell this gentle man that she'd called my father woolly-minded and dreamy and associated Bible reading in Gaelic with indecision? I would get mired in explanation and he would not listen. My father had spiritual qualities that all could see, hers were hidden by a practical and pragmatic, deliberately flighty nature. The two of them balanced each other. She was not one to suffer hellfire—she'd take heaven by storm, for goodness' sake. I was shocked at my father's fears for her. She was all love, difficult though that might be, and he couldn't have succeeded in being so much himself without her. He must have suspected that when he worried about her soul or he wouldn't have sought and accepted guidance.

After the funeral and burial in driving rain that was attended by nuns from the Brigantine convent whom the extreme Calvinist had happily tended when they were ill, my brother and his wife and son and our two remaining uncles and eldest aunt and some cousins who'd come down from Scotland drank whiskey and ate fruitcake in the icy house while the baby lay upstairs on my dead father's bed, tended by the bank manager's wife. The elders told stories of my father's childhood. When he was the same age as the baby Fergus upstairs, the river by the old house and forge at Broadford in Skye flooded and entered the house, and the children scrambled up the stair to watch the new baby carried past the stairway on the raft of his baby clothes. His mother snatched him from the waters just before the clothes got sodden. "Did you hear that story, Mairi?" his brothers and elder sister asked joyfully, one after the other, and then again, to confirm that I understood he'd been spared by God's grace. My father was the youngest of the eight, the last baby, the favorite.

He'd divided his fortune between my brother and me, and with a special proviso left money for Peter's education to equal what he had spent on my brother's child, and he left me the best of his furniture, because we had so little and Iain was well provided for.

The day after the funeral—it was still cold and raining—I drove the baby in my father's car to a photographer's to have his picture taken, and then to London to get him a passport with the tiny photo from the U.S. consulate so that he could reenter his own country with me when we flew home. My brother was of no help to us. The death had destroyed him. He'd said long ago that we could never leave our mother and father, and I'd gone off all the same. How painful that must have been, when he thought I was the preferred one. It was sad he felt that, and felt it to the point of madness. We were sitting together in our parents' drawing room about then, feeling odd without them, when the phone rang. "That'll be for me," my brother said, expecting a summons from his surgery. "Who is it? What did you say your name was?" He repeated the name of a boy I had known at school in Norton many years before and my heart leapt up. He had become a doctor like his father. "You'd like to speak to my *sister?*" asked Iain. "You read my father's *obituary?* Yes, my sister's here, but she doesn't want to speak to you now." And he put the receiver down. "Denis Bowman. Says you were at school with him in Norton."

"But I would like to have talked to him!"

"Too late now. I don't know how he got this number."

"We were *friends*. I would so much have liked to speak to him!"

"Then you should have answered the phone, shouldn't you. I can't keep up with all your friends." And he began to ramble from one subject to another to cover up his extraordinary behavior. Among other things he recalled how my father had behaved at my mother's death, when he had run through the night shouting that he could have done more for her when she was ill, and he didn't, in the terrible guilt of the survivor of a long and devoted marriage.

"Not *English* behavior," I said, to keep the peace, and wondered if Iain's behavior could be called English in its weird rectitude. He had pointed out to me before the funeral that he was the chief mourner, and would be the first to follow the coffin out of the church, the rest of the mourners to tail along afterward. He quoted Lady Troubridge on etiquette to make his point clear.

It was hard to reconcile these concerns of his with that picture of our father running through the night, crazed with grief, so I told Iain that on the last occasion when I'd seen her, our mother had made a point of telling me that whatever had happened in their marriage, no one could have done more for her than our father, no one, and I had to remember that, for he was a good man, the best who ever lived.

My father had always driven like Jehu, and he was still the terror of the roads and practicing medicine part-time when he died, and he hadn't put his house on the market or bought a new topcoat. The new baby may have decided him not to join us in New Jersey. He didn't say. He knew he might die any minute, and he may have decided to leave things as they were, and the time of his death to his Maker. His death was no shock. He had warned me long before of his condition. He died by himself, in his own house, with his things about him, probably as he wished. It was otherwise for Owen.

It had been of course before my father's death, in the early spring of 1965, when my little daughter was about seven months old, that I found myself pregnant for the last time. John was abroad.

"I'm going to have another baby," I told Owen as he came gliding through the house in his wheelchair. The pregnancy was an accident, but after all, babies are good news.

He braked aghast. "Oh no!"

He was not a warmhearted man and he didn't take much notice of the children, or of me, or of John even, though they watched baseball games together, so why the dismay? He didn't feel sorry for me when I once had to iron twenty-one shirts, or every day cook and clean and organize and rush off to work after getting the baby-sitter, and return in the evening to take back the baby-sitter and cook and clean once more, although John always helped me. Displacement by an infant may have reminded him of hard days in Ontario when the family scrabbled to get by. His only delight as far as I could see was to hobble on his crutches down the dirt road to the trailer and talk to the man and woman there. They weren't people I warmed to, and I don't think they thought much of me, since without explanation and like a rebuke they took in a dog that the vet had given me; the dog had sought them out and I made only halfhearted attempts to fetch her back because she was a sad little thing. I felt they were nicer and more in touch with Owen than I was, and blamed myself for being so hard pressed that I couldn't put on a show of friendliness, though it wouldn't have been easy. One morning a fox had trotted under my kitchen window, all lithe and brilliant in his golden brown fur and black legs, the tip of his brush pure white, and I was still excited when a moment later there was a bang from the trailer and I knew the fox had been shot. "It was a fox!" Owen shouted at me when I burst into tears.

When Fergus was two and Antoinette three he bowled out of his room raging that the babies had been stealing his money, and he brandished his crutches to show what he'd do to them if he caught them. It was absurd, but frightening. So we found him a room with a nurse in the village, and when he started threatening her too, and kept walking away along the highway and being picked up by the police and returned, his doctor had him admitted to the state hospital. There John visited him regularly. On one of the rare occasions when I went, he looked at the nurses and orderlies coming and going down the central aisle of the old men's ward and said to me that they were members of the circus and had been sent to entertain the patients. He was not joking.

He died of pneumonia as he'd always dreaded, with that pneumonia in mind from which he had suffered in 1920, when his wife, John's mother, had died, pregnant with his unborn brother. Jonathan came, and Peter, and after the funeral we buried him on the hillside of the cemetery in Flemington. The priest, who wore one black shoe and one brown, referred to him as our sister. John thought that was a punishment for his not going to mass. More likely the priest was old himself and past caring.

Now that the two grandfathers were gone, my vision of a matriarchy could no longer be sustained. We were merely a two-generation family, a couple with four children, one away at Yale. It is true that the crates of furniture from England lent a certain solidity and suggested a family past and future and a responsibility. Yes, it was very nice, some of it actually beautiful and all of it valuable. Ah, the tyranny of things! I'd rather have had a room of my own. I moved my typewriter to my bedroom and then I moved it back to the sitting room.

"Ah," said the visitor, advancing, "and what are you at work on now?" He'd peer. I'd scream a faint un-English scream. "Oh, sorry. Just curious, and it was all laid out, it didn't occur to me you'd mind, sorry. So what are you at work on?"

So many possessions made me want to bolt. Since I couldn't bolt, I longed for abstractions, the next best thing, or those abstractions like the absences of Rilke's which became angels to his mind as it waited and waited for poems to appear. Quiet and leisure: the two qualities the mother of young children cannot possibly enjoy without a good deal of cunning and foresight, those were what I needed, and instead there was all this furniture from my childhood, beautifully polished and serviceable, a pleasure to the eye, a solace to the heart.

From the birth of our daughter and the move to Springtown Road, life became less a series of episodes and more of a play with a particularly long middle act. During this middle act John was often offstage. He was able to say at one time that he managed to visit Spain every year. Once someone kindly asked me how *I* enjoyed Spain, and I had to murmur that I'd never been there. People looked to me for an explanation. I smiled and shrugged. The justification for his absences was that they were to his professional credit, testimony to grants and fellowships and commissions to write about the bullfights for *Sports Illustrated*.

It is pleasant that our children, who are now approaching middle age, look back nostalgically on those years in Springtown Road and intend to duplicate them for their own children somehow, at some time: the games in the yard, the progeny of Polly the cat scrambling through the cherry tree, the roses and lilacs by the house. I'd add to the list sights in the everyday—water in a pail as I wash the floor, a small fat hand on my face, a held-breath kiss, rather sticky, the eyes looking over my head; the gathering of pears from the tree, the discovery of Polly's kittens dangerously placed under the hood of the car to keep warm, geese migrating half a mile up and uttering cries like a hallucination, neighbor children straddling bikes, preparing for some jaunt, coffee taken on the terrace with Owen, his rambling speech; the intense concentration of a small child as its hands are inserted in sleeves and feet in trousers, and its clear eyes close up, the iris perfectly greeny brown or else gray-blue, the white faintly tinged with blue, each eyelash curved perfectly and clearly; Fergus teasing his sister by pretending to run down to the forbidden pond, one foot forward, and she screaming at last, her nerve broken.

Lovely to remember, the deepest pleasure. I remember the satisfaction of hanging the wash outside by the lilac hedge, and cooking for friends, glancing through the kitchen window at the newly mown lawn, and talking to Maria, who had come to us through the good offices of a domestic agency run by a doctor's wife from Philadelphia who had pull in Washington and scouts in South America.

"Oh, the señor! *Qué precioso!*" Maria's voice screeched. "How delightful he always looks, so gentlemanly, so well turned out, a delight!" John was walking past the kitchen window along the drive, with the backdrop of the big pear tree, the lilac bushes, the smoke bush, the black walnut, and the other trees and bushes that our predecessors had obviously bought from catalogs and planted at random in the old farmyard. Yes, he always looked nice. The extremity of Maria's admiration surprised me just the same. She couldn't have designs on him herself, short and squat and hairy of face as she was, her best features the sweetness of her smile and her very dark eyes. My little children loved her looks, but they weren't glamorous. And John clearly found her repulsive. So what was behind her enthusiasm?

Maria had come from Uruguay, which was bankrupt. She had been a cook in a fabulously wealthy widow's house in Montevideo, and we represented a comedown. Nevertheless she was enchanted by the children, and by the señor from time to time, as now.

"Yes, he's lovely," I agreed.

"And so well dressed."

"True."

"Unlike you, señora. *Muy fea.* Those ugly shoes. Your hair."

Her dispiriting message had something to do with a souvenir glass ashtray John had brought back from Madrid. There was a black-and-white photograph reproduced on it of four people at a restaurant table, one of them John, two of them a young married couple we knew, and the fourth a heavily made-up woman with pearls and a becoming coiffure. At the sight of this ashtray Maria had exploded with laughter and derision. "Oh, señora!" When I accidentally dropped the ashtray and it broke, John was cross, but Maria shook with laughter for days.

To please, I had to dress up to the nines and wear fine stockings and high-heeled shoes every day. Then I, too, came in for cries of approval and delightful compliments. I was supposed to spend a lot of time mulling over my wardrobe. It would have been fun if

I'd had the time and the money to indulge her and myself. Our friends, too, were scrutinized and generally condemned on the grounds of race, taste, and deportment. When she condemned, food was made bad to suit. When she approved, as with the slim, graceful, and elegant, it was delicious and lavish. One Russian Jewish friend was served her homemade pasta, but with ketchup instead of a proper sauce. One New England couple with gentle manners were served on the best silver tray with my mother's silver coffeepot and cream jug and sugar basin, unearthed from the back of the cupboard and polished like the moon and stars. American academics are not remarkable for their style, still less their beauty. John alone was held up as a model. There was a strong hint in the air that if I didn't look sharp he would be lost.

She took Antoinette on one hip and Fergus on the other up the dirt road and round by the village store, miles, and came back complaining of the *bichos*.

"What *bichos,* Maria?"

"Oh, señora, *hay siempre bichos.*"

Bugs. Vermin. Flies. This was a woman from the city. She was lost in the remoteness of our country district. She proved incapable of pronouncing a single word of English. I spent an hour trying to get her to say *yes*. Her reading and writing even in Spanish were precarious. I took her to New York and she insisted on walking three paces behind me. A man called after us, "Don Quixote y Sancho Panza!" Maria fell apart with laughter but never drew level. I put her on the New York bus alone after that and she found parts of Manhattan where she could chat and buy and eat and meet other women who'd come for jobs from Montevideo, and into Manhattan she vanished after a year and a half, crying her eyes out, to be housekeeper to a woman with one son, whom she pronounced on the telephone to be *precioso.* I think she was happier there. By that time she and John had become openly hostile. There was something lovely about her to my mind, as well as something unpredictable and crude, and she gave me a little leisure and a calmer mind and relief from the isolation of a woman with young children. For when he returned from his absence, monthlong or six-month-long, John was not only eager to write up his discoveries but also anxious to busy himself about the property, painting the house, putting a new roof on the carriage house, or making a tennis court for rough tennis, or planting a vineyard. People said he was a Renaissance man, capable of turning his hand to anything, a rarity among scholars in being also a worker with his hands. I saw more and more clearly that I'd have to live my own life and not batten on his if I were to prosper. But even with Maria's help it was hard work running the house and caring for the small children and their older brother while conscientiously carrying out various tasks for the Center, and I often thought I'd collapse with the effort to keep calm and not die of exhaustion.

After all, going away might have been worse than staying behind. Before my daughter was born we'd visited Saul Bellow and his then wife, Susan, at Tivoli on the Hudson, and she'd broken down in front of me when the men were absent and complained in a flood of tears that Saul demanded that she go everywhere with him. She was always to be at his side, she had no life of her own, no time to write letters, or chat on the telephone, or sew her clothes, let alone pursue whatever other task she might have in mind, such as to write a book or make a garden or even walk along the river by herself.

At least John went off to live his own life. He had said in Mexico that I wanted us to do everything together. No, that was not it at all. Some things, possibly. And then not even those things. What was the point? What had we in common? We were unlike. Once when he received a celebrated fellowship, he said to me immediately, "How would you like to spend Easter in Venice?" "Yes!" I cried. But that was that. The suggestion was left as he first made it, stuck in the past like a nail hammered into a wall for some picture that has been hung elsewhere.

At the end of one academic year some friends held an embarkation party on the *Michelangelo* before sailing for a holiday in the Mediterranean and a sabbatical year in London. We went up to Manhattan and found the quay on the Hudson from which the huge beautiful ship would sail in a few hours. On the quayside, before climbing the gangway, I stopped, overcome with a shattering grief. This was a surprise to both of us. "Why are you crying? Tell me what's wrong." I didn't know.

The absences were made worse by this unacknowledged longing for the land where I'd grown up and which I missed more keenly year by year. John saw that land in my place, but he didn't see it with my eyes, and he didn't think I missed it because there was no place he missed.

"You want me to stay home and rot," he repeated each time he went off.

One day when driving to work I switched on the radio and Dr. Joyce Brothers's call-in program.

"Dr. Brothers, I am very unhappy," said a woman's voice.

"Yes, what is your problem?"

"My problem is this, Dr. Brothers: my husband is a photographer and often he goes abroad on assignments, leaving me at home with our little girl. I get very lonely, Dr. Brothers, you know?"

Dr. Brothers admitted nothing about knowing or not knowing, and the caller began to describe a situation like mine, with the interesting addition that the photographer husband took her along on an assignment in Hawaii. And was she happy then, inquired Dr. Brothers. No, she was not, said the caller, she was miserable. Her husband was far too busy to keep her company, and she spent her time on the beach or at the hotel by herself, as lonely as at home, while her expenses canceled out his earnings. Moreover, she'd parked her child with her mother, and that hadn't worked out well either, as the grandmother complained the child was spoiled. So she was worse off than before, when a polite fiction

had love burn bright at least when the man came home. So what
should she do, Dr. Brothers? She was so unhappy that she was
thinking of leaving her husband.

By this time I'd pulled off the road and was listening agog.

"Leave your husband? And what good would that do?" asked
Dr. Brothers, laughing a clear bright sensible laugh. "Then you'd
have nothing, would you? No disappointment and no husband,
just loneliness!" Oh silly goose, caller! Find yourself a job! Learn
tennis! Join a club!

I rejoined the traffic and went to work. Nothing new there.

At last during one sabbatical we all went abroad.

We started out by renting a villa from an American woman in
Spain, on the Mediterranean shore. She said it had four bedrooms,
a swimming pool, bathroom, study, and the usual equipment.
Not far from a beach; simple, idyllic, sunny. It sounded right for
us. John went off to a bullfight in northern Spain, taking Peter
with him, and I arrived at Alicante with the two little ones after a
hot, slow, hungry journey by train from Algeciras, and took a taxi
along the coast to the village of Alfaz del Pi. From there a rocky
path led to the villa a mile away. It was a half-built brick bungalow with an empty swimming pool beside it and a garden of sad
roses undersown with carrots and onions and a few potatoes. In
the garden stood several women from the village ready to show me
the ropes. Water, they informed me immediately, was off. No
water. Only at night was there water. I paid the taxi driver and we
tottered into the hall. The women had brought milk and eggs and
bread. We ate and put the toddlers to bed unwashed, where I soon
followed them. In the morning I noticed that the groves of olives
and oranges round about us were watered by concrete channels between the fields tapped by wooden sluice gates raised at certain
hours through the week, and this irrigation in the eroded landscape demanded every drop from the reservoir on a nearby hill.
Hence the swimming pool could not be used. As for provisions,

only flour, rice, butter, and a few other staples were available in the village. The rest had to be sought down the coast. After a few days the water supply was cut to a couple of hours in twenty-four.

It turned out that the bungalow stood in an expatriate community of Britons, Canadians, Dutch, and Germans, who spent their time gossiping and squabbling and flirting in unappetizing fashion, and I could see no point in remaining there. So we abandoned the place and rented an apartment in Madrid. It, too, was far from ideal, but at least there was a reasonable school in the city for Peter to attend and a kindergarten nearby for the little ones.

Yet glorious as it was to live in Madrid, it was difficult for John to write his book in our narrow apartment in the frequent presence of three children, and eventually he made no bones about his extreme frustration and despair, swearing, shouting, cursing, day after day, week after week. This was of course behavior that I had never been permitted, and its unthinkable nature, for all its comic aspect, had to be faced. At last I could bear it no more and asked for a divorce. That evening, I said I didn't want a divorce after all. Too late. He developed the same appalling headache he'd had when I first was pregnant, in London, when he had no job. He was admitted to hospital, vomiting and sleepless, hiding from the light. When the headache lifted, we resumed our old ways, more circumspect now, politer, more distant. Better not to have left America. Better for him to have enjoyed yet another absence, to have written his book in the peace of home when he got back.

Better for me too, since the Center for Alcohol Studies had not kept my job for me as they said they would. For some time I had been acting as an editor, since the compilation of the dictionary had long ago gone as far as I could take it, and the manuscript had lain for months on the desk of Bottleneck, awaiting his attention. I'd meanwhile become used to working on articles submitted for publication and making abstracts of material published elsewhere, for inclusion in the archives of the Center, and these arrangements had been foreseen in the original terms of my engagement. When I was away, another colleague saw the dictionary through the press. My two pregnancies had not made any difference to my work. If anything, I had worked all the harder at home and in libraries to maintain a right number of hours and of effort in the nine-out-of-twelve-month academic schedule. And of course it was illegal to penalize a worker for taking time off to deliver a baby. But a younger woman research assistant who'd become pregnant was not reinstated, which showed the director's covert point of view. As for my working from home, the same rules applied to me as to a fellow worker who appeared with her work only once a month. In other words, she provided a precedent. Nevertheless Bottleneck declared that no more money was available to employ me. The Center was heavily funded by public and private means, and my work had met with congratulation. Shabby treatment, then, unrelieved by explanation. This was shortly before the tribunals were besieged by people who had been treated in the same manner.

John, too, returned to bad news. His graduate department had been placed in a new college not of liberal arts but one devoted to raising the educational standards of the poorest, particularly the black poor, who were raging and rioting to obtain a better life. Students who applied to a college and who hadn't managed to reach the standard for entrance were now admitted anyway and given lavish tutorial assistance, financial grants, and every conceivable help so that they could learn to benefit from everything the university had to offer. With this praiseworthy enterprise a graduate program in foreign literatures had nothing in common, and so it was perceived. Someone crossed out "Department of Comparative Literature" on the index in the elevator and wrote over it "Honky Studies." Within a year it was admitted, as was obvious from the start, that the teaching of literacy belonged in schools, not colleges, and in primary schools, not high schools. Nevertheless the founding idea of the college persisted. The first graduates took their degrees into the marketplace and found jobs that many could not hold down because their reading and writing were inadequate. Meanwhile the admittedly scholarly and refined studies that John presided over were ridiculously out of place, as anyone might have seen who was not totally absorbed in missionary enthusiasm. But those were iconoclastic days, when fine things were attacked because they were fine. In imitation of student rebellion in the streets of Paris, students took to the streets in New Jersey too. There is always reason to revolt. The horror of the war in Vietnam to which they might be sacrificed led to sympathy for the opposing side, which of course was Marxist. Marxism in that climate looked more just than capitalism. It was not yet everywhere apparent that Marxism does not work or may lead to greater injustice than capitalism. It was enough that the present order was questionable. "We didn't know what we were demonstrating for," one of John's most delightful students told me later. "We'd heard that everyone was demonstrating, so we demonstrated. We were amazed when the president gave us what we asked for and said to come and see him whenever we liked." That was Mason Gross, one of the wisest and most human presidents any university ever had. Later, when young men were regularly drafted into the armed services against their will in order to fight the appalling and shameful Vietnam War, things got very much more serious. Jonathan was at Yale enduring the prospect of being called up. A psychiatrist friend offered to certify him as insane to prevent his going. His work suffered and he was told to drop out of the university for a year. He spent it teaching at a boys' school in Canada. So what was the value of the long and difficult syllabus John and his colleagues devised, and who prized it, in those unhappy times and in that unlucky college where his department had been assigned during his absence for a year abroad? If he'd stayed at home for at least part of the sabbatical year, he could have kept it intact for those students who liked its demands and astringencies. We did not have each other cheap, John and I.

THE WAY IT NEVER USED TO BE

He learned
You add to, you don't cancel what you do.

—THOM GUNN, "Duncan"

So I found work as an English instructor in a county community college. Like the university college to which John's department had been assigned, it was one of those institutions set up in the sixties and seventies to play down civil unrest by easing unqualified citizens into higher education. They varied from excellent and serious Vietnam veterans to lazy seventeen-year-olds who'd barely finished high school and adults returning to school for qualifications as nurses or policemen or automobile engineers or telephone operators or sports instructors, or retired people out to complete unfinished business in the arts or psychology or the social sciences, or women moved by feminism to burst the confines of the marriages that had once been their trophies. I taught them some sections of freshman English and an option implausibly called World Literature. Freshman English was unpopular. In my eight o'clock morning class the back row was filled with slumbering forms made up of those coming off night shift, or those on drugs who hadn't yet had their first fix of the day, or those recovering from the previous night's fixes. Nearer me sat the diligent, usually very young, writing notes on elaborate stationery, or the cocksure, who doodled. In the front row sat the desperate, smiling insanely at me or clenching their brows. Over a third of each class would drop out during the first year, some in shock, some in despair, some in apathy, some in disbelief. I was walking through crowds of students one day when someone shouted "Hey!" from a distance and seconds later I felt my arm grabbed. "I was shouting at you," said the grabber, annoyed. "You didn't stop. You give me a bad grade there. You tell me why. I'm just a farm boy. I deserve an A."

Such cheek stupefied me. Yet the majority thought poorly of themselves and required an equally implausible amount of encouragement. Others didn't believe encouragement worked fast enough, and were prepared to cheat. They commissioned work from relatives and friends or bought from the anonymous campus essayist whose same efforts showed up year after year. There also existed essay agencies where you could acquire something of the standard you stipulated, for a graduated fee. It was easy to con me, hopeful as I was of natural virtue. Moreover the showdown was always hateful, with its lies and tears and tales of woe. One man even threatened me when I found he was cheating. He was an ex-convict who wanted to become a policeman. "I have reformed," he shouted at me in my office. "I have done my time. You should give me a break."

"No one can trust you," I said. "How can you possibly become a policeman?"

I was leaving for home when he jack-started his car in the road where I was walking and roared it close to my shoes, scattering me with grit.

Even that was better than the case of a pleasant woman who had spent five years as a nurse's aide and now presented herself as a candidate for the registered nurses' program. The gross disparity between her classwork and stuff she wrote at home made me give her an essay to write in my office. It turned out to be barely literate. "A nurse has to be able to write intelligibly, or someone might die," I said. "And you must be trustworthy." She cried as if that were news.

On the other hand, a colleague pressed me into raising the grades of a man who supported a large family, though he missed classes and his wretched work was always late.

Of course there was compensation when the mountains of writing turned in every week included genuine efforts or thoughtful work, or the work of those who simply loved words.

Because the community college represented the last ditch in education for many people who'd failed to be accepted into the state university, its administration was strict. Writing classes were kept on track by big expensive anthologies that the students couldn't afford. Once, tired of the limited material and the footnotes that went with them, I found a photocopying machine in an office and ran off some verses of Stevie Smith's and distributed them in class. The class was electrified. It so happened that an irate administrator, the natural enemy of all teachers, caught me visiting the photocopier again. Who was I? Someone off the street? What did I think I was doing?

Later I discovered that if I taught World Literature I could choose the texts myself, avoiding anthologies, photocopier, and gauleiter administrators alike, for it was a subject not many instructors wished to teach, and only one section was on offer. One of our number who had recently acquired a doctorate of philosophy and taken to wearing a suit and hat even asked me if I had a qualification in comparative literature. No, I said, and added humbly that we were simply reading a few books. Which added up, I thought. Scholarship didn't enter the picture. Our literature was in translation. There was no need to fear I would lead my flock astray. New conventions could be studied. If anything, I said, I was imparting confidence to those who were frightened of books, their unknown territory.

The doctor listened to me gloomily. I was as good as telling him his degree was useless. And so it was really, on the required level. It was difficult to find the titles of any works of literature known to the students of the community college.

Yet by their second year, the ignorant, stupid, drugged, and lazy freshmen had somehow undergone a metamorphosis into reasonable people. My first class in World Literature was composed of about thirty students, mostly young: would-be nurses, engineers, prison officers, policemen, secretaries, and three Vietnam veterans; the old included three retired people; the middle-aged included two Hungarians exiled by their uprising and a Greek woman called Cleopatra; there were black people, white people, Latinos, a single Chinese. In the first class I distributed copies of the *Agamemnon* of Aeschylus and asked them to read it at home. I talked about Greek drama, about tragedy, and the nature of kingship, and the role of women. I made them repeat the names of the characters in the play over and over till they were fluent in them. Everyone was smiling. This was adventure. "But what is this about?" asked one of the nurses sweetly. "I want to know what I am doing here."

"*What are you doing here?*" repeated a Hungarian. "You are having a wonderful time."

"We are here to read this book, this play, because it is beautiful," said Cleopatra. "We need beauty."

"Beauty?"

"We need to know what it tells us," I said. "There's only so much we can learn from life firsthand. The rest we have to learn from legends, and fairy tales, and movies, and plays, and newspapers—"

"—television—"

"We need beauty," repeated Cleopatra.

"It is a privilege—"

"Privilege?" said the nurse.

"You will see the relevance," I said. "It tells us about ourselves."

"Yeah?"

"*Now,*" I said. It was ten years since the siege of Troy began. *That* was the year in which the prophets said Troy would fall. Agamemnon, leader of the Greek armies, was expected home any day in Argos, where the watchman was on the walls watching for the beacon that would give warning of his approach. "Are you ready?" I asked them. "We are going to speak of Iphigeneia." I nodded at Gary. I'd commissioned several students to look up the identity of characters, and he was the first to give his brief report.

Gary was a tiny man with a beard and glasses, twenty-two or twenty-three years old, though he looked ten years older. He'd dropped out of high school with some serious illness, recovered, and was returning to pick up his education. He always wore a woolly hat and scarf and a cardigan under his parka in spite of the warm classroom. Community colleges were a godsend to people like him, and he was a godsend to me as I tried to herd my heterogeneous students in the same direction.

"Iphigeneia was the daughter of Agamemnon, King of Argos, and his wife, Clytaemnestra. When the war with Troy broke out, she went with her dad and his army to Aulis, where the Greek fleet was going to set sail for Troy over the water. But the winds were always contrary, and a prophet said they wouldn't change till Agamemnon made a sacrifice of his own daughter. It was a kind of exchange for all the innocent children who would be killed by the Greeks at Troy. So he kills her on an altar, and the winds drop and the Greek fleet takes off for Troy."

"This is really stupid," said the nurse. "You don't sacrifice your own daughter."

"Sure you do," a young woman screamed at her.

"It's monstrous."

"Gods often demand sacrifices," I said.

"Yeah, like Abraham and Isaac. But that didn't happen. I mean, God stopped Abraham at the last moment. He said a ram would do instead."

I dragged them back on course. So Iphigeneia was sacrificed, the Greeks besieged Troy, and eventually Troy fell to the Greeks. There were brief reports on Helen of Troy, Hector, Achilles, Agamemnon, Menelaus, and the hour drew to an end.

"How come Clytaemnestra let her daughter go with her father to the war? I wouldn't let my daughter go to the war like that."

"And how come Clytaemnestra let her husband go off for ten years? That's a long time."

"Good point," I said.

Afterward Karen, a woman in her mid-twenties, came to see me and say how much she had enjoyed herself and how she intended to keep coming, though her husband disapproved. She wouldn't say why. She was young and childless and bored, with something old-fashioned about the way she defended her wish to go back to school. Was it the community college he objected to, I asked.

Oh yes, the drugs, she said. The dealers in the bushes near the car park. The undercover policemen. There was more, though. Not just leaving the house. Not qualifying herself for a job, if that's what she might have in mind eventually.

Not just displacing him from the center of her life, then?

That too.

And couldn't she get her priest, her rabbi, or some similar authority to speak for her?

No, he had these ideas all his own. He wouldn't discuss them, not with anybody, not with his mother even. His mother was a good friend to her, wanted her to follow her own line.

Driving home afterward, I asked myself what the *Agamemnon* of Aeschylus had to do with Karen, and what the young husband could object to. And what had it to do with me, come to that? Why had I chosen it to teach above other tragedies? Simply because I longed to know it better? It had been years since I'd read Aeschylus. There was more, though: when you have something on your mind, incident after incident in your life appears to refer to it, one coincidence after another occurs, with an apparently secret message for you alone. And yet you know that the perception of coincidence is unreliable. I don't know what Karen found of her predicament in *Agamemnon,* but when I look back I see the apparent coincidences as a second chance: bungle your circumstances the first time round, coincidence lets you sort them out later. Even this memoir may be a way of sorting things out. So I see myself examining the *Agamemnon,* which reflects my experience back at me. "Look, there I am! I wasn't so stupid after all! I told you how it was, didn't I? And you didn't believe me!"

One must be careful, all the same, to distinguish between getting a grip on the past and changing it in order to borrow a little dignity from a masterpiece.

I taught at the community college four mornings a week, preparing the classes at home and reading submissions at home also. Two things concentrated the mind: one was the pleasure of the World Literature class and the other was wonder at the aspirations served by the community college in general. Very little in the humanities was studied for its own sake. Reading and writing were simply tools to work on the better life. The forebears who wanted nothing more than to fill their stomachs had been forgotten. Since they weren't hungry, their descendants looked around and saw what else there was to be desired. The realization of their great scope was essential in the American character.

Even the elegant and gentle young woman who now ran my house and looked after my children in my absence had come to America for more scope. Her name was Patricia, and before she'd come to us she'd been working as manager of a dress shop in the small town of Ayr in Scotland, where she'd learned the rag trade from start to finish. The big department store of Lord & Taylor in Philadelphia had offered her a job as buyer as soon as she obtained a visa. If she worked for us as housekeeper for a year, that visa would be hers. In fact she stayed with us two years, going off every weekend in my car to relatives in Pennsylvania, and at the end of two years getting the position she wanted in the wider world, with (I imagine) a decent salary and all the benefits of a good job. By the time she joined us, Peter had gone off to board at the excellent Hill School on his grandfather's legacy and Antoinette spent her mornings in kindergarten. Only Fergus was at home all day. Again, as in the editorial job at the Center for Alcohol Studies, I was able to work efficiently at home, while nearly everything I earned went toward paying Patricia and maintaining an extra car. The real reward came in my sense of freedom. The children were as well off as if I'd been there the whole time, and the house ran smoothly, and there was some sort of desirable distance between me and the small children one loves so much and who can be so exhausting. Patricia even listened sympathetically to my complaints about freshman English.

And once she and I and the two small children arrived home from some expedition and found John, crowbar in hand, dismantling the bigger of the two staircases, the entire house covered in a pall of plaster dust, the carpet deep in splinters and planks, and dust casting a pearl light over the windows. We stood speechless. Eventually Patricia said only, "Well! I've never seen anything like that before!" in that sharp moral voice that goes with the Scottish personality. So that was that. We close a door and move off. We take off our coats, I prepare supper, the children settle down to play.

"What are you singing, Fergus? Is that a hymn?"

Pause. "No, it's a her."

A car passes on the dirt road. The pear tree in full blossom waits to be admired.

"It will be much more spacious in there now. We don't need two staircases." John is disheveled and triumphant. We may even laugh.

With Patricia in place, I can think about Clytaemnestra.

———

"How come Clytaemnestra let her husband go for ten years? Wasn't that kinda long? You were going to say something about that."

"No one asked her what she thought," I said. "Agamemnon thought he should go, so he went. You might say, *He didn't want to stay at home and rot.* The question of his staying is never raised. He was called, he went. I suppose it was a matter of honor. Remember that Helen started the Trojan War when she eloped with Paris, the Trojan prince, and her husband, Menelaus, had to get her back, as a matter of honor. Well, Agamemnon is the brother of Menelaus, and they are joint kings of Argos. What affects one affects the other. In a way all the Greeks had to get her back. It was a necessity. You have to accept the terms of the play, and not read our customs into it. Today a woman can run off with a lover and her husband will sue for divorce. That will be all."

"You mean, he won't come after her with an army," remarked one of the former dropouts.

"No way, man," said a veteran.

"But we can compare those conventions with ours," said a Hungarian.

"I think so," I said.

"The way I think of it, it's like a mirror," said Gary. "You look in the mirror and you see the meaning you naturally place on it, and at the same time you see superimposed the image of what is meant in the book."

"Right on, man," said one of the veterans.

"She got to let him go so there'll be this story," remarked one of the older men.

"*Well . . .*" A spanner in the works. A wrench in the works, I should say, and bit my words back. "The action arises out of the circumstances. It's just as Gary says, what is meant in the book is the meaning you must put first and foremost. Helen is stolen from her husband and the insult to his honor must be avenged. That's the given. That's the way things are in the story. I don't think there's a *moral* to the tale. It's not *improving*. We're not in *church*. Every story has its own logic, not necessarily educational. Suppose Agamemnon had stayed at home, Iphigeneia would not have been sacrificed, Aegisthus the lover wouldn't have got his foot in the door: all hinges on Agamemnon's going off to the war for ten years. *He didn't want to stay at home and rot.* Mind you, if he hadn't gone, the whole of Greece would have laughed at the cowardice and weakness of Agamemnon, and the Trojan War would have dragged on a bit longer than in fact it did. And certainly Aeschylus would have had to choose a different subject for his play. But Agamemnon went to the war, sacrificed his daughter, and the tragedy got under way. Yes, it was a very long absence indeed," I said. Then it struck me that I had let some inconsistency into the argument. "The tragedy hinges on that departure for Troy, and then the sacrifice of his daughter is added to that departure, so it can be followed to its conclusion."

"Then when he come home, she kills him. What kind of homecoming is that?"

"Nasty, man."

"Justice called for it," said Gary.

"Tooth-for-a-tooth justice? Revenge, like?"

"He away ten years, he *deserve* to die," said a large woman at the back who hadn't spoken before. Her name, amazingly, was Cassandra.

"The leader of the chorus says, 'You're caught in the net of doom.'"

"Yes. Doom is necessity. Agamemnon had to go to the war. He had to sacrifice his own daughter. But he had to be punished for that too. And his punishment is about to happen. He is about to die at the hands of his wife, Clytaemnestra. But he makes everything worse by bringing home as concubine the princess Cassandra. She is a Trojan princess. And she is the priestess of Apollo. A prisoner of war, a slave. And he's desecrated her by making her his mistress."

The Cassandra in class was black. She shouted, "A slave, like, no more than a slave. And he got no shame, he brings her home."

"True," I said.

"But Clytaemnestra still loves Agamemnon," said one of the older women. She put on her glasses and read out Clytaemnestra's speech to the chorus in which she describes her love and loneliness.

"Is she speaking the truth?" I asked. "Remember, she's going to kill him in a minute."

"I don't understand this Agamemnon, bringing this girl home to his wife. I mean, first he kills his daughter, then he brings this girl home. Of course his wife kills him. And the girl. Mind you, I was sorry for the girl."

"Cassandra," said Cassandra.

"Remember Cassandra's story? She has the gift of prophecy. But her gift has been made useless, so that no one believes her. Did you know that, Cassandra? It's an excellent dramatic device, because the audience understands, but the other characters in the play do not. That's dramatic irony. She says, 'There will come another to avenge us, born to kill his mother, born his father's champion.' And the audience understands she is referring to Orestes. The characters on the stage, however, fail to understand. They fail to believe her prophecy."

"Oh my Gawd," said the heedless older man. "What sort of play is this?"

"That Orestes," said Gary, "he comes in the next play."

"So he's *doomed,* Agamemnon is doomed, Orestes is doomed. . . . All these gods, they get you in deep trouble."

"What's this, *stay home and rot?*"

"That's what my husband says when he wants to be off," I said.

"Yeah, I understand that. He don't want to wash dishes, he leaves them to you."

That was not quite fair. John was an assiduous dishwasher.

And then there was an explosion from one of the younger students who had been pursuing his own train of thought: "They got to have all those gods so they could have an argument and carry the narrative along, this Zeus and his wife Hera and Artemis and Apollo and all, they argue, and all the issues get tossed around, like. And that's why human beings offend one or other of those gods whatever they do, that's why they're doomed."

"You got to put up or shut up," said one robust woman. "Or put up and explode."

"Yeah," said Karen, "like my husband give me a black eye if I come to your class. Yesterday he hit me real hard. I'm living a lie, I see that." Everyone turned to look at her. It was true, her face was bruised.

"You tell him, watch out," cried Cassandra. "You tell him, Agamemnon, he *die*."

"Remember," I said, "we have to put first and foremost the original significance of the play." If our husbands went off for a spell, we might not take lovers just because Clytaemnestra did, that would be childish and subvert the whole idea of the play, which was a moral one, meant to warn us of evil consequences following such an act. I contrasted Clytaemnestra's behavior with that of Penelope, who kept her suitors at bay during her husband's absence. And the class came to an end with one of the Vietnam veterans, who looked about twelve years old, declaring that he had returned from the war to find his wife in bed with another man, and the other man had jumped out of the window. The wife had eventually gone off after him. "Couldn't blame her, I guess," said the veteran. "Away two years. Not like Agamemnon, but long enough, I guess. And she didn't try to kill me in the shower. She took my car, though."

As I'd expected, Karen followed me out. She was leaving her husband and moving in with a friend while she worked out how she was going to live. It was the sort of outcome my mother feared when she spoke out against educated women, quite as unreasonable and equally unexplained. And yet there was a kind of justice in Karen's reading *Agamemnon* and on the strength of it (if that's how it was) deciding to leave her husband. The disinterested use of words must have impressed her. Or the portrayal of conflict as legitimate. It eased her into life, the way no priest or rabbi could. She had to be at least equal to the book.

It was several years after this that John won a second Guggenheim Fellowship and went off to Italy by sea on a dirty little Greek freighter, which caught fire in an Atlantic gale. He and the other half-dozen passengers were rescued by a sister ship after being towed behind the burning stern in a lifeboat for two days. They lost all their possessions. John also lost the early chapters of the book he was drafting and his notes.

The news was relayed to me in a garbled cable read over the telephone by Western Union, then in its last throes. When I'd at last grasped what had happened and where John was—the passengers had been landed on Madeira—I went down to tell the younger children. Peter was away from home, working as a copyboy on the *New York Times*. "I have bad news about Father," I said.

They looked up cheerfully. "I've just had some bad news. News about Father. His ship caught fire at sea."

To my amazement they burst out laughing.

"Why are you laughing?" I don't think they knew. Had they taken a look at my soul and seen its contradictions?

"You must admit it's funny," my little daughter said.

"No, not funny at all."

"*We* think it's funny, don't we, Fergus?"

I was appalled. They were still laughing when I told them he was safe, so it seemed they did not hear.

Four or five days later John flew home from Lisbon and I drove out to JFK to meet his plane. I did not share his enthusiasm for ships or hatred of air travel. It was a long drive to JFK and the plane was late. Of course he had no luggage and was the first to pass through customs into the waiting crowd. He gave me a shock. I suppose by that time I'd got used to the few facts Peter, using the resources of the *New York Times,* had extracted from the shipping agent and other sources—that the passengers were not safe in Italy but in Madeira and then Lisbon, that the ship was not intact and on its way through the Mediterranean but a half-burnt hulk in Gibraltar, that the cargo had not been harmless but so dangerous and illicit as to call for lie on lie. The exhausted figure with salt marks on his clothes and shoes too: he wasn't a Guggenheim fellow, he was someone who'd nearly died, who'd come back from the borders of death.

With this return the long middle act of my life drew to a climatic conclusion. Patricia had gone to work as a buyer in her big beautiful department store in Philadelphia, and I'd become resigned to unsatisfactory casual help who were constantly late or ill or disinclined to help me out. Again there was no quiet or leisure. John recovered from his fire at sea, re-created the missing notes and rewrote the first chapters, and set out again for Italy, this time by air. He had been concerned by Fergus's constant colds and made me promise to have his chest X-rayed. When our doctor saw the X rays, he noted that the boy's heart was enlarged, and referred us to a cardiologist. The cardiologist looked at the X rays and listened to his chest intently and after half an hour's examination pronounced him to have two holes in his heart. There was no immediate danger, but Fergus should undergo open-heart surgery in a year's time so that the holes could be patched.

This was news so appalling and unsettling that I could barely take it seriously. Fergus was a vigorous well-grown little boy. His lips were never blue, he was never short of breath, and apart from the usual colds of a small child who was gaining immunity, he was never ill. Jonathan had a friend whose father was a cardiologist. Through him we were referred to a child cardiologist at Columbia Presbyterian Hospital in New York, who with the greatest tact confirmed that the child's heart was normal. Children's hearts enlarge when they are ill, she said. She could detect no holes.

In the interval I had resigned from the community college. If Fergus were seriously ill, I wanted to look after him myself. Onerous though it had been to teach freshman English, however, and often though I'd talked of resigning, I was sorry to leave. It was the last good job I had, as when I tried to return, fortified by the excellent news about my boy's heart, it was too late, the job had been snapped up by one of the many Ph.D. candidates who crowded the true universities in those days, taking refuge in scholarship from call-up to the infamous Vietnam War, which still dragged on.

None of this story would be sayable on two accounts: were it not, first, for John's making up for his absences a thousand times over by his loving-kindness in later years; and, second, for my life's transformation with the publication of a second collection of my verse, twenty-five years after the first, and a subsequent award of a fellowship from the National Endowment of the Arts, which led to another book and another fellowship and yet others. Silence about marriage is seemly when things do not go well, and silence can be broken only when they go right again. Ridiculous: because contradictions are life-giving, and the just and the unjust may balance each other in a single life as in an *Agamemnon*. So grants and fellowships enabled me to drive up the coast of California as far as the state of Washington, and on another occasion to visit South Uist, in the Outer Hebrides. Both were places I'd dreamed of visiting. In California there were sea lions on the reefs to be marveled at, and on the machair of South Uist, near an outcrop of rock between beach and sea, a seal came in and beached himself high on the sand, and a rabbit that had been hiding in the rocks came out and ran toward the seal, an extraordinary conjunction to my mind. Once that kind of sight became possible, and the writing that they indirectly allowed, John's absences no longer mattered. With such a freeing of thought, also, you see significance everywhere.

Years later, I heard Jean Redpath the folksinger singing an old old song about the gray selchie of Sule Skerrie that spoke to the thoughts I had long since put away. It was a lament, such as you don't hear nowadays because laments are thought improper for women of great pitch and worth, and though it is imaginative, it told me something that seemed important about my life. A selchie (or silky) is a seal. The word comes from the Old Scottish *selich,* from Old English *seolh,* a seal. Sule Skerrie is a rock in the Atlantic fifty miles southwest of Orkney, in the far north of Scotland. The song begins: "In Norway land there lived a maid," and she laments:

> *I know not where my baby's father is*
> *Whether by land or sea he does travel in*

One day she wakes from sleep to find a gray seal at the foot of her bed, who says he is the father of her child.

> *I am a man upo' the land,*
> *I am a selchie in the sea,*
> *And when I'm far frae every strand*
> > *My dwellin' is in Sule Skerrie.*

Well, so, it struck me, I have married a seal.

In the song the young woman laments:

> *Alas, alas, this woeful fate!*
> *This woeful fate that's been laid on me,*
> *That a man should come from the Wast of Hoy*
> *To the Norway lands to have a bairn wi' me.*

Hoy refers to a place in Orkney. West of Hoy is Sule Skerrie. Or it could be Minnesota.

And the song spins itself out like this. After seven years the seal returns for his son and they go off together. The Norway maid marries a gunner, who in due time shoots the seals, the father and the son, who is wearing the gold chain his mother put on his neck when the father took him away. The mother is brought the chain, sees what has happened, and feels her heart break. The melody that goes with the words is very sad, and matches the inexplicable sadness with which I saw my husband go off year after year without me. I had married one whose nature belonged in a different element from mine and who had his true life elsewhere.

I am a man upo' the land,
I am a selchie in the sea.

And my sort of life, the human sort, would kill him just as the gunner, an ordinary human, kills the changeling seal. I'd have liked to be a seal myself, but that was not my destiny. I had only the one world to play with, alas, alas.

Likewise I found myself Penelope, the faithful wife, not Clytaemnestra with her lover and her vengeful sword, who pushed the common experience well beyond the common scope and so created a tragedy and a masterpiece. Not that I thought for a moment of killing my Agamemnon on his return. Not that I entertained an Aegisthus in his place, though I thought about it. But then I understood something very simple: to make things happen, you have to go away.